In praise of Kristen K. Brown's

THE BEST WORST THING

"If you have ever loved and lost, or have loved and can't begin to imagine such a loss, you will fall deeply for *The Best Worst Thing*. Kristen Brown opens her tattered heart for all to see, then shares her rocky road back from the edge, as she finds the woman she was meant to be."

— Julie Bauke, author of
Stop Peeing On Your Shoes:
Avoiding the 7 Mistakes That Screw Up Your Job Search

"*The Best Worst Thing* is a must for anyone facing adversity. Kristen Brown's deeply human account of her own loss and healing—and its unexpected pathway to helping others to transform their lives—will touch the depths of your heart and ignite your own inspiration."

— Lauren Mackler , best-selling author of
Solemate: Master the Art of Aloneness & Transform Your Life

"Kristen Brown's *The Best Worst Thing* takes the reader on a powerful journey of love, loss, rebirth, and self-discovery. Kristen has a gift of keen insight, provocative imagery, and raw authenticity that places us ringside into her heart-wrenching story of unimaginable grief while allowing us to witness her ultimate transformation. After reading *The Best Worst Thing*, I found myself overwhelmed with gratitude for the many gifts in my own life. Thank you, Kristen, for taking us with you!"

— Theresa Rose, award-winning author of
Opening the Kimono: A Woman's Intimate Journey
Through Life's Biggest Challenges

"You will be captivated from the very first word and may not be able to put this book down, as I personally experienced! Kristen is a gifted writer and she tells her incredible story that will move you emotionally in many ways. I highly recommend this book. As I was reading it, I thought of several friends I intend to buy a copy for."
— Peggy McColl, New York Times Best-Selling Author

"Too often we appreciate what we had only after it's gone for good. Let Kristen Brown be a clear reminder to us all to cherish what we have while we still have it."
— Jeff Cohen, author of
The Complete Idiot's Guide to Working Less, Earning More

"In life we rarely see someone who learns from every lesson given to them by life. In *The Best Worst Thing*, Kristen Brown takes readers along with her on her emotional journey through the end of life as she knew it, her transformation and her new beginning. To see Kristen rise from the flames of the tragic hand she was dealt to become a better, happier person not only for herself, but also for her daughter and everyone she touches on a daily basis, is inspirational to say the least. Kristen's life story is told in a way that, not only captures the difficulty of it all, but also leaves the readers feeling that reaching their dreams and full potential is something they too can achieve."
— Jina Schaefer, author of
Fountain of Youth

If you've been searching for answers when it comes to the challenges of life, search no more. Kristen has been there and done that. She has got it together. Why don't you get it together and read her latest book.
— Senator Holland Redfield, host
Straight Talk with Redfield-US Virgin Islands

THE BEST
WORST THING

ALSO FROM KRISTEN K. BROWN

The Happy Hour Effect
Training & Education Series

Go to www.HappyHourEffect.com to get Kristen's articles, tips,
training books, DVDs and CDs on stress management, work/life
balance, overcoming challenge, widowhood, and single parenting.

Listen to Kristen's radio show:
The Happy Hour Effect with Kristen Brown
http://webtalkradio.net/shows/the-happy-hour-effect/

Coming Soon:

The Happy Hour Effect Balance Plan:
Minimize Your Stress, Maximize Your Life

THE BEST WORST THING

A Memoir

Kristen K. Brown

BALBOA
PRESS
A DIVISION OF HAY HOUSE

Balboa Press books may be ordered through booksellers or by contacting:

Balboa Press
A Division of Hay House
1663 Liberty Drive
Bloomington, IN 47403
www.balboapress.com
1-(877) 407-4847

Imagery by www.erinandiphotography.com

Because of the dynamic nature of the Internet, any web addresses or links contained in this book may have changed since publication and may no longer be valid. The views expressed in this work are solely those of the author and do not necessarily reflect the views of the publisher, and the publisher hereby disclaims any responsibility for them.

The author of this book does not dispense medical advice or prescribe the use of any technique as a form of treatment for physical, emotional, or medical problems without the advice of a physician, either directly or indirectly. The intent of the author is only to offer information of a general nature to help you in your quest for emotional and spiritual well-being. In the event you use any of the information in this book for yourself, which is your constitutional right, the author and the publisher assume no responsibility for your actions.

Any people depicted in stock imagery provided by Thinkstock are models, and such images are being used for illustrative purposes only.
Certain stock imagery © Thinkstock.

ISBN: 978-1-4525-3310-0 (sc)
ISBN: 978-1-4525-3311-7 (e)

Library of Congress Control Number: 2011903299

Printed in the United States of America

Balboa Press rev. date: 4/22/2011

For Brooke, the best gift Todd could have given me and the best memory of him I could ask for.

In loving memory and honor of Todd Brown, a portion of proceeds from the sale of this book will support heart health research to fight America's #1 killer of both men and women. Please support the cause!

PREFACE

When I put pen to paper in December 2007, I had no intention of writing a book. My pen flowing across the page was simply an outlet for the emotions that were trapped inside me after my young husband's unexpected death left me a widow mom. And yet, here I sit, three and a half years later with a book in hand.

And while the process has been therapeutic for my own healing, my first wish is that it provides a ray of hope for other young widows who don't have many resources or points of connection as there are only a few thousand of us out there under the age of 40.

My second wish for the book is that it shifts people's perspectives so they appreciate and cherish what they have before it's too late. Anyone who is in a relationship and trying to balance multiple roles can and should relate to my conflicting emotions of regret, guilt, sadness and anger as I progress through my grief.

And finally, my third and most important wish for this book is to provide my daughter with context and understanding of how her mom made it through a challenging time in her life to come out on the other side a better person. I want her to know that she too can overcome any obstacle and achieve any dream she sets out to pursue in her life. My most important job is to be a role model for my child and I hope this book is a testament to my resolve, resilience and drive to improve the world one person at a time just as I hope Brooke does someday.

Kristen K. Brown

"Let no one ever come to you without leaving better and happier."
Mother Teresa

PROLOGUE

I open my eyes to impenetrable darkness. The air feels thick and heavy with electricity, and my body is soaked with perspiration. I strain to see through the shadows. My bedroom is filled with a suffocating heat that burns my skin; yet I shiver, chilled to the bone, alone under the blankets, hoping this might finally be the night he shows up. The hot, oppressive air pins me to my pillow. As my vision adjusts to the night, my eyes see that the room is empty, but my instincts say otherwise. The hairs on my arms stand on end, and I stare into the blackness, sensing him and straining for a sign, some hint of his presence. My pulse pounds. I can feel my heart thumping and racing in my chest, anxious and confused, excited and hopeful. I am not breathing for fear that any exchange of air will disrupt the flow of energy in the room—Todd's energy. I am not afraid. I feel his particles vibrating around and through me, his spirit hovering over me, yet I still see nothing. But I feel it and know it's him. Finally, after months of waiting, he's showing himself.

"Todd, are you here?" I whisper, my eyes welling up with tears. I wait anxiously for a response, a shifting of light, a faint breeze, something to know he's acknowledging me. "Are you okay?" I whisper again, hoping I'll get an affirmation that he is happy on the other side. The heat in the room intensifies as I wait for him, missing him so badly. I scan the room.

Did I see the curtain move?

Was that a sound?

I listen and look, willing something to happen.

The air changes suddenly—an abrupt cooling and calming. The feeling of electricity relents, and I sense him leaving.

"That's not enough!" I sob, my heart breaking. But he's gone. Then, like a bittersweet kiss goodbye, Brooke babbles in her crib next door, and I know he's with her now. She's just a year old, awake and cooing as her daddy makes his presence known to her. Moments later she is quiet, and silence punctuates the fact that he is gone and I am alone again in our bed with only emptiness filling the space beside me.

Knowing I won't sleep again this night, I get up. I walk by his closet, and my heart leaps: the bifold doors are ajar. They were shut when I went to bed just two hours ago. As on most other nights, I had squeezed inside the tiny space to inhale his scent, letting the familiar, sweet musk of his body and cologne wash over me. I would curl up on the floor on top of the clothes stacked there—sometimes for a few minutes, sometimes for hours—and then pull the doors shut, not wanting to let any of his smells escape. But now the doors are open. Todd was here, trying to communicate with me, to let me know he's okay.

Todd, are you still here? I've spent so many nights waiting and longing for you to visit me somehow—as a ghost, in a dream—hoping for any sort of connection or sign to prove you're still with me. I wanted to apologize and make peace. To let you know of all my regrets about our relationship before you died. To express my frustrations with how you changed—and how I changed. And now you've shown that you were here, and I feel worse than ever. Like I've lost you all over again. The pain and regret I feel are eating me alive, and I don't know what to do.

Regret. That bitter feeling has haunted me and kept me awake night after night for months. How do I reconcile my past wrongs against someone when he's dead? That's the question I can't answer, the puzzle that has stolen my sleep since Todd died. Every night I lie in bed, unable to close my eyes, wondering how I can possibly move forward. I know I wasn't the best wife I could have been to him, and he wasn't the best husband he could have been to me. How do I get past the regret of what was and what could have been? How can I find the words that I didn't get to say before he left so suddenly?

ONE

We staggered through the dark parking lot, laughing and stumbling, the air frosty and crisp, typical of Minnesota weather two days before Christmas. My black, high-heeled boots wobbled over snow-encrusted pavement peppered with gravel that provided just enough friction to prevent a wipeout. My breath left thick plumes of condensation in the air, and I pulled my black wool peacoat, which was not even close to being warm enough, tight around me to block the shocking cold creeping under my clothing. Once again, I had sacrificed warmth for fashion, wearing a thin blouse, jeans, and no gloves or hat. For years, I had dressed inappropriately for the frigid climate, hoping to lure an unsuspecting man—and to impress other women with my fashion sense (usually unsuccessfully)—and that night was no exception.

The heat of bodies and warm breath fogged the windows as my friends climbed into Rob's red extended-cab pickup. My feet slipped off the shiny chrome step rail, the vodka-cranberry cocktails I had been overserved earlier demonstrating their effect on my coordination. Laughing, I shook my head, embarrassed. Rachel, already in the back seat, grabbed my hand to heft my one hundred and twenty-five pounds up next to her in the truck. Her cleavage-enhancing, black wrap sweater gaped open, giving me a view of more than I needed to see—although I had seen it many times in situations just like this. We had been friends since elementary school, partying together through high school, college, and into our early twenties, and we always knew what the other was thinking—which was useful when an unsavory suitor was making his move. But tonight, Jake, our third backseat mate, was an invited partner. He and Rachel had been flirting all night.

1

As I slid onto the gray leather seat, Jake pulled a can of Busch Light from inside his ski jacket, ready for our drive along the familiar country roads that ran through our little hometown. In front, Todd Brown, tall with blonde, curly hair, shook his head in amusement, seemingly wondering how he had ended up on a road trip with this group of misfits. Although we had all gone to the same high school, Todd and I had never talked. All I knew about him was that he had been in the class after mine and was a bit of an egotistical jock. Todd, Rachel, Jake, Rob, and I grew up in a small, rural farming community about two and a half hours west of Minneapolis, called Montevideo. Yes, Montevideo—like Montevideo, Uruguay, which is, in fact, its official "sister city." I've always found it comical that a predominantly Scandinavian farming town in Minnesota is twinned with a South American metropolis in a third-world country.

Just minutes before, my friends and I had been inside the warmth of the Hunt Bar and Grill, a hot spot in our hometown—if a farming town with a population of fifty-five hundred can have a hot spot. It was nearing closing time, and the one hundred or so people in the bar were thinking about where to go next. Holiday weekends in Montevideo always meant a reunion between those still living there and those who had left after high school. Although I was among those who had left, seven years later at age twenty-five I still thought of Montevideo as home, and I loved going out and getting crazy with everyone I hadn't seen in a while.

As we were thinking about what to do next, a buzz arose.

"Brian's having an afterbar," someone announced.

"Who's going to Brian's? I hear he has a keg," someone else said.

Brian, another friend from high school, was going to keep the masses entertained by hosting a gathering at his house for further socializing and drinking (as if we needed more of the latter). But he wasn't going to leave the bar until the last minute, while Rachel and I were ready to head out. As we discussed what our plan should be, Rob approached us.

"A couple of us are going road-tripping before heading to Brian's; want to come?" he asked, spinning his keys around his finger.

If you think *road-tripping* is an innocent term used to describe exactly what it sounds like—a trip on roads—you are sadly misinformed. With few entertainment options in Montevideo, the concept of "road-tripping" long ago evolved to include roadies—alcoholic beverages consumed while on said road trip, otherwise known as "bar-in-the-car" or "auto-drinking." Yes, we were aware of the dangers of drinking and driving, but that added to the allure. (We're talking about twenty-somethings in a small town, remember?) Just hearing Rob propose a road trip made our eyes light up.

"Totally. We'll road-trip with you," Rachel and I replied. Buttoning my coat, I checked the pockets for my money and ID. I never carried a purse in Montevideo. You never knew where you would end up, and keeping track of a purse was just the sort of inconvenience you didn't need when an opportunity like road-tripping arose.

I got situated in my spot behind the front passenger seat, and Jake handed me one of the "secret" beers from his jacket pocket. I cracked open the Busch Light and held it down below window level as Rob pulled away from the bar en route to the dark country roads that would obscure our illicit activity. I took a sip and cringed. It was warm from Jake's coat pocket, where he had probably put it before going out that night "just in case." But I drank it anyway. That was another of the risks of road-tripping—dealing with subpar beverages desperately obtained after the liquor store closed by either swiping swill from a parent's liquor cabinet or buying lightweight 3.2 beer or wine coolers at a gas station. I leaned over the front seat as we drove, the radio cranked up, drinking, talking, and singing to AC/DC and Guns N' Roses, belting out the anthems of our youth like we were Axl Rose. When the slow songs came on, Todd and I sang together in true monster ballad style, leaning toward each other with our beer can microphones in hand, despite having just officially met.

I felt a jab in my back and looked over my shoulder to see that Rachel and Jake were no longer drinking, talking, or singing; they were kissing. And not just innocently smooching in their own little corner, but thrashing and bumping around like caged snakes, writhing all over each other and pushing against me in the process. I had seen this type of drunken make-out scene before and knew nothing could stop it once it started. I shifted forward toward Todd, our shoulders touching now. I nudged him and moved my face close to his ear so he could hear me over the music.

"Check out the lovebirds in the backseat. I think their saliva is getting on me." My cheek was so close to his mouth that I could feel his breath.

"Wow!" Todd grinned, shook his head, and took a swig of his beer, leaning closer to me. "I'm glad I'm not back there. Awkward! We should probably get to town so you don't have to sit next to that anymore." I still felt his warm breath on my face. I searched for something clever to say and tilted my head and laughed in what I thought was a seductive manner, but due to the vodka-cranberry cocktails was actually more snorting than seducing.

"Yes, please. Let's head back to the afterbar," I said to Rob, not just because I wanted out of the backseat, but because I needed to pee from all the beer and bumpy roads, and so that Todd and I could get back to our bonding over song.

As Rob turned down the next road to head back to town, something happened. One second I was leaning over the front seat facing Todd, our heads mere inches from each other to avoid the flailing bodies beside me, and the next, the space between us disappeared. We turned toward each other at the exact same moment, my brown hair brushing his cheek and his light blue eyes meeting mine for an instant. And then—I turned into a writhing snake myself. I kissed Todd right there in front of everyone. And he kissed me back!

Now, historically I have been extremely against public displays of affection in my own relationships. But something, some combination of magnetism and fate and vodka-cranberries, made me kiss a guy I barely knew while driving the back roads of our small hometown—our warm Busch Lights in hand, not spilling a drop. We pulled away from each other, giggling like preteens who have just exchanged their first kiss in the bleachers at a football game—or maybe that was just me. We looked down at our beers and took another sip. Rob was fiddling with the radio, probably disgusted by all the hormones flying around in his truck without any to go around for him.

After the kiss, Todd and I maintained that connection to each other. We talked over the seat for the fifteen-minute trip back to town, and when we got to Brian's house for the afterbar, no one else mattered. It was as if just the two of us were there, not forty other people, and we wondered why we had never even talked with each other all these years.

The party wound down, and we suddenly realized it was three in the morning. While we weren't far away from our own childhood beds, neither of us felt sober enough to drive, nor did we want to leave each other, although we didn't say that out loud. So we both opted to stay overnight at Brian's house. We could easily have snuck into a bedroom together, but we didn't. Our moral compasses and something blooming inside both of us prompted us not to. I took the couch while Todd stretched out his long, lanky body on a recliner nearby. Even though I didn't have all my wits about me, I remember this as if it happened just last night. I curled up on the couch with my boots still on, my eyes shut, playing coy and pretending to sleep yet fully aware of Todd's presence just feet from me. As I started to doze, I sensed him moving off of his recliner, but I kept my eyes shut, not wanting him to know I was "monitoring" him.

My heart pounded in my chest.

Was he going to come over and make a move on me? Part of me hoped so.

My mind raced, working through the possible scenarios of the next moment: Maybe he was just getting up to go to the bathroom. Maybe he was going to the kitchen to get a late-night snack. Or maybe in a minute we would be making out like crazy teenagers!

A second later, I heard a gentle swoosh of air and fabric and felt a fuzzy blanket being gently tucked around me. Then Todd's hands lifted my feet, slowly eased my boots off, and lightly covered my feet with the blanket before tiptoeing back to his recliner. I feigned sleep, my heart swelling with emotion. This guy was someone special and I knew at that very instant that I would marry Todd Brown.

TWO

The next couple of days went by quickly as I celebrated Christmas with my family, and soon I was back at work in Minneapolis. But my mind wasn't on my job, it was on Todd. He worked for a bank as a mortgage lender on one side of the city, and I was a national accounts manager for a small gift bag company on the opposite side of town. That first day back at the office, I felt like a schoolgirl, wondering if Todd would call. I checked e-mail, kept my old-school giant cell phone on, and stayed near my desk just in case he called me at work.

By the end of the day, I was convinced he wasn't going to call and that our kiss and subsequent connection had just been a vodka-cranberry/ Busch Light-induced moment that didn't mean anything to him. At 5:05, I picked up my bag and started down the hallway to leave the building. Just as I was about to walk out the door, I heard my office phone ring. I turned and sprinted as fast as I could back toward my cubicle, raced around the corner to my phone, and grabbed it. The line was already dead. Crap! How could I blow it like that? I knew in my gut it was him. I stood there for a moment, catching my breath and cursing myself for missing his call. Dejected, I started to leave once more, but I saw the message light on the phone begin to blink. I anxiously picked up the phone and dialed the voice mail code, crossing my fingers that it wasn't just a work contact.

"Hi, Kristen, it's Todd Brown. You gave me your card but it only had your work number on it, so not sure how else to get ahold of you." (Those damn vodka-cranberries again!) "I wanted to see if you maybe wanted to grab a bite to eat this week sometime. Anyway ... so call me if you get a chance."

"Aaaahhhhh!" I was squealing like a lovesick teenager, jumping up and down, waving my hands in the air. Fortunately, the coworkers who sat near me had already left for the day. Why was I acting like this? What was wrong with me? Since when was I a giddy, sappy girl? My mind suddenly kicked into typical Kristen over analytical mode. Okay, game plan time. What should I do? Do I call him back right now, or will that seem too desperate? But if I wait, will it seem like I was screening my calls? Do I call from home tonight? What if he's busy? Do I wait until tomorrow so I don't seem too anxious? Or will that give him enough time to fall completely out of love with me? What? Love? Who said anything about love? That's just crazy; we had a total of five hours of interaction time!

So I waited … the fifteen minutes it took me to get home. Then I practically sprinted up to my apartment, threw down my bag and jacket, and grabbed the cordless phone off the wall. I sat down on the edge of my lavender (yes, lavender) couch and stared at the phone in my right hand. In my left hand I held the scrap of paper with Todd's phone number. I had been carrying it in my pocket all day, so the ink was smudged and the paper was crinkled pretty badly, but I could still make out the number. But paralyzing fear kept me from dialing. I stood up and began pacing. I am a master at pacing—back and forth, back and forth—while I work out problems or situations in my mind. I walked into my bedroom, then back to the living room, through the kitchen, and into the bathroom.

I looked in the mirror, leaned against the sink, and lectured myself.

"Kristen, you can do this. Just call," I said out loud, trying to give myself a confidence-building pep talk. "The worst that can happen is he says he changed his mind and thinks you are an unattractive, crazy chick who kisses random guys in pickup trucks." Breathing deeply, I picked up the phone and dialed.

"Hello?" Todd answered.

"Umm, hi, it's Kristen … Larson from Montevideo," I stammered. Real smooth. He obviously knows I'm from Montevideo.

"Oh, hey!" He sounded happy to hear my voice, which gave me the courage to keep talking.

"Hi. I got your message just as I was leaving the office. Sorry I missed you." I scrambled to think of something more interesting to say so he wouldn't hang up on me. I started to pace.

"Sorry I had to call you at work," he replied. I didn't have any other numbers to call you at. But I wanted to see if you'd like to get something to eat one of these nights." I could tell he was nervous. How do guys handle that pressure of asking girls out? The fear of rejection would send me right over the edge.

"Sure, that would be great. When are you thinking?" I tried to sound casual and breezy. Please say tomorrow! Please say tomorrow!

"How about tomorrow night?"

Yes!

"I think that should work," I answered, trying to sound calmer than I felt. "What time do you work until?" I silently lunged towards the floor, doing fist pumps in the air.

"I should be home by six. I was thinking a little place over in Edina, called Two Guys from Italy. Want to try that?" Finally, a man with a plan. This was getting better by the second.

"Sounds good. I can come to your house, and we can go from there if that works," I suggested, but then cringed, worried it sounded a little forward. But Todd seemed thrilled.

"Yeah. Perfect. What's your e-mail so I can send you my address tomorrow?"

We exchanged information and hung up. After all that pacing, I had ended up in the guest bedroom/office perched on the edge of the daybed. I set the phone down next to me, out of breath and buzzing with adrenaline. Content, I took a deep breath and hoped for good things to come. Tomorrow night couldn't come fast enough.

THREE

As the end of the next workday drew near, I could hardly contain my excitement. My coworkers laughed and tried to calm me down as I paced around the office, unable to concentrate, just waiting until I could go and prep for my first date with Todd. At four o'clock, I couldn't take it any more, and neither could my office mates.

"Why don't you just go home already?" my boss said, poking her head around the corner of my cubicle. She knew about the impending date and had seen me walk past her office door about fifty times.

"Really? Are you sure?"

"Yes; get out of here and have fun!" She smiled and walked back to her office shaking her head as she laughed.

I shut down my computer and quickly gathered my jacket and bag. I drove as fast as my lead foot would allow, parked in the spot nearest my building entrance, and bounded the steps two at a time up to my apartment. With much care and thought, I had chosen my wardrobe after getting off the phone with Todd, leaving me time now to freshen my makeup and style my hair just right. You only get one chance to make a first impression, I thought to myself (even though this really was my second chance, since the vodka-cranberry kiss had been the first—and it obviously *had* made an impression). I double-checked my appearance in the full-length mirror, feeling perfectly casual yet put together—just right for a first date. I grabbed my coat and purse and headed back out to my car for the twenty-minute drive to Todd's house.

I sped down the freeway, my nerves starting to unravel. I hadn't been on a first date in years because I was always in a long-term relationship. What would we talk about for the duration of an entire dinner? Maybe we should go to McDonald's—short and sweet. But we had spent hours together that night at Brian's, talking about anything and everything. I could do that again, but maybe it would be easier after a glass of wine or two. Liquid confidence, that's what I needed.

I pulled up in front of Todd's house, which he shared with three roommates. There were no cars in front, so I didn't know if anyone was home. Maybe Todd was just parked in the alley behind the house. I sat for a moment, deciding what to do, when he pulled up behind me. Through the rear view mirror, I saw him wave, and I gathered my senses and prepared for our first actual date. I stepped onto the snow-covered street, taking care not to move too fast for fear of falling. I'm not the most graceful person on or off the ice. Todd smiled at me, shuffling over in his dress shoes.

"Hey. Sorry I'm running a little late. I got stuck at work. Let's just run in, and I'll change so we can go." Allowing me to walk in front of him, we went up to the house, he opened the door, and I stepped into a stereotypical version of any place occupied by four mid-twenties guys. Sports magazines, *Playboys*, chew cans, playing cards, and dirty dishes were scattered about, and a basketball game was on television. It didn't even look like a game from that decade, as I thought I saw Larry Bird. But I would come to learn that, a game is a game, regardless of its actual importance to today's world. If there was competition, it mattered to Todd.

Todd hurried down the hall to his room, slowing just enough to introduce me to his roommate who was lying on the couch completely cocooned in a blanket, a full chew wad in his mouth and the remote control on his chest.

"Hi. Nice to meet you," I said, trying to make polite conversation.

"Hey," he mumbled.

I felt relieved when Todd quickly returned, his dress pants and tie replaced by jeans and a navy blue V-neck sweater that perfectly complemented his blue eyes. He grabbed his coat off the back of the couch and opened the front door.

"See ya," he said in his housemate's direction, as he again held the door for me and we walked down the sidewalk toward our cars.

"Whose should we take, mine or yours?" he asked.

I looked at the two cars—Todd's rusting, tan Mazda 626 with the "Chick Magnet" bumper sticker, and my new, black-cherry-colored Nissan Maxima with heated seats, sunroof, and leather interior.

"It's up to you. You pick." I didn't want to make him feel bad.

"Okay, I'll drive." He moved toward the driver's side door. "Wait there. I'll pull away from the curb so you don't have to step in the snow."

I smiled at both his gallantry and his complete lack of concern about his car. Not that I cared what we rode in. I'm not one of those girls who measures a man by the car he drives, but it was comical that when faced with the decision between a brand-new vehicle and his own rather dilapidated one, he chose the latter. I stepped inside the car, which to my surprise was immaculately clean. He obviously paid attention to cleanliness—an important trait in a man. We pulled away from the curb and drove the ten minutes to the restaurant. We chatted about nothing in particular—the weather, his job, the restaurant we were going to—all nervous, first-date talk to warm us up for the real conversation to come. In the parking lot, Todd came around to open my door. As I slid past him, I could smell his cologne, a warm, musky, clean scent like fresh laundry, soap, and Old Spice (don't knock the Old Spice!). I was completely dazed by the cologne trance he had put me in as we walked to our table.

"Hi. I'm Lisa, and I'll be your server tonight. Can I get you something to drink?" The waitress looked at us, wondering if we'd be drinkers and add to her tip potential for the night. Luckily for her, this was a first date, which meant at least two glasses of wine for me.

"Yes, I'll have a glass of Pinot Grigio please," I replied, thinking a vodka-cranberry might be a little too aggressive for a weeknight.

"Sure. Can I see your ID?"

I pulled out my wallet to prove I was of legal drinking age.

"And for you, sir?"

"I'll have a Newcastle please." He dug into his coat pocket. And then his other coat pocket. And then his jeans pockets. He started to look a little frantic at not being able to find his wallet, and after a moment looked up, embarrassed. "I guess I'll just have water."

The server looked at him pitifully. You could tell she felt bad for this poor guy who forgot his wallet and now couldn't get any liquid confidence of his own. She walked away to get my wine and Todd's water.

"Damnit! I forgot my wallet in my work pants at home. I changed so fast I didn't even think about it." He slumped down in his chair, his shoulders sagging in defeat. "Oh, wait, my checkbook is in the car. I'll be right back." He jumped up and bolted out of the restaurant. A minute later he was back, triumphantly holding his black-covered checkbook.

"Sorry about the ID. We can get it when we're done here if we decide to go anywhere else," I suggested, suddenly afraid it was too forward of me to presume we would go anywhere else. What if dinner sucked? What if we hated each other? What if we couldn't think of anything to say?

But none of that happened. We spent our dinner talking about growing up in our small town and how funny it was that we never knew each other yet shared so many of the same friends. Our high school wasn't large; there were about five hundred students when we attended. I was a grade ahead, but I played sports and was in a lot of activities with many of his female friends, and he played sports and hung out with many of my guy friends. We compared stories of sporting events, school dances, and parties that we both attended, yet we couldn't recall seeing each other there at all. It was as if we were describing the same events from different vantage points just a few inches apart. We were amazed at how our lives had been on parallel tracks back then and had never crossed until now.

When we finished dinner and the server brought the bill, Todd snatched it off the table. "I'm paying." He waved me away as I tried to give him money.

"Let me give you something, or the tip at least," I protested, trying to slip some bills into his hand.

"Nope. I got it." He pulled his checkbook out of his pocket.

"Okay, but I'll buy you a drink at the next place, if you want to go somewhere else." I hoped we would indeed be going somewhere else next.

"Yeah, after we go back to my house for my ID." He laughed, opening the checkbook. Suddenly, the laughter stopped and his face fell.

"What's wrong?" I leaned toward him.

"I'm out of checks." He looked defeated again. Poor Todd. No booze. No money. For him this must have been the worst first date ever.

"Well, lucky for you I brought my purse tonight." I smiled, hoping to pull him out of his funk, and took out my debit card to pay for the meal and my wine (which only seemed fair since the wine cost more than my dinner).

"I cannot believe I did that. What an idiot!" Todd folded his arms and shook his head while I mentally noted the irony. I had been nervous all day and here we were, me feeling cool as a cucumber and Todd about as anxious as a guy could be on a first date. After I had paid, we walked out to the car, Todd quietly fuming.

"It's really no big deal," I said, trying to comfort his bruised ego.

"I feel like an ass. I'm getting our drinks at the next place *and* paying the next time we go out."

Did I hear that correctly? The next time we go out? Does that mean he likes me? Suddenly I saw a vision of us on a porch swing, old and gray, grandkids playing in the front yard, a couple of dogs lying at our feet. Stop it, I said to myself. Stop thinking like a crazy person. I shook my head to clear the image and climbed back into Todd's chick magnet, ready for anything.

FOUR

After four or five weeks of dating, one Saturday Todd offered to come over to my apartment and make me dinner. I expected a typical man meal of spaghetti or steaks, but he showed up carrying a giant, silver stockpot.

"What's that for?" I asked him.

He didn't reply, just smiled, took the lid off, and started unloading ingredients onto the counter. Inside were potatoes and four butcher-paper-wrapped packages.

"Check this out," he said, unwrapping the first. It held two plump sausages.

"Yum!" I exclaimed, not letting on how much I loved any type of sausage, bacon, or other processed meat. The next package held a handful of shiny, black mussels. "Oh, I'm intrigued."

Next was a packet of fresh shrimp—even better! Todd knew that seafood is one of my favorite foods, so his thoughtfulness in using it in our first home-cooked meal completely melted me.

"But wait, there's one more," he said, doing his best impression of an infomercial. He took out the last package, slowly pulled back the paper, and ceremoniously unveiled two enormous lobster tails.

"Oh my gosh, you had me at the sausage, but this is even better."

Todd pulled out a bright yellow package of seasoning. "Have you ever had a seafood boil?"

"No, but by the looks of this spread, I am going to like it!"

As Todd went about the work of putting together the meal, I started pacing nervously. "Can I help?" I felt my type A control freak starting to emerge.

"Just sit down, have some wine, and talk to me while I cook."

THE BEST WORST THING

So I did. I stopped pacing, and for half an hour, I just sat.

Todd assembled the ingredients in the pan and set it on the stove to cook. When the water started to boil, he dumped the packet of seasoning into the water, and my apartment was filled with a spicy aroma that smelled delectable. But within moments, the aroma became an odor that quickly worsened, burning our noses.

I picked up the package of seasoning and read the instructions. "'Use one to two tablespoons to taste.' You just put at least half a cup in there!" My eyes started to water from the pungent spices permeating the air. We both laughed hysterically as the burning smell intensified. We raced to the balcony door, tore it open, and launched ourselves into the brisk January cold for a breath of sting-free air.

"I guess I should have read the directions." Todd was barely able to contain his amusement with himself.

"What are we going to do? Can we still eat it?" I felt bad that all his planning, hard work, and thoughtfulness had been ruined.

"Yes, we can still eat it. I'll just scoop some of the seasoning out and add more water and a bunch of lemon slices. That will take away the bite." He tried his best to fix it, but as we ate, our noses ran, our eyes watered, and we drank three bottles of wine, choking down that super-spicy attempt at our first romantic home-cooked dinner. Although that one didn't turn out the way he'd planned, there were many successful meals to come. We spent the next three years experimenting with cooking, traveling together, and learning to be each other's best friend.

FIVE

Todd and I went back to Montevideo regularly to see his parents and our friends. My parents had moved away but I had grandparents and relatives in town too and we both called it home. One such trip home took us to a party that involved karaoke. Now if you had asked Todd, he would have said he should have been a professional singer, but in reality, he was good, but not rockstar worthy. Nevertheless, during every car trip we took he would sing away, even if not always quite on pitch. Even if he wasn't a great singer, he was fearless; and although I wouldn't admit it to him, I was jealous. I didn't have the guts to sing out loud if anyone else was within earshot. (Well, not unless my vocal chords were lubricated with plenty of alcohol.)

When we arrived, the karaoke deejay was in full swing, luring singers of all abilities on stage. I didn't want to go up; I hadn't hit the inebriation threshold that would allow me to embarrass myself like that. But after a couple of drinks, that changed.

My mom's friend, Darla, whom I had known forever, staggered up to me.

"Hey, wanna sing 'That's Amore' with me?" she slurred. A duet of drunken voices trying to sing a classic probably wasn't the best idea, but at the time it seemed like a genius plan. If you're familiar with this song, you'll recall that although it has a simple melody, the notes have a rather expansive range, making it not for the faint of heart. But I had consumed just enough adult beverages to think I could pull it off, so I agreed to join Darla. The deejay called our names, and we approached the stage. I grabbed the microphone, preparing to dazzle the crowd with my vocal stylings, confident that my six-note vocal range would expand to at least twelve to hit the notes required in the song. The music started, and the screen with the word prompter counted down the beats to the first notes. Then the words appeared, and I belted it out.

"When the moon hits your eye like a big pizza pie that's amore." So far so good. But then Darla broke into soprano, throwing off the velvety smoothness of my should-have-been-a-rock-star voice. I panicked, fear taking over my vocal cords, perspiration rising on my upper lip. Suddenly I was struggling to find the notes, and my female alto voice somehow became a male bass. I looked around the room; the crowd was laughing at the scene they were witnessing.

"Tippy tippy tay, tippy tippy tay," Darla, my costar, sang in operatic form. Oh my god, what am I doing up here singing this song? I tried to regain my vocal bearing but with no success, so I figured it was time to quit trying to sound good and start milking my sucky performance for all it was worth. At least I could give the audience a good show with my performance quality, if not with my voice. So I just let loose and— thanks to the five or six vodka sodas I'd consumed earlier (I had evolved from the vodka-cranberries)—I was able to pull off what I considered a solid 4 out of 10, driven strictly by showmanship and not singing talent. I certainly can't say that the crowd went wild, but at least they didn't boo me off the stage, and I was laughing at myself as much as the audience was.

As I walked off the stage, Todd was cringing, his face a mixture of amusement and embarrassment for me. He came toward me, and I could just see the snarky comments forming in his brain. I rested my head on his shoulder, still giggling at the spectacle I had created. He put his arm around me and laughed.

"Well that was interesting, James Earl Jones," he teased.

"So I was off key a bit. I just couldn't get past Darla suddenly singing soprano after the first verse." I knew there was nothing I could say to stop him from making fun of me, but I didn't really mind. That was how we were: we could tease each other and also take it—one of the things we always said we loved about each other.

"I'll go get you another drink, Mr. Jones." He started walking away, still chuckling.

"Very funny, Mr. Montreal," I called to him. "Just keep laughing."

He stopped abruptly and turned. "You said we'd never mention that story." He feigned a hurt look, but I knew he was a bit amused that I'd brought up one of his many karaoke adventures.

We had been in Montreal a year earlier for one of my business trips, and we fell in love with the culture and vibe of that beautiful and friendly city. On our first evening there, we were out exploring the nightlife. We'd had dinner and were working our way through the entertainment district when we walked by a busy bar with a sign announcing that karaoke would be going on for the next few hours. We both looked at each other and immediately decided to go in. We approached the bar and ordered a couple of drinks—Todd his usual beer, and I was still in my vodka-cranberry days.

"Go put your name down," I prompted, nudging him toward the sign-up sheet by the stage.

"No, I don't know anyone," he answered.

"Exactly. Go up and do it. You know you want to." I could see he was already on board. He liked being the center of attention, even if he didn't like to admit it, so I knew it wouldn't take much encouragement to get him on that stage.

"Okay, if you're going to make me." He maneuvered through the crowd to sign up. While we waited, we sat at the bar, oblivious to those around us. We laughed and talked and cuddled. It was early in our relationship, and we were still pretty lovey-dovey.

"Todd Brown, come on up here for 'Runaround Sue,'" the announcer called.

Todd hopped up, pecked me on the cheek. "Wish me luck," he said, sauntering up to the stage. The song began, and he was really hamming it up in this crowd where no one knew him, twirling the microphone, bopping to the beat. I have to say, he was fantastic. He hit every note and choreographed every dance move perfectly. I sat there at the bar feeling proud.

"Is that your husband?" the bartender leaned over and asked.

"No, he's just my boyfriend."

"Well, he is one fine piece of meat." The bartender winked, and I whipped around. Finally taking in my surroundings, I noticed there were suspiciously few women in the room but a lot of men, hooting and whistling as Todd worked the stage. Then it hit me: We're in a gay bar! I felt simultaneously amused and panicked, wondering how Todd would react once he realized where we were. Don't get me wrong: Todd had no problem with people's lifestyle choices. But knowing that he was in a room full of men lusting after him would have made him extremely uncomfortable. What should I do? The song was almost over, so I decided to just let him finish and then clue him in.

Todd ended his performance with an exaggerated dance move and then hopped off the stage, obviously proud of himself as the crowd hooted and cheered for him. He approached the bar and took a swig of his beer.

"Gotta run to the bathroom. Be right back." Before I could warn him of who or what he might meet at the urinals, he disappeared into the crowd. As I stood there wondering if I should go after him, he came back with a perplexed look on his face.

"Two men were making out in the hall, and a guy looked at me funny in the bathroom."

"Well, I don't know how to tell you this ... but we're in a gay bar."

"What?" He looked at me, stunned for a moment, then scanned the room. "Let's go," he commanded, grabbing my arm and leading me out into the street. Entertained by the whole situation, I laughed as we stepped out onto the sidewalk.

"What's so funny?" he asked.

"Come on. Don't you think it's pretty comical that you just performed probably your best rendition yet of 'Runaround Sue,' and it was for a bunch of men? The bartender told me you were a fine piece of meat!" Todd looked at me intensely, then broke into a smile.

"Yeah, that is pretty funny. But don't tell anyone I sang at a gay bar."

And since then I've told this story at least twenty times.

SIX

It took me awhile to get used to dating a guy like Todd. He always went with the flow, taking whatever came his way without fighting for or against it—not wanting to rock the boat or upset his own world. I, on the other hand, was always needy, demanding more and more all the time. Not that I was dependent on others for survival; I felt that I could take care of myself and handle whatever life threw at me. But when it came to relationships, I always needed and wanted as much of my partner's time as possible, relying on him for my entertainment and happiness. I'd get sucked into his world, abandoning mine, and demanding every moment of his attention—as much as I could get. So when I met Todd, my borderline insomniac tendencies kicked into overdrive, and I lay awake at night thinking about him. What is he doing right now? Who is he with? Is he thinking about me? It was a lot of work for my type A personality to plan and analyze (or more accurately, overplan and overanalyze), and all that thinking kept me up many nights.

As time went by, it didn't get better. It was a hard transition for me to be with a guy who spent so much of his time playing sports, hanging out with his friends, and watching every televised athletic event imaginable. I couldn't understand why he didn't want to be with me every spare moment. Eventually, I got used to the dynamics of our relationship, realizing that he was a guy's guy and I wouldn't always be his number one priority. But I still nagged and bugged him for more time, more attention. After the puppy love period ended, the early romantic gestures that had reeled me in ended too, and as our relationship solidified, I pestered him for more attempts at romance.

I always wondered what made Todd tick. I don't know if I'll ever figure it out. Sometimes it felt as if I knew him better than anyone in the world, and other times it was as if he were a complete stranger. Todd was always "that guy"—that guy who would walk into a room and all heads would turn. The crowds would part, and people would flock to him. I watched it happen at bars, weddings, family gatherings, sporting events; he was always a star. Even when he was growing up he was "that guy," doing well in school without even trying, always the star athlete and fierce competitor, attracting friends and girls without expending an ounce of effort.

I knew of Todd during high school, but I didn't know him. I remember thinking he was egotistical, as most spoiled golden boys are. He'd always disagree with me when I teased him about it.

"You just thought you were too good for me back then," I would joke.

He would just shake his head. "No, I really didn't." And that was probably the truth. He was just "that guy"—the spoiled kid who always got his way. The boyfriend who seemed to spend more time with his buddies than with me. But I got used to it and found ways to keep myself happy when he spent weekends at softball tournaments or dawn-to-dusk golfing. I still couldn't imagine anyone else being more perfect for me than Todd. We were like yin and yang, opposites in every way yet fitting together perfectly. This "oppositeness" was our strength—and sometimes our downfall. His laid-back, almost lazy attitude balanced out my take-charge behaviors, while my proactive planning balanced out his unscheduled, fly-by-the-seat-of-his-pants existence. And I don't think he'd experienced a moment of insomnia in his life. If he was horizontal or even slightly inclined, he could sleep and nothing could wake him. I heard stories about him falling asleep on tiny patches of floor during weekend softball tournaments. And at WE Fest, a huge outdoor country music festival, I once found him sleeping in a tent in the middle of the day where it had to have been over one hundred degrees with ninety percent humidity.

Todd and I brought out the best in each other and helped one another overcome our negative traits. At the same time, we drove each other nuts a lot of days. I couldn't stand his aggressive driving, and he couldn't stand my nagging about safety and traffic laws, both written and unwritten. I can't count the number of times we'd be in a full-on fight by the time we arrived at our destination. But mostly we kept it peaceful, each of us knowing we would be miserable without the other.

Because of our undeniable connection, we spent our weekends and most nights at one or the other's house. I had purchased my first home and he had purchased one with some friends as an investment. But despite our separate residences, we *needed* to be together if even for a few hours of sleep in between work and his sports leagues and outings with friends. We would lay awake long into the night watching movies, cuddling, and talking about our goals and dreams. And as time passed, our individual plans became more and more intertwined and soon, they were inextricably linked for the foreseeable future.

SEVEN

We sped down the freeway toward downtown Minneapolis and our favorite restaurant, Sophia, for our six o'clock dinner reservation. It was early July in 2004, and the air was heavy and damp with humidity. The late afternoon sun blazed down on the roadway, the air conditioning inside the car betraying our senses to the temperature outside. While he drove, Todd was uncharacteristically quiet.

"What's wrong?" I asked.

"Nothing, just excited for our night." He smiled, his blue eyes crinkling.

"What's going on? You're being a little mysterious." I eyed him suspiciously as he fiddled with the radio.

"What? I can't be excited to go out for dinner with my favorite person?"

I knew something was up, and his corny answer confirmed it. Then the events of the day started coming together in my mind, and I realized what was happening. Todd had mysteriously left my house in the middle of the afternoon for a "quick errand." He had been pacing and nervous all day. He had taken an especially long shower and gotten himself extra spiffed up for our night out, spending an additional five minutes on his hair and putting on a little more cologne than usual. And now he kept fidgeting and digging into his pants pocket. It could only mean one thing: He was going to propose tonight! After nearly three years of dating and plenty of waiting and hoping, the moment was finally here. We turned the corner, and I squinted as the sun slanted into the car. I hid my excitement, turning my gigantic grin away from him, pretending I was shielding my face from the glare. I could feel a crazy, teenaged-psycho-girl scream rising in me, but I held it back; I didn't want to change his mind before it even happened. Outside, I kept up a calm façade, but inside, I was squirming and jittery, wondering how he would do it.

We arrived at our destination, Todd parked the car in the garage, and we descended a stairway through the historic building that housed several restaurants. The smell of floor polish and years of musty wood and dust enveloped us, the summer heat bringing out the odors of the old building. These were soon countered by the pungent aromas from an Asian restaurant, and my stomach gurgled with hunger as we walked past. A moment later we entered the dark, gleaming, wood interior of Sophia. On one side of the room a long, polished bar welcomed those coming for a drink or quick bite. The middle of the space was dominated by a raised stage featuring a grand piano and several chairs for the night's live performance.

The hostess escorted us to one of the exquisitely set tables at the back of the restaurant and winked at Todd. I had seen that happen before. He was a good-looking guy that women flirted with often, even in front of me, but he typically didn't catch on to what was happening. Tonight, though, he shifted nervously in his chair, and I wondered if she was in on the proposal plan. As the evening went on, though, I began to wonder if I was wrong. I counted at least a hundred "perfect moments" when he could have done it, but we ate our meals, drank our wine, and talked—and nothing happened. When the bill came, I thought for sure the time had come, but he merely put down his credit card and stood up to go to the restroom. I was convinced I had been wrong and tonight wasn't the night. Todd returned to the table, looking happy again, his nerves seeming to have calmed.

"Let's go. I think I saw that a band is playing outside at a bar down the street." He held my hand and led me outside. From the dark interior of the restaurant we emerged onto the cobblestone streets that lined the Minneapolis riverfront where the Mississippi River flowed through the city, its domineering size powerful even from shore. We strolled the familiar street hand in hand as twilight and the faint sounds of music mixed with the rushing of the current along the riverbank settled around us. Todd pulled out his cell phone and started dialing.

"Who are you calling?" I asked, irritated that he needed to make a phone call during our romantic evening.

"I have to call someone quick." Todd said turning away from me as I heard a voice answer on the other end of the phone.

"Hi, Mark?" he said quietly with a tremble in his voice. Mark? He doesn't have any friends named Mark that I had ever met. My dad was Mark, but why would he call him? Wait a minute!

"It's Todd. I'm here with your daughter, and I have something important I need to ask her, but I wanted to check with you first to make sure it's okay."

I turned toward him, stunned. Was this really happening? After a minute of what I presumed to be my father giving his approval, Todd smiled and relaxed.

"Okay, will do. Thanks!" He turned to me and smiled shyly. "Well, you've known this was coming. It's taken me a while, but I've always known it would happen. So...." Todd took my left hand in his and slipped them both into his pocket where we grasped a small box. "Do you want to see it? I designed it myself."

That crazy-girl scream I had been struggling to contain finally erupted. "Aahhhh! Yes!" I squealed, drawing the attention of passers-by on the path. I couldn't see what was happening, but with both of our hands still in his pocket, I felt him pull the ring from the box, shift my left hand gently, and slide the ring onto my finger.

I pulled out my hand, and there it was—a perfect, sparkling diamond ring, exactly as I had always imagined my dream ring would look: antique-y, simple, elegant, and timeless. I bounced up and down, knowing I looked like a dork but not caring what anyone thought. My heart thumped, and Todd finally said it: "Will you marry me?"

I threw my arms around his neck, not caring how long I had been waiting for this moment because now that it was here, it was perfect. I looked down at the ring and up at his crazy-curly hair and blue eyes gazing at me with so much unconditional love.

"*Yes!*"

EIGHT

I had always dreamed of a Christmas wedding in Montevideo—the sparkling lights, the beautiful white snow, the festive atmosphere that awakens our senses and our spirits. Happily, Todd shared my enthusiasm for the idea. But having already waited three years to get engaged, I wasn't waiting another year and a half to get married. No way! Immediately after Todd's proposal, everything went into overdrive as we planned a wedding for just five months later.

Todd really only cared if there was a bar and good food so the planning of the décor and theme were left to me. It was a beautiful, if somewhat gaudy, winter wonderland that I created for our reception at the Hunt Bar and Grill, where we had met three years before. I wanted to capitalize on an already beautiful time of year and let it complement our marriage celebration, so I went crazy with holiday decorations, going as far as to include multiple full-size Christmas trees. Everything was red, gold, and ivory with a lot of pine garland. It may have bordered on tacky, but we both loved it.

The morning of the wedding, December 18, I awoke early, a bundle of nerves and happiness. At about nine o'clock I ventured out from my warm hotel suite into the frigid cold to get my hair done and returned a couple of hours later to relax. My personal attendant had given me a bag of goodies, and late morning I raided it for snacks, cracking open the energy drink she had included for a little extra boost. I had never had an energy drink before. I don't drink coffee and rarely drink soda except for the occasional Diet Coke because caffeine does things to my system that aren't pleasant. So I don't know what I was thinking, slamming down a caffeine-laden, sugar-filled beverage on the biggest day of my life.

Within fifteen minutes, I started sweating and felt my stomach churning. Not making the connection with the energy drink, I assumed it was just anxiety. But as I lay on the couch, the symptoms escalated and—well, I'll spare you the details, but I was in the bathroom every twenty minutes for the next six hours. But I sucked it up and enjoyed every minute of our wedding day. I was the happiest I could remember ever being and wasn't going to let a little thing like stomach problems ruin my day.

Before going to the church, Todd and I met for my wedding gown reveal at the Hunt in front of one of the Christmas trees I had brought in for the occasion. As Todd stood in his tuxedo with his back to me, I walked into the room in my form-fitting, ivory lace and beaded dress and veil. I'd never felt more beautiful in my life, and when Todd turned toward me, I'd never seen him look more handsome. The Christmas trees and holiday decorations and the photographer all receded into the background, and we hugged each other, realizing we weren't just having a wedding but were marrying our other half.

At the church, and throughout the ceremony and reception (and between my trips to the bathroom), I felt completely at peace, happy and content. I knew my life was finally starting with the man I wanted to be with forever, the man who would father my children, the man I'd grow old with, the man who would be by my side until death do us part. As I walked down the aisle, my nerves disappeared as I approached Todd and our lives began as husband and wife.

NINE

Todd and I spent the first year of our marriage traveling and having fun together, but I felt like something was missing. I could hear my biological clock ticking every time I passed a pregnant woman in the hallway at work or on the street, or saw a baby in the grocery store. Todd seemed ready too. We talked about kids often—we both wanted three—and when that clock and our conversations couldn't be silenced, we knew it was time to start our family.

At first we were casual about it, not really trying but not preventing it either. But inside, I was ready; I wanted to get pregnant more than I had ever wanted anything. We had planned a March trip to Mexico with some friends and decided we would officially start trying to get pregnant after that. But apparently, margaritas, jet skis, and sunburns are the right mix for baby making. Nine months later, our daughter was born.

I never truly understood the words *home* and *family* until Brooke arrived on December 1, 2006—exactly halfway between Todd's and my birthdays. She made us into a family, permanently connecting the three of us by her simple arrival—and through her DNA. She is a Sagittarius, one of the fire signs, befitting her entrance into this world and her existence so far. At 7:05 p.m. she was still physically a part of me; at 7:06, after one last, painful push, her tiny lungs screamed to the world that she was here.

"She's so cute," I said as the doctor laid her slimy body on my chest.

"Look at her little fingers," Todd whispered with tears in his eyes. "She's adorable."

Of course she was. She was our baby, so precious to us. A miniature, blue-eyed cherub with a perfectly round little head covered in white fuzz that was barely discernible as hair.

From that moment on, my life was all about her well being and happiness, my livelihood "lively" because of her existence. Not that those first few months after she was born were easy. Although I didn't have to struggle with balancing motherhood and a career for the three months I was on maternity leave, it was still the most difficult time of my life. I was surprised at how challenging it was for us as a couple to navigate life with someone else as our focus. For me, it felt like a never-ending rollercoaster ride as I veered between the high of watching her grow and develop and the low of constantly arguing with Todd—mostly over his spending time away from us to watch or play sports and be with his friends.

Todd was a great dad when he was with Brooke, always greeting her when he got home from work by sneaking to the top of the steps and playing peek-a-boo. He was good with her when I was around, less confident when I wasn't, but seemed willing to learn about fatherhood and the steps involved in caring for an infant. I tried to teach him without being bossy, using my previous nanny and day care experience to impart the knowledge he needed. Maybe he felt like I was preaching to him, or there was just too much information for him to absorb so quickly. Whatever it was, I struggled getting him to fully engage, and several times he made choices that completely confounded me.

When Brooke was only two or three months old, Todd went out of town with friends for a golf trip. Brooke got sick with a high fever and ended up in the emergency room in the middle of the night, but instead of coming home, Todd opted to stay with his friends. A few months later, Brooke had to go to the emergency room again for another high fever and congestion. It was 1 a.m., and Todd was scheduled to leave for another two-day golf outing that morning. He accompanied me to the hospital, and I assumed he would cancel his trip. But when we arrived home at five o'clock—after driving around for two hours in desperate search of an all-night pharmacy—he packed his bag and left, leaving me to care for our very sick infant daughter.

I started questioning our viability as a married couple. I just couldn't understand why Todd didn't want to be with his family. He didn't seem to want to take responsibility as a husband sharing duties for parenting and needed constant reminders or he would forget the simplest requests. I didn't have the energy to take care of two kids, which is what it often felt like.

The sleepless nights that most parents face after the birth of a baby were most definitely a reality—for me, anyway. Todd's ability to sleep through anything continued, and rarely did he awaken when Brooke cried needing food, a diaper change, or a cuddle, even when she slept in the same room as us. And the more tired I became, the more my annoyance with him grew; my nagging increased, and my expectations of him started wearing both of us down.

So Todd retreated. He became quieter and more solitary, spending hours alone in his basement bachelor den, watching sports.

I had often heard about couples whose relationships went downhill after they had a child. They didn't get along as well, they would fight about money, and the kids took up all of their time, leaving them exhausted and without enough time for each other. I never thought that would happen to Todd and me, but after Brooke was born we started to grow apart. We became strangers living together under the same roof, feeding the same dog, caring for the same child, but not caring for each other. I knew that I still loved him, though, and that our paths would change. I was certain that once the stress of new parenthood wore off, we would find our way back to each other.

TEN

It was August. My younger sister, Audrey, was getting married in early September, and I was her maid of honor, planning the showers, my dress fittings, and the all-important bachelorette party. To my horror, Audrey wanted to go dancing for her party. As an ungraceful, world-class klutz, I assure you that dancing is not my strong suit; in fact, it isn't even a weak suit. On a scale of one to ten, with one being Urkle and ten a "Dancing with the Stars" champion, I rate a negative five. So when Audrey suggested the partiers take a dance class together before going out on the town, I felt a little relieved, thinking that would be a good way to alleviate my fears of embarrassing myself. But when I read the description for the class she selected, I didn't know whether to laugh or cry:

This will be an evening you will never forget! With a club-like atmosphere and state-of-the-art sound system, our sensual and spacious studio has eleven dance poles to accommodate up to 25 guests. Get ready to learn some hot new moves and dance the night away! Includes a 1-hour private party, warm-up and stretch, and striptease and pole dance lesson.

Umm, what? Striptease and pole dance lesson? Not only do I not dance, but I've never felt especially seductive or sexy—so I was about to be completely out of my element. Todd, of course, loved the idea, thinking he would benefit in some way despite my having zero intention of using any pole dance moves in real life.

When the day of the party arrived, I strategized with my sister about wardrobe options for the evening. After registering for the dance class we had received some follow-up information saying we could bring wine and beer (thank god!) and any type of clothing that made us feel comfortable and "in the mood" for the class. As Audrey and I discussed our clothing selections over the phone, we got the giggles.

"Do a big, old T-shirt and capri sweatpants count?" I asked, digging through my closet.

"I don't think so, but how about a button-down plaid shirt that I've had since eighth grade and some tight-rolled jeans?" I could hear her opening and shutting her dresser drawers.

"Ooohhh, I've got it—these are perfect!" I pulled out the black patent leather, pointy-toed, stiletto boots I'd purchased in Germany several years before but had only worn a handful of times since.

"What is it?" Audrey asked curiously.

"Not telling; you'll just have to wait and see." As I hung up the phone I spied a pink feather boa that I'd bought for a costume party and shoved it into a bag with the boots, then headed to the kitchen to add a few bottles of wine and some snacks.

When we arrived at the studio, we encountered an unmarked security door where we had to buzz to be let in. Really? Is that much protection needed for a dance studio? We proceeded up a narrow flight of stairs into a brightly lit reception area where a skinny blonde receptionist sat at a desk. In a way-too-over-rehearsed voice, she said, "Hi and welcome. Please sign in and fill out a waiver form, then feel free to come on back to our lounge area and kitchen to hang out. You have an hour of relaxation time in the lounge, and your class will start after that." A waiver form? I knew I was injury-prone and figured if someone was going to get hurt in a dance class, it was even more likely to occur when a pole was involved. I signed the release and entered the lounge area. It was a comfortable space of leather chairs and couches with a small adjoining kitchen in which to set up our drinks and snacks.

I needed to get some wine in me if I was going to enjoy this dance debacle even a little bit, so I opened a few bottles and brought them out to the group of my sister's friends. Apparently we were all in the same mindset because we went through several bottles in that hour as we laughed and mentally prepared for what was about to occur. To get us "in the mood" for a striptease and pole dancing class, a monitor played Pussycat Dolls music videos, and a stack of *Playgirl* magazines lay on a table nearby—and actually, it worked. Well, the Pussycat Dolls music did, but not the *Playgirls*. After a minute of paging through them, we all decided they could stay on the table out of sight. By the time the instructor popped her head through the door and said, "Five-minute warning, girls," we were all tapping our feet and ready to go—maybe from the music, maybe from the wine, maybe a little of both.

We entered the dimly lit studio, and immediately I became self-conscious. The mirrored walls reflected the eleven stripper poles permanently installed throughout the room. No space was safe or hidden from view. I had seen poles in movies and caught glimpses of them through the doorways of strip clubs when quickly walking past, but never had I seen one up close, let alone made actual physical contact with one. Everyone scattered to the perimeter of the room, as if in fear of the poles, and I wondered how so many of us would be able to navigate just eleven of them.

I opened my bag and pulled out my boa and patent leather boots. "Audrey, here are my stripper shoes," I called to my sister, holding them up for everyone to see.

"Oh my god," several of the girls yelled back. "Those are awesome!" Just then the instructor walked in, a curvy, tall brunette oozing confidence in a skintight, black leotard and black stilettos. She gestured towards a shelf on the far wall that housed a variety of high heels.

"Pick out some shoes to get you in the mood," she directed. I had my boots, so I hung back as everyone else tentatively edged towards the shelf, clearly a bit apprehensive about donning the six-inch clear Lucite heels. After laughing and trying them on, they hobbled in their ankle-breakers back to the poles.

Because there were more of us than there were poles, some of us were forced to double up (all men reading this, quit fantasizing!). I shared a pole with my sister's soon-to-be sister-in-law, Lana, whom I discovered was as apprehensive as I was. I approached the pole, getting my first look at it up close. It was smeared with finger- and handprints, and I felt disgusted imagining all the other hands and bodies that had grabbed and spun around it. Like a true uptight prude, I used the edge of my T-shirt to wipe the pole off—as if that would actually help. Lana seemed to have the same abhorrence to it, but we both took a deep breath and mounted that pole like we were professionals. I don't know if I've ever laughed as hard as I did for that hour while we gyrated and grooved to the song "Umbrella" by Rihanna. The first half of class was devoted to learning how to work the pole, integrating arm twists, leg gyrations, and full body spins. I know those aren't the stripper-correct terms for the moves we did, but I was laughing so hard at my own unsexiness that I missed the actual names.

The second half of the class focused on lap dances, with my sister the bachelorette serving as the lap-ee and the rest of us designated to take turns as the lap-ers. The instructor demonstrated the moves first, using my sister as her seduction target—and holding nothing back. Audrey was obviously uncomfortable but was a good sport. She clearly did not expect to have a spandex-clad butt an inch from her face. I have photos of this scene, and my sister's expression is a mixture of fear, amusement, shock, and disgust as she leans back into the chair, trying to put as much distance between her face and the instructor's ass as possible.

While the whole experience was a bit mortifying, it was also a lot of fun as we were all pushed out of our comfort zones. We learned a little about that world of stripper poles and lap dances that we thought existed only in the inner sanctums of the strip clubs downtown or in the bedrooms of those confident, sex-crazed couples you see in movies. But after that class, I realized that anyone could use the tactics we learned, even if only for a good laugh. (And now every time I hear the song "Umbrella," I mentally do the routine in my head, while people around me wonder why I'm laughing so hard.)

That night when I got home, Todd was lying in bed, watching a game on TV. "How was the party?" he asked as I sat at the edge of the bed, pulling off my shoes.

"Well, I learned a few good moves at the stripper class."

"Oh yeah, that's what I'm talkin' about; let's see 'em!" He sat up, grinning.

"No frickin' way. You know my skills at dancing suck; I am not doing it." I started walking out of the room towards the bathroom.

"You just have to have confidence. You're a good dancer, but you get too nervous." I could hear the hope in his voice and knew he was being playful, but I was already in the bathroom and had no intention of demonstrating the moves I had learned. He always said the same thing whenever I'd complain about how awful I was at dancing and how I had no rhythm: Just have confidence. Well, that was easy for him to say—he was a fantastic dancer. Todd could spin people around the dance floor like a professional, and he loved the show "So You Think You Can Dance"—although he'd never admit that to his male friends. I know he wished I would have just let my lack of confidence go and danced when he encouraged it, and now I wish I had too—especially that night. Why didn't I do a private dance for my husband? It would have made him so happy. But my self-consciousness and selfishness took over, and I will always regret that.

ELEVEN

A week before Audrey and Matt's wedding, I turned thirty-one. Todd and I were on our way to downtown Minneapolis for my birthday dinner at Fogo de Chao—a predominantly meat-based, Brazilian restaurant, so it should have been a dream night for me. But we had spent the day helping my parents move into a new townhouse, and between that and the stress of parenting, wedding planning, and feeling older, I was tired and crabby. Instead of being thankful and happy that Todd was taking me out to celebrate, I was acting like a child, pouting as we left the house. Merging from one highway onto another, Todd pulled one of his common driving moves, accelerating way too fast past several slow-moving cars in the right lane and then at the last minute pulling in front of them to exit the highway.

"Why would you do that? What did it save you—like three seconds?" I sniped at him, turning our dinner outing into a battleground.

"What's the big deal?" he responded—one of his most frequently used phrases.

"Really? Was it necessary to cut off those other drivers and cause a near accident? It's rude and dangerous." A lump formed in my throat; I knew where this was going, but I felt helpless to stop it.

We drove the rest of the way in silence, and when we got to the restaurant we ate with barely a word passing between us. After our meal as we waited at the valet stand for the car, Todd broke the silence.

"Look, there's Joe Johnson." He pointed to a group of middle-aged men smoking by the valet stand. I had no idea who he was talking about.

"So?" I snapped back, rolling my eyes and turning away instead of being nice and asking who Joe Johnson was.

"He's an old Twins baseball player. It's just kind of cool to see him out and about."

I could tell that Todd was taken aback by my uncalled-for nastiness, but I didn't relent. "Like I'd care about a sports star." I was being an ungrateful brat after he had taken me out for my birthday. That was a common occurrence with us—a small thing turned into a big thing that would ruin our alone time together.

When I woke up the next day I felt bad that I had been so crabby to Todd the night before. We had a rare Saturday night out without the baby, it was my birthday, we were going to a new restaurant and I had ruined everything with my crankiness and stubbornness. So I decided to make it up to him and serve him breakfast in bed. Since the beginning of our relationship, I had always made sure that Sundays were "Todd's day" to do what he wanted—watch football, nap, or play golf. I almost always made him breakfast in bed on Sundays. He would smile when I'd walk in with the tray of food, read the sports page while eating, then curl back up for another couple hours of sleep. I was usually the romantic one in our relationship; Todd wasn't very good at the grand romantic gesture. I didn't have a "Kristen day," but he would bring me tulips often, even in winter when I knew it killed him to spend the extra money for an out-of-season flower.

That morning, I cooked him bacon and eggs and brought it to his bedside. It seemed to bring some peace between us, and as the day progressed we found a calm place again and even went to the movies that night. But although we weren't sniping at each other anymore, the next few days were tense. My sister's wedding was that weekend, and I was getting ready to leave for Detroit Lakes with my mom to help with preparations; Todd would make the three-hour drive north with Brooke and my dad a couple of days later. In the days before I left we barely spoke, hardly even looked at each other. When he went to work the morning of my departure, we didn't hug and kiss goodbye like we had done almost every day since we met. Since Brooke was born the hugs had gotten fewer and farther between. The kisses were nonexistent. We were drifting. It worried me, but I figured I could fix that later. I had to focus on the wedding first.

THE END

"What a day may bring, a day may take away."
—Thomas Fuller

TWELVE

Saturday, September 8, 2007

"Man, I'm stiff and sore today," Todd complains. He turns over, sits up slowly, and stretches his legs off the side of the hotel pullout's mattress. I roll my eyes.

"Maybe it's because you slept too long," I say in an exasperated tone. I have been up for a couple of hours already, tending to Brooke, and I'm tired and annoyed.

"It must have been this damn pullout." He stretches his body from side to side, willing the knots and stiffness out of his back and shoulders. It's true. Like most sofa beds, this one has deep ravines and poorly placed metal bars that shimmy our bones and joints into unnatural curves and bends as we sleep.

"Can you take Brooke? I need to finish getting ready." I'm telling more than asking as I hand her to Todd. He pulls her close for a morning cuddle and kiss, and I turn, stepping over the toys strewn about the hotel room floor and going into the bathroom to finish primping for Audrey and Matt's wedding day. Unzipping my makeup bag, I hear the television click on, and the all-too-familiar theme of ESPN's *SportsCenter* meets my ears. That music grates on my nerves every time I hear it—which is at least once a day. I kick shut the bathroom door to block the commentator's voice and go back to applying my make-up, being sure to accentuate my brown eyes—my "good features" as I've been told. I'm about to get my hair done up in a style I found in a celebrity gossip magazine. It was a picture of Jessica Alba with rolled ringlets all around her head—very big and complicated. I don't know why I think a small-town hairstylist will be able to pull it off, but I'm willing to take my chances. After finishing my make-up, I grab my raincoat, purse, and the Jessica Alba inspiration picture, give Brooke a kiss goodbye, and start issuing commands to Todd.

"Don't forget to feed her a midmorning snack, and if you go to the pool be sure not to get too much water in her mouth. And give her a bath before you get dressed to come to the wedding if I miss you when I get back. And don't be late for the pictures. Her dress is hanging in the closet, and her tights and shoes are in her bag. And make sure there are plenty of diapers and her bottle supplies in the diaper bag when you come." Now it's his turn to roll his eyes at me as I spout off instructions as if I'm leaving Brooke with a babysitter instead of her daddy. But if I don't remind him, he'll forget. I've learned that the hard way over our six years of courtship and marriage.

Audrey and I go to the salon, and my hair looks a little bit more like Medusa than a celebrity, but what did I expect? A few hours later, we return to the hotel to finish getting dressed before going to the church for pictures. I am exhausted from being up so early with the baby but have to rally to support my sister on this important day. Todd's in our room with Brooke. They have just come back from the pool, and he's feeding her lunch.

"Todd, make sure you don't give her too big pieces. And make sure her cereal and fruit are mixed up well but not too thin." As usual, I'm assuming he won't do it right.

"Yeah, yeah, I know," he replies in an exasperated tone. "I've done it plenty of times. I know how to feed her."

I feel my shoulders tense as another exchange between us escalates into a silly spat within moments—our modus operandi lately. "Fine. Just make sure the pieces aren't so big that she chokes."

Todd shakes his head, turns back to Brooke, and continues offering her the bread, cheese, cereal, and fruit from her plate.

I walk into the adjoining room where I had moved all of my bags earlier that morning, gather up my dress, shoes, and jewelry, and go into the bathroom to change for our afternoon and evening of pictures and wedding festivities. The dress is Dupioni silk, strapless and knee-length, pale aqua with a brown organza sash that ties in a knot on the hip. I love it and know I will wear it again, unlike most bridesmaid dresses out there.

When I come out, Todd whistles. "Hot stuff!"

"Yeah, right. I've still got baby weight, and my hair looks like a helmet." I shake my not-quite-Jessica-Alba-styled head while fiddling with the bow on the dress.

"I think you are smokin' hot." It's the trademark compliment he always gives me when I dress up, but in my mind it's usually an exaggeration. He spanks me on the butt as I come over to give Brooke a hug.

Audrey walks into the room. "I'm ready to put on my dress," she says. "Can you come and help?"

I grab my bags to follow her out. "Bye, Brookie. See you at the church for pictures." I rub her fuzzy head. "Todd, don't forget all of her supplies and a change of clothes for later after the reception. Everything is all laid out by her diaper bag." I close the door behind me.

At the church, I stand for pictures with the rest of the wedding party, and then Todd and Brooke arrive for the family portion of the shoot. Brooke looks like a little doll decked out in cream and brown silk with her almost-bald head. I promised myself I would never dress her in such obnoxious and impractical baby fashion, but here she is in a non-machine-washable frock that cost more than most of the clothing in my own wardrobe. But she looks adorable. And Todd is handsome as always, his tall, lean frame accentuated by his sharp, navy blue suit. He always looks great in formal wear, and seeing him reminds me of our wedding day just three years ago. It had been one of the best days of our lives, second only to the day Brooke was born, and we often talk about it and how glad we are that we ended up together.

As I think about our own big day, the annoyance I felt with Todd earlier this morning disappears. I look at him and Brooke and feel happy we're all together, excited about what lies ahead for us. Despite the challenges and frustrations we've had with each other, Todd and I have been talking about trying for another baby next summer, and I'm eager to give Brooke a sibling and add another child to our family—maybe even two more. I've always wanted three kids, and although Todd is on the fence about that, I know he'll want to try for a boy he can mold into his mini-me athlete—so at least one more child is in the cards for us. At this moment, posing for pictures before my sister's wedding, I feel secure in what our future holds: no questions, no doubts, just a clearly laid-out plan we will follow until Todd and I walk our kids down the aisle at their own weddings—after which we will spend our retirement traveling and spending time with them and our grandchildren. It's a sixty-year plan, and we are only six years in; ninety percent of our lives together left to go.

After pictures, Todd and Brooke go out to mingle with the arriving guests in the entryway while I head downstairs with the rest of the wedding party to await the processional. The music starts, and I am again reminded of my own wedding day, of Todd standing at the altar, waiting for me to walk down the aisle to him. Today, he is in the congregation, holding our daughter as I come down the aisle as maid of honor. I smile at them as I pass, and Todd winks back. I know he too is thinking about our wedding.

I stand near my sister, holding her flowers as she recites her vows and exchanges rings with Matt. I think about my relationship with Todd and how it has somehow deteriorated over the last few months. The happiness and excitement of a few moments before are tempered by feelings of sadness and regret. I don't want us to continue as we are now. I have to change things. I have to make sure we don't become one of those couples who end up as a divorce statistic, sharing visitation rights for our child, fighting over our house, dog, and possessions, and always wondering why things didn't work out. I catch his eye and smile, determined to get us back to where we had been in the early days, each doing our part to make the other happy. I know we can have that again; we just need to make an effort and take time to reconnect.

After the wedding ceremony, a bus takes the wedding party barhopping before the reception. Todd leaves Brooke in the care of relatives and joins us. It feels just like old times. We hold hands, laugh, tease each other, and have some drinks, relaxing and getting along like we used to. Climbing back onto the bus to go to the reception, I vow to myself: From this moment on, things will be different. When we get back home, I am going to do everything in my power to make things right again. I will give Todd the space that he needs to do what he wants to do so that he doesn't feel smothered or trapped, and I'm going to help him understand that I need to feel like I'm a priority to him. I am going to work my damndest to be the best wife and the best mom I can be to Todd and Brooke so they will always know how much I love them. I will never have any regrets over my relationships with either of them.

We arrive at the reception and immediately go find Brooke. Todd watches her while I go about my maid of honor duties—giving my toast, running the photo slideshow, and making sure everything is going smoothly so that Audrey doesn't stress out. Once my official duties are over, all I have to do is relax and enjoy the rest of the evening. But now I am so exhausted I don't have the energy to even stand up anymore. My feet hurt. My head hurts. All I want to do is go back to the hotel. Brooke left with relatives earlier, and I decide to join her. No one will miss me; this evening isn't about me. I find Todd on the dance floor, his typical location at wedding receptions. I pull him aside.

"I'm going to get Brooke at the hotel and go back to our room. I'm exhausted." I tug at my dress, which has started to feel uncomfortable.

"Should I come with you?" He takes a sip of his whiskey and Coke.

"No, no, stay and have fun. We'll be fine."

"Are you sure? You won't be pissed if I stay?" He questions me suspiciously, not used to my being so agreeable.

"No, just stay and have fun." I hope he'll change his mind and come back to the hotel without my having to ask for his attention and time, but I know he won't.

"Okay, see you later." He turns away, walks back to the crowded dance floor, and melts into the crowd. I can see his blonde head above the other dancers for a moment, then he disappears from my view.

I turn to leave, feeling bitter because Todd had chosen to stay, and feeling guilty because I have chosen to go. Oh how I wish we had both chosen differently.

THIRTEEN

Sunday, September 9, 2007

I hear the door to the adjoining hotel room open. Rolling over, I glance at the alarm clock. Two a.m. Voices come from the next room, each fighting to be the loudest. I've been asleep for only a couple of hours, but not deeply, just dozing like I always do when Todd is out. I have to know he's safely back before I can fully relax.

The door to our side of the suite creaks open, and Todd enters the room. I think he might pull his typical late-night-out habit of crawling into bed, waking me up, and wanting to talk about his outing or fool around, but he doesn't. A few seconds later he leaves, the door closes, and I am left in silence, feeling relieved. Relieved that he's back and relieved that he's chosen to sleep next door so he doesn't wake Brooke or me. I snuggle deeper under the covers and go back to sleep, unaware and uninterested in where Todd is sleeping in the next room, just glad he's there.

A few hours later, I awake to Brooke's hungry whine that will only intensify if I don't feed her right away. I make my way through the dark to the door connecting my room with the one where Todd, my parents, and my younger brother James are sleeping. Brooke's formula is in their refrigerator. I knock, hoping for a quick response, but no one answers. My back tenses up. I knock louder. Still no answer. I know they got back late. I know they're hung over from the typical wedding dance drink-fest. But seriously, can no one hear me knocking? My fist is throbbing from pounding so hard, so I resort to kicking the door, rage rising in my chest. After several fruitless minutes, I give up. I'll have to brave the cold and get the backup bottles and formula from the car. I throw a pashmina over my pajamas, wrap Brooke in a blanket, and take her outside.

It's just before sunrise, and the world is dark and still, the air thick with mist. I feel like I am in a dream state. I pull the blanket tighter around Brooke as the chill penetrates my lightweight clothes. I spot our SUV, its gray exterior the same color as the muddy parking lot and the damp, murky sky. I open the rear hatch and manage to balance the metal formula cans, a bag of bottles, and Brooke without dropping anything. Retracing my path, I return to the hotel room to calm Brooke's hunger and my agitation.

After she finishes her bottle, I go about the mundane business of getting ready for our drive home to Minneapolis. I've been in Detroit Lakes since Wednesday and am looking forward to returning to some normalcy and a regular schedule again. I haven't forgotten my resolve to work on my relationship with Todd and get us back to a good place. Brooke plays on the floor, and I pack our suitcases and bags. I put her fancy silk dress on a hanger, adding it to the plastic garment bag where I hung my bridesmaid dress the night before. In the bathroom I find at least fifty bobby pins that had held my hair in place, with strands of my hair stuck in them. I slide the pins into my makeup bag, not sure when I will ever need that many again, but not wanting to leave anything behind either.

When I'm nearly finished packing, the door to the adjoining hotel room finally opens. I shoot an evil glare in its direction, aiming at whoever is unlucky enough to walk in—all occupants of that room deserving of my anger for not hearing me earlier and forcing Brooke and me into the cold.

My mom comes in fully dressed, chipper as always. "Should we go down and get some breakfast?" She scoops Brooke into her arms.

"Really? That's all you have to say? Didn't you hear me knocking earlier?" The annoyance in my voice is obvious as I stuff the last of my clothes into my open suitcase on the bed.

"What? No, I didn't hear a thing. What did you need?" she innocently replies, bouncing Brooke on her hip.

"Only Brooke's formula and bottles. I had to tote her outside to the car in the dark and the cold to get the backups."

"Sorry, I didn't hear you. But James and his buddy are sleeping right in there on the pullout where you and Todd slept last night. I'm surprised they didn't hear you either." She's still not grasping that I'm peeved.

"Yeah, me too," I respond sarcastically. I grab the room key, and we head downstairs to get breakfast.

Brooke destroys a piece of toast, and I devour a bowl of cereal, starving after the long night before and the morning so far. "How did you guys get back last night?" I ask my mom as we eat.

"We took the shuttle bus and then hung out downstairs in the party room for awhile." She brushes toast crumbs from Brooke's chin.

"How was everyone? Super drunk? Under control?" I'm not sure if I really want to know the answer. Todd has a tendency to overdrink at shindigs like this, especially when I'm not around.

"No, everyone seemed fine. We got back to the room and went to sleep. But Todd sure snores. I heard him making some crazy sounds this morning."

"I know. He's bad. He doesn't normally snore, but he always does when he drinks. Was he as bad as Dad?" I snicker, knowing my mom has to put up with my father's obnoxious bedtime noises every night.

We finish our breakfast and head back upstairs so Brooke can take her morning nap before we have to check out of the hotel. We enter through the other side of the suite. The room is dark, but through the veiled light of the window shade I see my dad sleeping in one bed, Todd in the other, and James and his friend on the sofa bed. I gaze at Todd, his mouth slightly ajar with his typical nighttime look. I feel slightly annoyed that he's still in bed while I've been up for hours taking care of the baby, but I expected nothing else and decide to let him sleep in, serious about implementing my vow not to be so demanding of him. Plus, he's going to be driving us home, so the least I can do is let him get his rest. I walk by, Brooke perched on my hip, and jiggle his foot. "Brookie, look at Daddy. He is out! He looks dead." I navigate through the duffel bags, clothes, shoes, and boxes of wedding paraphernalia scattered throughout the room, past James and his buddy, both still clothed, the odor of a brewery wafting from their sleeping forms. I can't help feeling a little envious of their carefree existence with no real responsibilities yet. Brooke and I lie down on the bed, and I fall asleep almost immediately, knowing that everyone is where they're supposed to be.

* * *

I'm snapped awake by my mother's voice yelling frantically. My body tenses, and I know something is wrong before I hear her next words.

"Todd! Todd, it's time to get up. Todd! *Todd*! Oh my god, Mark … call an ambulance!"

"Todd! Todd! *Todd*!"

I spring to life, quickly glancing at Brooke still asleep beside me. I run toward the shouting. My heart is pounding, my mind is racing. What's happening? What's wrong? I charge through the doorway to where Todd is lying, looking just as he had when I touched his foot an hour before.

"Kristen—he's gone," my dad murmurs.

I stare dumbfounded at Todd, trying to absorb the situation; then I go into autopilot. "Someone go sit by Brooke so she doesn't roll off the bed. Did you call an ambulance?" I move toward the figure of my husband, lying just as silent and still as Brooke had been when I left her a moment ago.

I scramble across the bed to Todd's side, tip his head back, listening for breath, pry his mouth open to check for anything that might be blocking his throat, put my ear to his chest, praying for a heartbeat, any sign of life in my husband's body. But there is no response. Nothing.

Audrey rushes in. "No, no, Todd, no!" She flings herself onto the bed, her fingers covered with the wedding cake frosting she had been tasting with her new husband just a moment before. I mourn for both of us as the happy memories of the previous night are replaced by this horrific scene. Her life is just beginning while mine as I've known it is ending.

The paramedics arrive, hauling equipment and clearing a space on the floor, and a momentary glimmer of hope spikes through me. Todd is only thirty years old. Surely they can save him.

"Did anyone perform CPR?" one of them asks. No one answers because no one has, somehow understanding that it won't make a difference in the outcome; yet I'm still holding out hope. They lift Todd's body off the bed, and the comforter slides off to reveal urine-soaked sheets. I see his bare legs and arms, his pale body mottled with blood. I feel my stomach flip and I swallow, holding back the vomit that threatens to emerge. The premed classes I took years ago come back to me at this moment, and I remember the term "pooling"—when a body lies dead for a period of time and the blood settles into the lowest points.

Something shifts inside of me, and I know that I am looking at a dead man. My husband is dead. His body is slack and lifeless. It does not respond as the paramedics begin forcing air into his lungs. It's too late; he can't be saved. My eyes sting with tears as I try to comprehend what is happening. Todd is no longer alive, and there is no hope of reviving him.

"We need to clear the room," one of the paramedics commands.

"I'm his wife. I'm not leaving him." I cross my arms across my body, unconsciously trying to hold myself up. I sit heavily on the bed, four feet from Todd yet feeling as far away from him as I've ever felt. I sit there in a stupor, watching silently as they try to breathe life into an already dead body. I don't cry. I don't yell. I just sit there in disbelief, watching every pump of the paramedics' hands and every breath they give him artificially raise and lower his chest. Shock overcomes me, and I am paralyzed on the corner of the hotel bed in which he was lying just moments ago—where he'd been sleeping just hours before. I look at the bed—the wet mattress, the tangled sheets—and feel a scream gather in my chest, panic threaten my breath. What is happening? The mattress still shows the contours of his body. The pillow still has the imprint of his head.

The scream rises to my throat. A paramedic asks, "Was he diabetic? Did he have sleep apnea?"

"No," is all I manage to say. Inside, I'm shouting, "No, he had zero health problems and no previous symptoms. What the hell is happening?" The scream is now in my mouth, and as it is about to escape, I feel my body get heavy. I go completely numb, my brain clicking off to protect me and keep me from self-destructing.

Todd's silence is punctuated only by my own—silence from shock and pure horror as reality sets in and I see my husband, my best friend, my soul mate, lifeless on a hotel room floor, his body limp, his spirit already gone.

* * *

What would I do if I had to relive that experience? Would I again sit silently, glued to the corner of that bed, watching, not able to make a sound, or would I scream in pain as that terrible scene played out in front of me?

I can't count how many times since that day I've wished I had taken that pillow where he dreamed his last dreams and breathed his last breaths. Or how many times I've written and talked to Todd about how he left this world.

Todd, what were you dreaming in those last moments before you died? I hope you were dreaming something good, something to usher you out of this life on a hopeful note. I hope you didn't suffer—or wake up knowing that something was wrong but unable to call for help. I will always regret not calling for you when you came home that night. Instead, I continued sleeping, oblivious to your spirit ebbing away just twenty feet from me.

* * *

The paramedics wheel Todd out on a stretcher and ask me to go to the hospital. No one says it is to identify the body, but my gut and heart tell me that's what I have to do. My dad stays with Brooke, and my mom and I walk to the elevator. People line the hallway and stand in doorways, gaping at us. I feel like I'm in a time warp with no sound, just blurry streaks of light, jumbled faces, arms reaching out to pat my shoulder.

I make my way outside, unsure of what I'm supposed to do next. My throat remains tight, holding back the scream that still threatens to erupt. As we drive to the hospital, I have no feeling, no reaction. I don't say a word, just hold my purse on my lap, try not to throw up, try to absorb what is happening, the taut straps of the seatbelt all that keep me upright.

We walk into the frigid emergency room. The nurses and doctors look at me in pity. I know Todd is officially gone. I knew he was dead in the hotel room, but I thought and hoped that some medical miracle would occur and the machines and drugs might conjure him back to life, even for a few minutes so I could have a last goodbye. But that was just a fantasy; reality slaps me in the face as a nurse ushers me to a room to see him. She pulls back the white curtain. Todd is lying on the stretcher, looking like he is asleep, but with tubes in his arms and throat.

"We can't remove the tubes and equipment yet. He was so young, and we need to investigate his death more thoroughly. The office in St. Paul will do an autopsy later this week and hopefully find out more."

It's all so surreal. I touch his hair. He feels alive—so warm and soft. I can smell him, that familiar, yummy, sexy scent of his cologne mixed with deodorant, soap, and skin. But he is dead. On a September Sunday morning, in a heartbeat, he was gone.

I don't know why, but I feel compelled to make the calls to his family and friends myself. I have to break the news even though I haven't absorbed it fully.

"Come with me. I'll get you a phone. Do you need any water or coffee?" The social worker from the hospital leads my mom and me to a room with a phone and a recliner. She and the nurses hover, not sure what this young widow is going to do, not sure if I'll start screaming and become violent, or fall to my knees crying and helpless. But I am numb. The numbness is what allows me to deliver the worst news any parent or sibling can ever receive.

I don't know what compels me to do this, but first I call Todd's parents' best friends. "Joel? It's Kristen Brown. Can you go to the Browns' right now? I have to call them and give them some very bad news and don't want them to be alone."

"What happened? Is everything okay?"

"Todd died this morning, we're not sure how or why." I collapse onto the armrest of the recliner.

"Oh, Kristen. I'm going now." He hangs up, likely sprinting the six or eight blocks to Todd's parents' house. I sit staring at the phone, dreading the call I am about to make. I dial their number, and Todd's mom, Mary, answers the phone.

"Kristen, hi. I don't get calls from you very often." She sounds surprised and cheerful.

"Is George there?" I ask.

"Yes, he's here." The cheerful note has changed to concern.

"Todd died this morning."

"Who?"

"Your son, Todd," I say loudly and slowly, as if that will make it clearer that she has just lost her oldest child. The rest of the conversation is lost in fog; I'm only aware of Mary's voice quivering as she tries to understand what has happened.

I hang up and call Todd's brother John, who is at a Vikings football game with his wife, Kara. It's their first wedding anniversary, and now it will also always be the anniversary of his brother's death. I dial the number for Todd's best friend, Derek, finding him on the golf course. Later he will tell me he made a long putt that he never would have made on a normal day, and he felt that Todd must have already been there, helping him. I call Tom, one of Todd's best friends from college, and ask him to contact everyone else.

No one can believe it. Everyone wants answers, and I have none. The doctors won't know what happened until after an autopsy is performed. My first thought is that Todd drank too much the night before, but everyone who saw him says he wasn't out of control. Maybe it *was* sleep apnea; maybe he slept so deeply that he didn't wake himself up. The paramedics had asked about diabetes—but that's unlikely since he hadn't had any diabetic symptoms. I am at a loss and can only hope that the autopsy will provide an answer and it won't end up being one of those deaths with no explanation.

I sit silently during the drive back to the hotel. I keep thinking that I don't want Todd to be alone. I don't want to leave him in this town where no one knows him and where they will treat him just like any other corpse. I don't want his body to have to travel alone to the coroner's office in St. Paul for the autopsy. But I need to go to Brooke. She is the only thing I want if I can't have Todd—the closest thing I have to him now that he is gone.

At the hotel, people flock around me, offering comforting words. I am also met by two police officers.

"Ma'am, I'm so sorry for your loss. Can we ask you some questions?"

"Sure," I mumble, not comprehending their presence.

"Can you tell us what happened?"

I suddenly understand. They aren't just "asking me some questions." I am being questioned—like a criminal.

I describe the events of the morning.

"When was the last time you saw him?"

"At the dance, about eleven or twelve. I came back to the hotel with the baby. He came home later and slept next door in the bed next to my parents." I feel like I have done something wrong and they are trying to find my weakness.

"Was he drinking a lot?"

"Not any more than he had in the past at weddings. I don't know." I am confused and scared. Maybe he *had* drunk too much. I should have stayed at the dance. Was this my fault? If I had stayed I could have monitored his drinking. Or should I have made him come back to the hotel? Maybe then this wouldn't have happened.

"Okay ma'am. We'll let you know if we have any other questions, and please call if you think of anything else." One of the officers hands me his business card. I look at it blankly.

What else will I think of? That I put a pillow over his face while he slept? That I poisoned him at dinner? At this moment, I feel as if I had done those things, that Todd's death was somehow my fault, that he would be alive if only I had done something different in the last twenty-four hours. But what? What did—or didn't—I do? Why can't I pinpoint the exact moment I screwed up?

In my parents' room I pick up Todd's clothes from the night before and put them into his duffle bag. The smell of his toothpaste and deodorant is familiar and strong as I gently tuck them into his travel kit. Somehow I manage to get everything packed up for the long ride home. My parents guide me into the front seat of my SUV. My dad drives while my mom sits in the back with Brooke. Todd was supposed to drive Brooke and me home. What if he had died while he was driving? What if he had died when he was in the pool with Brooke yesterday? Questions start to flood my mind as I stare out the window. Questions and emotions: regret, guilt, anger—and denial. This isn't really happening, I keep thinking. I consciously take deep breaths, fearing I will forget to breathe if I don't focus on it. Please let this be a dream. Please let me wake up tomorrow and none of this will have happened. I silently plead, over and over, pinching my arm, hoping to wake myself from this nightmare. My phone rings.

"Hello, Mrs. Brown. I'm Jill from the organ donation center, and I'll be your care coordinator. First of all, I am so sorry for your loss. I know you must be in shock right now, but because you have chosen to donate Todd's organs, it's important that we do this right away to ensure we can use as many viable organs as possible. I will be asking a lot of questions about Todd's habits, health, and history. Some may be difficult to answer, but do your best."

I try to gather my wits in order to think clearly and speak intelligently. How has she gotten my phone number—and so quickly? When did I say I would donate his organs? Yes, we are organ donors, but I don't remember actually telling anyone. I sit lifelessly on the leather seat, responding to questions about Todd—everything from his height and weight to his mental state to his exercise habits to his sexual history to previous alcohol and drug use. My shoulders tense into tight rocks as the questioning continues. Finally it's over, and I breathe heavily.

"Again, I'm so sorry for your loss, Mrs. Brown. And please don't hesitate to call me if you have questions or just need to talk. We are here to support you. Thanks for your time."

I shut my eyes and lean back against the headrest, exhausted, my phone still in my hand. I sigh, long and deep, but it isn't a sigh of relief; it is of defeat. Todd can now be "processed," and I have no chance of winning the argument I have been having with God to let this all be a mistake or a dream. I have lost.

* * *

After driving a while, we all need to get out and stretch our legs, shake off the anxiety that's been growing in the silence. We pull into a rest stop and climb out of the vehicle that has housed our grief for the past two hours. I take my turn in the bathroom while my mom plays with Brooke in the grass. When I come out, I slump down next to them, watching my daughter as she plays with the grass blades. Suddenly, she starts shifting her weight back and forth and lifts her belly off the ground. My mom and I look at each other in surprise, and then she does it—Brooke puts one hand and one knee in front of the other and crawls, really crawls a few inches through the grass. After months of sliding around on her belly, kicking off with her left leg and slithering to where she needed to go, she has finally crawled.

Todd had been working on getting her up on all fours, demonstrating the correct position, his long limbs covering the room in two or three strides. It took all the effort she had to drag herself across the floor, and she couldn't quite get that fourth "kickstand" up underneath of her. Seeing her move through the grass, I knew that Todd was there, supporting her and cheering her on. They say children have a sixth sense and can sometimes see things adults can't because their creative, open-minded brains haven't yet been "turned off" by societal pressures. Was he there, demonstrating the right moves? Did she see him and want to follow him? Did she wonder why he wasn't coming home with us? I would later think of that moment in the grass as one of only a few instances of brightness during a time of such darkness—months when I felt that all light was gone. Any light that did manage to break through was always the result of something Brooke did to make me smile again.

* * *

When we finally arrive at my house, Audrey, Matt, and Rachel are already there. The last time I had this kind of reception was ten months earlier when Todd and I brought Brooke home for the first time. That day we had been met by pink balloons on the mailbox, congratulatory phone messages and a fridge full of food. But today, there are no balloons.

I open the front door and walk inside. Pain sears my body as I realize that Todd isn't there and never will be again. He isn't there to carry his one small duffel bag, my gigantic, over-packed suitcase, and all of Brooke's supplies into the house. I don't know who does, but somehow our stuff ends up where it needs to be. Through my mental haze I realize that he will need the suit he had worn the night before. I find it hanging in his closet along with his duffel. I pull out the suit, burying my face in the fabric and inhaling deep and long. The smell of his musky cologne and soap-scented skin still saturate every fiber. He had been wearing it less than twenty-four hours ago, still alive, dancing and laughing. Now it's just a limp garment that he will wear again, but as a corpse, a piece of meat that will soon be transported, cut open, and manhandled. The least I can do is make him look as good as possible after all that impersonal treatment. I carefully fold the suit over my arm and carry it to Audrey in the kitchen.

"Can you have this dry cleaned for me?"

"Sure. I'll drop it off when they open tomorrow."

"I don't know what will happen, but if he's going to be in an open casket, he would want to look perfect." I start to teeter and sit down on a barstool near the wooden island that dominates the center of the room. The scream is in my throat again. I rest my head against the island. Again, I exhale a deep sigh of defeat.

"Go and lie down for awhile," my mom says, walking into the kitchen with Brooke.

"Okay, I'll try." I shuffle into my bedroom, feeling emotional exhaustion settling into my bones and hoping sleep will find me. I can see that Rachel and Audrey have been at work here. The bed is made, the pillows fluffed, Todd's closet is shut—not like the usual mess, where Todd's towel hangs over the open closet door, a stack of laundry waits to be put away, and at least two of his white T-shirts litter the floor. This is too clean. This isn't right. A surge of anger courses through my body.

I tear the covers off the bed, toss one of the pillows onto the floor, open a dresser drawer, and survey the room. This is better. This is more like normal. I crawl into my side of the bed, still fully dressed in the jeans and tan cardigan I have been wearing since morning. I stretch out and instinctually slide my foot across to Todd's side of the bed. We slept like that most nights—our feet intertwined, keeping each other warm. But now his space is cold and empty. Another surge of anger rises but manifests itself as tears—the first real tears I have felt all day. And instead of holding them back, I let them fall. I slowly slide my body to the middle of the bed and reach for Todd's pillow. I hug it to my chest and then fully move into his spot where the slight indentation from his body on the mattress holds me, just like Todd used to do. The tears continue to come: tears of confusion, tears of anger, and tears of sadness as my heart breaks. I don't sleep. It's hard enough for me to sleep on a normal night, and now, things aren't normal. They aren't right. And I don't see how they ever will be again.

FOURTEEN

Monday, September 10, 2007

I'm up early, tired from a restless night of going over the events of yesterday again and again, trying to figure out where I screwed up. I get out of bed, throw on a sweatshirt and jeans. Our big black Labrador, Cosmo, follows me around, unsure of what's happening. He snuggled up close to me as I cried through the night, sensing my need for comfort and closeness, his furry head and floppy ears resting on my chest, his moist eyes looking at me in mute sympathy. But he wasn't in bed when I got up. I find him in the laundry room, lying on a pile of Todd's dirty clothes, missing his master who didn't come home with the rest of his family. I call for him, petting and hugging him close. He follows me to the kitchen and stays by my side, probably wondering if I'm leaving too.

I sit on a barstool next to the phone, Cosmo curled up by my feet, offering me the support I desperately need. I call Todd's office, relieved when I get his boss's voice mail. I don't want to talk to anyone right now but know I need to deliver the awful news.

"Hi, Ed, it's Kristen Brown, Todd's wife. I'm not sure how to say this, but Todd passed away yesterday. I don't know funeral details yet, but I'll let you know when we finalize things. Thanks." I'm surprised at how straightforward and businesslike I sound, but this morning I'm all business. I do everything I can think of to stay busy and focused on something other than the fact that my husband died just twenty-four hours ago. I log into my work e-mail and respond to messages in my inbox. I call Todd's credit card companies, his car loan bank. I need to feel useful instead of the way I really feel—lost, confused, angry, and hopeless.

Todd's boss calls back, obviously upset. He had asked Todd to leave another bank and come to work for him, and Todd thought of him as a mentor and a friend.

"Kristen, I am so, so sorry. Let us know if there's anything we can do to help you. I'll have HR go through all of his benefits and get them processed." He tries to be professional and not let his emotion show, but I can hear his voice breaking. For the first time, I realize that Todd's death doesn't just affect our families and me. There is a whole network of friends, coworkers, former classmates, and teammates who haven't heard yet, whose worlds will be upended by Todd's unexpected death. The business mode I have affected suddenly disappears, and my heart breaks.

"Thanks, Ed. I really appreciate that," I manage to squeak. I hang up, tears stinging my eyes. What was left of my strength dissolves, and I collapse into a chair and curl up into a ball.

Throughout the morning I'm vaguely aware of my parents moving about, cooking, cleaning, doing yard work, and watching over Brooke and me. As I sit there lifelessly with no makeup, no shower, no motivation, I know they are going to be watching over us for quite a while.

In the afternoon, I find myself on the living room floor, staring up at the ceiling while Brooke plays next to me. My parents, Audrey, and Matt sit on the couch and chairs surrounding me, their bodies tensed, their faces somber. It is as if they are keeping vigil, making sure I won't self-destruct or snap in some way—watchful guardians keeping Brooke and me safe.

I lie within their protective circle, the light from the picture window too bright for my overloaded mind to handle, but my body and spirit too spent to move. Just like last night, I keep reliving the weekend, trying to figure out what I could have done differently to prevent what happened. Did I miss something? When Todd said he was stiff and sore Saturday morning after sleeping on the pullout couch, was that really an indicator of something more going on with him? Why didn't I insist he come back to the hotel with me, where we would have been in the same bed? I would have known something was wrong if he had been sleeping mere inches from me—wouldn't I?

I stare into space for hours, wondering what crime I committed for which I need to pay such a terrible price. Was it because I occasionally take sick days at work when I'm not really sick? Was it because of the time I bad-mouthed a friend in high school? Was it because I was mean to Todd on my birthday? Was it because I was a constant last-minute canceller of plans? I know I'm not perfect—far from it—but I can't think of anything that warrants the magnitude of the punishment I have received.

In the evening, our closest friends come over, the people Todd and I spent almost every weekend with for six years, most of whom he had known since his days at Gustavus Adolphus College. They hug me as they filter into the house, but I can sense their uneasiness in being here, and their uneasiness around me—especially the guys. They've been over more times than I can count, but always to visit with Todd, usually playing poker and watching sports in his basement man cave. We gather in the living room, all of us unsure of what to say or do next. At some point, the television is turned on to *Monday Night Football*, and the guys settle into their normal guy routine of cheering touchdowns and filtering out any non-football talk. I don't mind them watching the game. I understand it's hard for them to communicate how they feel—and besides, that's what Todd would have been doing tonight. I go to the kitchen with the girls. I have no idea what we talk about, but somehow we manage to fill up two hours of time.

When they leave, the house is still and my mind and body tell me I have to rest. Earlier today, I had called my doctor and told her what happened. She began to cry, which took me by surprise and restarted my own tears. She didn't hesitate to call in a prescription for a sleep aid, but the pill doesn't keep me from waking during the deepest, darkest part of night.

I can't stop crying, and I'm on the verge of throwing up. Todd would always tell me to have some soup whenever I didn't feel good. I would laugh and say that's just an old wives' tale, but right now all I want is to follow his advice. I stumble to the kitchen and find the familiar red and white label of Campbell's chicken noodle in the cupboard. The broth splashes my hands as I pour it into a bowl, not bothering to add the required can of water. The microwave hums, and I slump against the countertop, barely able to stand. As the normally comforting smell of the soup meets my nostrils, bile rises in my throat, reality crushing me. I don't even feel the burning hot bowl that balances precariously it in my trembling hands. Maneuvering it onto the counter, I dip my spoon into the steaming soup, but I can't swallow; the noodles lie heavy in my mouth, the undiluted broth like acid as it drips off the spoon onto my lips. All self-control is now lost, and I begin sobbing and heaving, realizing that soup isn't going to make me feel better.

My dad appears from the guest room and puts his arms around me. Neither of us says a word. All I can do is sob and sob until my chest and throat hurt. My dad just stands there, holding me. And I finally realize what has happened: Todd is gone, and no amount of my overanalyzing, second-guessing, or self-recrimination can ever change that.

FIFTEEN

Tuesday, September 11, 2007

"Hi, Kristen, it's Maria from Crown Bank. I'm so sorry about Todd. He was such a great guy." I frown, trying to figure out exactly who is calling me and why. After a moment I realize that Maria is the Human Resources manager from Todd's company.

"Thanks, Maria. It's been a shock, that's for sure," I manage to say, my common response to pretty much everyone who has called or come to the house during the last two days.

"I'm going through all of Todd's benefits, and it looks pretty standard," Maria continues. "We can do most of the legwork for you on rolling over his 401k and other investment accounts. But we need you to sign some paperwork sometime in the next couple of weeks to process it all. It's no rush, but I wanted you to know we're working on everything for you."

"Okay. Is there anything else?" I ask, feeling a little better because I can cross something off of my to-do list.

"Well, it looks like Todd had the standard company life insurance, and then he signed up for some extra insurance earlier this spring. And he has a checking account we can close out." She starts outlining terms and numbers, but all I can think about is the life insurance. I remember when Todd had me sign the authorization form. He wanted additional insurance in case something happened to him, so that I could pay off the house. At the time, I didn't want to think about the possibility of anything happening to him, but he insisted. "Can you sign this form," Todd had asked handing me a sheet of paper. He had just walked in the door from work. I was in the kitchen making spaghetti for dinner, while Brooke played in her baby gym.

"What is it?" I asked taking the paper from him.

"It's an authorization to get some additional life insurance. If anything happens to me I want to be sure you can at least pay off the house." He answered as he reached down to pick Brooke up out of her play gym.

"That is just silly. We don't need to have extra life insurance now. Nothing is going to happen." I exclaimed shaking my head not wanting to think about the possibility.

"You never know. I might walk into the backyard and have a tree fall on me." He said as he laughed and cuddled with Brooke.

"How much more does it cost? Is it worth it?" I asked stirring the noodles on the stove.

"Not that much more. It'll come right out of my paycheck. We won't even know it's gone–and if something does happen, you won't have to worry about the house payment." He replied adamantly.

"OK–it's probably a good idea. It just seems a little premature." I said as I grabbed a pen from the counter and signed the form.

"Thanks–I'll give it to HR tomorrow." He tucked the signed form under his arm and walked out of the kitchen to change out of his work clothes.

While I should be relived that the policy is there to keep Brooke and me secure, I can't help feeling it's cursed—that by getting the insurance, he had tempted fate. Maria finishes her recitation of the details of Todd's benefits, and my mind, overtaken by memories and anger, shuts down to preserve my sanity.

The rest of the day is devoted to planning Todd's funeral. How do you commemorate a life that should never have left us at so young an age without being overcome with anger? For me, the only alternative to anger is numbness. I exist on autopilot. I do what I have to do, plan what I have to plan, and show up where I have to show up—but inside, I don't care. I just want to curl up and die myself.

After dropping Brooke off at day care, my parents drive me to the funeral home in Montevideo two hours away where we meet Todd's parents. Todd isn't there yet; he's still in St. Paul awaiting the autopsy. I feel completely apathetic about what is happening. My head and eyes burn with exhaustion, and my muscles ache from the constant tension that has knotted up my back and shoulders. But I know Todd would want a big celebration to commemorate his life, so I force myself to do this for him.

Troy, the funeral director, shows us in. He knew Todd through sports and growing up in Montevideo. My parents and I sit down next to Todd's brother John, and his wife Kara and Todd's parents. We all look awful with bloodshot eyes, slumped shoulders, and somber expressions, dreading the difficult conversation we are about to have.

Over the next two hours, my mind drifts and my body stiffens as we discuss every detail of the visitation and funeral—where to hold the services, where to send the flowers afterwards, what the funeral program should include, the obituary wording, cremation versus burial. I don't retain a single detail of the discussion. I keep wanting to turn to Todd to ask him what to do, but then I stop and remember that it's because he is gone that all of these decisions need to be made. So I just nod, agree, and say a few words to appear as if I am engaged. But it really doesn't matter. I just don't care. All I want is to be alone and out of this horrific situation where I have to do things and make decisions and put forth effort.

Our meeting ends, but there is still work to be done. Todd's parents agree to handle the funeral program. My task is to use the wedding slideshow I put together for our big day to create pictures and music for what I can't help but think of as Todd's big day.

Finally, my parents and I drive back to Minneapolis, where I immediately crawl into bed, even though I know I won't actually sleep. I just need to get away from the details and the planning. My mind can't process it all, and I wonder if I will ever care about anything again.

SIXTEEN

Wednesday, September 12, 2007

It's been three days since Todd died, and I am in limbo. We have planned the funeral; family and friends have been notified; I have contacted Todd's employer and credit card companies. Now what? Do I sit and wait? Cry? Shop for groceries? I am at a loss as to what to do with myself in this strange new world, not sure how to navigate anymore.

So I sit and sit, questions swirling in my head. Where is Todd? Why do I feel so alone? What will Brooke do now without a daddy? What will I do now without a husband? Who am I? The visitation and funeral will end this limbo—won't they? They will give me some closure so I can start forging ahead—won't they? The questions keep coming, and I can feel my grip on reality slipping. But I fight to put on a brave face for the two long days ahead. I am imploding inside while building a wall so that no one will be hurt by the shrapnel.

The doorbell rings. It's a few of my high school girlfriends who have come from Montevideo. I am surprised and touched by their visit; they will be coming to the visitation tomorrow but still drove two hours to see me. We have kept in contact over the years—we went to each other's weddings, hung out together in our hometown. But until this moment, I haven't realized how much they are an integral part of my life and how much they mean to me.

"Kristen, I'm so sorry," one of them says, handing me a basket full of goodies, wine, and some things for Brooke.

"Thanks. That is so sweet. I can't believe you guys drove all the way out here." My tension lifts slightly as we sit and chat. Their thoughtfulness is just what I need to get through this day of not knowing what to do with myself.

After they leave, I feel a little bit of energy and decide to pack Brooke's and my bags for tomorrow's trip to Montevideo for the visitation and the funeral. I stand in front of my closet, staring at my wardrobe, trying to decide what to wear to these two events that will be forever burned in my memory. I have already chosen Brooke's outfits—a brown shirt and the leopard print pants Todd loved so much for the visitation, and a brown velvet dress my sister bought for her for the funeral. But what should I wear to commemorate my husband's life? I would pick sweatpants and a T-shirt, but my duty as a grieving widow trumps my personal preference. Do I choose something Todd liked? Do I choose something I like? Do I go with typical funereal black, or with widow-wear as in the movies? But I don't own a black hat with a black veil, and where would I even get something like that? I settle on a combination of practicality, somewhat up-to-date style, and what Todd would have found attractive: For the funeral, a pale gray shirt, tailored black jacket, black pinstriped pencil skirt, black tights, and black round-toe patent leather shoes that I know will support me throughout the day. For the visitation, the same reliable shoes with black pants and a red sweater. Todd loved me in red. I own a pair of red pants that he really liked, but they haven't fit me since I last wore them at our groom's dinner almost three years ago. So I settle for a red sweater—the closest thing I have to a substitute.

As I pack the carry-on suitcase that we used countless times for our trips together, I feel as though I should be packing for Todd too. I always at least started his packing; otherwise, it would be a last-minute battle to get him out the door with everything he needed. And still he inevitably forgot something, requiring a trip to the nearest store. I think he owned about fifteen belts as the result of forgetting one for various trips. But this time, I don't have to pack for him. He has with him all he needs. When I put the last of my clothes into the bag, I realize it holds nothing *I* need to make it through this trip. Todd is what I need, and he is gone.

SEVENTEEN

Thursday, September 13, 2007

It's a cool autumn day, just perfect for a warm sweatshirt, a pot of chili, and an exciting football game—Todd's favorite kind of day. My dad drives Brooke, my mom and me to Montevideo. He drops me off at the funeral home, and they head to my grandpa's house where we will be staying. I walk up to the door, both nervous and expectant. Todd is finally here, and I am anxious to see him, to make sure he is okay. I need some private time with him to apologize, to be angry, to reminisce, and to cry. I miss him and want to hold my best friend's hand for the first time since I left him at the hospital the day he died. I need him to comfort me, even if he can't hold me back.

Troy meets me at the entrance. "How are you doin'?"

"Okay. How is he?" I respond, as if Todd actually has feelings about his situation. I'm sure it's not easy for Troy to organize Todd's funeral and make him presentable given that he knew Todd, but it's a comfort for me to know that someone who also cared about Todd will be helping to usher him out appropriately.

"He looks a little different, so just be prepared for that." Troy leads me through a doorway into a dimly lit room. As I see Todd for the first time, I am taken aback.

Todd lies in a wooden casket, as still and gray as a stone, hands crossed at his waist, his skin waxy and pale underneath orange-y makeup. His face, usually bright and smiling, is dull and slack, and his eye sockets sink unnaturally into his skull. "Oh, Todd, I'm so sorry," I whisper overcome with emotion.

"I'll give you some privacy," Troy says softly. "Take all the time you need. I'll be in my office."

I sit in a chair next to the casket, resting my head on Todd's chest for a few moments. Sitting up, I can't stop staring at his face. He looks nothing like himself. My shaking hands reach out to touch his. I'm surprised at how soft and warm they are. I hold his hands tightly, willing my life force to move into him. "I'm sorry. I'm so, so sorry. I know you'd hate this," I keep apologizing through my tears. After a long time, I compose myself, wipe my eyes, and switch into business mode. I check his tie to make sure it's straight. I smooth his curly hair off his face. I brush lint from his suit. Then, for some reason, I look under the bottom half of the casket where his legs are. He's not wearing any shoes; they're just lying there next to his feet. Later I won't recall if he even had feet at all. His connective tissue and cartilage were taken for organ donation, and I won't be able to remember what his feet looked like when I peeked under there. But it seems that at some point I ask for his shoes back, because I discover them in his closet a couple of weeks later.

I go about the business of making sure he looks as good as he can under the circumstances, talking to him as if he were still alive. "Here is a picture of Brooke for you to take with you, and one of all of us. And here is Cosmo's collar and the picture Brooke painted at school on Father's Day. See, it says 'World's Best Dad.' And I know some other people have things for you too. You'll get them later." I ramble on, trying to fill his silence with a voice. Finally, there's nothing left to do or say. I kiss his cheek, squeeze his hand, and walk out into the sunshine, the bright light and crisp wind shocking the dimness of the funeral home and the fog of tears from my eyes. I wipe my eyes and walk the six blocks to my grandpa's house holding back more tears as I compose myself for the events to come.

When I get to my grandpa's house, I try to stay busy until the visitation starts that evening. I'm ironing my clothes when my cell phone rings.

"Hello, ma'am. This is Chad Jutz from the Detroit Lakes police department. I have the results of Mr. Brown's autopsy."

Please, please don't let it be alcohol poisoning. I don't want his death to be caused by a self-induced condition. I think to myself. "I'm so glad to hear from you," I respond. "I was hoping we would know something before the visitation tonight." I feel my jaw tighten in anticipation of the results.

"Well, it was acute myocardial infarction, which is a heart attack."

I lean against the ironing board in confusion. "What?! Are there any other details?" I hope there will be something to explain why an apparently healthy thirty-year-old would have a heart attack.

"Yes, he had a ninety-nine percent blockage of the left descending artery." I will later learn that this artery is called "the widow maker." Officer Jutz reads some more medical terminology from the report, but I have heard all that I can absorb. By the time he hangs up I am relieved to have an answer but also incredibly angry. Todd was tall, thin, and athletic. He ate healthfully, exercised most days. And yet he'd had a heart attack? I'm angry with the healthcare system. How did we not know about the time bomb in his chest? Why wasn't he screened somehow? I'm angry with Todd. Had he known something was wrong but, like a typical male, didn't want to go to the doctor to get checked out? Was his family not important enough to him to prompt him to be proactive about his health and get physicals more often? But wait, he did have a physical not long ago and was given a clean bill of health. He'd been told he had slightly high cholesterol, but nothing requiring medication and nothing to be worried about. Nothing to worry about? Six months later he's dead of a heart attack. How did they miss this? How did I miss this?

My anger continues to build during the drive to the church with Brooke and my family. Why am I going to a church? What kind of a God would do something like this? We arrive, and a wave of nausea hits me. Todd is dead. His casket is in the front of the church, open for viewing. And I have to stand up there and greet people who come to pay their respects—and hug them. I have never been a hugger. I have a personal space threshold of about three feet, preferably five. I'm only comfortable hugging those who I feel closest to—Todd and Brooke. With everyone else, hugging infringes on my bubble of safety. At our wedding, we didn't have a receiving line for exactly that reason. Now, as Todd's widow, I'm already feeling vulnerable, yet I have to stand in front of a church with his parents and hug every person who walks through the visitation line, repeating "I'm okay" and "Brooke is the best medicine" seven hundred times while staring at my husband's dead body twenty feet away. It is pure hell.

Someone tells me how therapeutic it is for everyone to get to see me and show their concern. Why can't we do that without the hugging? Why can't I stand behind one of those velvet ropes and just smile and nod as they pass by?

When I get back to my grandpa's house, all I want to do is take a shower, wash away all of that too-intimate touching that made me cringe with every passing person. I peel off my clothes and scrub every part of me that had been exposed. I need to cleanse myself of all the grief and sadness that was transmitted by the huggers. I have enough of my own to deal with and don't need any more.

EIGHTEEN

Friday, September 14, 2007

They say everybody dies famous in a small town, and that definitely holds true in Todd's case. We had to rent the local auditorium to accommodate everyone expected for the funeral.

When I walk in, I am assaulted by the familiar smell of this space—a nostalgic blend of wood, carpet, sweat, stage makeup, and food. The school that was once attached was torn down years ago, but the haunting scent of sloppy joes, canned peaches, and raspberry bismarks remains. And I can still feel the heat of the stage lights and hear the rustle of the curtains as if I were once more onstage in a school theatre production.

The memories, the flowers, the anticipated crowd—it's all overwhelming, but also just how Todd would have wanted to be remembered: with a huge party. (Of course, he would also have wanted beer!) The only thing he wouldn't have liked was the open casket. I know he is pissed at me for that, but I took Troy's advice. He said that when a person dies unexpectedly, those who didn't have a chance to say goodbye want a body to see and talk to, so I said yes. Todd is now in the lobby, exposed to anyone who wishes to see him. I hadn't realized how different he would look, but no one mentions his appearance to me. Maybe I am the only one disturbed by it, having fallen asleep and woken up to his face almost every day for six years.

As people continue to arrive, I keep myself busy—pacing, circling the room, stopping only briefly to chat, avoiding anyone or anything that might set me off on a crying jag. It works until two friends Todd and I have known since elementary school walk onstage with their guitars, sit down in front of the microphones, and strum their first chords. All of my self-restraint dissolves, and I completely break down. I tried to be strong and brave, but upon hearing the music that signals the official start of the service I can't keep up the act any longer. We are at the funeral for my thirty-year-old husband. Todd is dead.

I walk out to the lobby to say goodbye for the last time. From our first date, no more than five days had ever passed without our being with each other, and now this will be the very last time I will see his face or hold his hand. I approach the casket, still not used to his appearance as he lies there motionless and unfamiliar. I place a white rose next to him, touch his hand lightly, and bend to kiss him—the last kiss we will ever share—my tears sliding from my closed eyes onto my lips as they softly meet his.

I step away trying to stop time so I have just a few more minutes with Todd, but the pallbearers close the casket then wheel it down the aisle through the audience to the front of the auditorium. I follow, my mind numb and my body overly erect, and take my designated seat. The pastor breaks the silence: "Let us pray." Many more words follow, but I hear none of them. I sit staring at my husband's casket in front of me, and my faith in God evaporates. All I can think is, fuck you, God. How could you do something like this? How could you take an innocent life? How could you let Todd leave me without a husband, Brooke without a dad, his parents without a son? I continue to silently curse God, my anger intensifying, my breath quickening. I am shaken into awareness by the pastor saying, "And now, Todd's wife Kristen and his brother John would like to say a few words."

I don't want to do this, but I know I need to. While planning the service with Todd's family, I had decided that I would always regret it if I didn't speak—to say how much Todd meant to me and how grateful I am to him for giving me our daughter. All week I struggled to find the right words. Last night, I scribbled my speech on a Bill's Supermarket notepad with a dull pencil I found at my grandpa's house. Now, walking up the steps to the stage, I'm struck by a random thought: I wonder if my butt looks big. What? Why would I even care about that? But I realize that I don't care what anyone else thinks; I care if *Todd* thinks my butt

73

looks big. Even though he's not really here, it's important to me that both Brooke and I look good for him today. I laugh to myself that such a crazy thought should occur as I am about to eulogize my husband, and that helps settle my nerves as I look out over the audience. I see familiar faces, strangers, family, friends – and every seat is filled. I can't stop on anyone's face for too long seeing the pity in their eyes. So I look down at my notepad and start speaking.

Todd, there are so many gifts you've given us—your smile, your charm, your wit. But one gift stands out above the rest: the beautiful Brooke Lucille Brown. She'll never know her dad, but we promise to remind her every day who you were and what you meant to us. We'll tell her about your love of life and how you never let much get to you. We'll tell her how you loved golf and softball and pretty much anything involving a ball. We'll tell her about your sense of humor—dry and sarcastic and playful. We'll tell her how you loved pasta al dente with salt and pepper, and rice and baked potatoes, pretty much all carbs. And how you loved family get-togethers—weddings, Corn Days, you name it, he loved it. We'll tell her how her dad made people smile and feel good and kept the world calm and sane, even during crazy times. We'll tell her how he loved his friends and always made time for them—classmates, teammates, colleagues. We'll tell her how nice his hair and his cheekbones and his pec muscles were, and how he always looked pulled together and handsome without really trying. We'll tell her about his dance talents, which we hope she inherits from him and not me. We'll tell her how she was the little light of his life for the nine months he had her. We'll tell her we don't know why daddy was taken to heaven. Maybe God needed a good golf partner, or they needed someone to lie in a hammock on the beach all day watching the weather, or maybe they needed a good book or movie reviewer. Right now the only sense I can make out if it is that his heart couldn't handle all the love pulsing through it, and now he's able to love us and watch us and protect us from above.

Brooke, your dad was a fantastic guy. Look at everyone here and how he's affected them. We were so lucky to have him as long as we did, and our lives are forever changed.

Todd, we love you and hope you love the party we're putting on for you. I racked my brain as to what I could do for you that would really be meaningful, and all I could come up with is to do everything you'd want us to do—have a big blowout with your nearest and dearest friends and family, make sure Brooke and I look cute, and keep it all upbeat and fun—just how you'd want it. I hope you're happy with our farewell to you, but it will never be over. We will miss you forever.

As I speak, I can't look at the audience without choking up. I interrupt myself several times, almost breaking down, but I get through it. When it's over I'm relieved and thankful I was able to pay tribute to him that way. I know he would have been proud of me for doing it and humbled by the words I said. John goes next, his emotions getting the best of him too. When we're done, we carefully walk down the steps and I move to my computer on the side of the stage to start the slideshow I had put together to memorialize Todd. The lights dim, the music plays, and I suddenly feel sick to my stomach, watching images of Todd flash across the screen. Todd as a baby. Todd in school. Todd with his friends. Todd playing sports. Todd and me on vacation. Todd at our wedding. Todd holding Brooke. Todd smiling. Todd laughing. Todd living. The familiar photos now remind me of Todd's lifelessness and the loss of my own life. They rip wider the hole that has formed in my existence by the lack of his. I sit silently for the rest of the service, tears sliding down my cheeks, but no sound arising from my throat. Fuck you, God. Fuck you. More bible verses, more readings, but I hear nothing as the anger and sadness boils inside me.

The pastor concludes the service, and Todd's closest friends join the pallbearers to escort the casket outside. I walk slowly behind, barely able to muster the energy to take each step. Emerging into the crisp September air, I take Brooke from my mom, hugging her tightly. The casket is wheeled toward the hearse that will carry Todd the four blocks back to the funeral home for cremation. The pastor lifts his hand and says a prayer for the hundreds of onlookers surrounding us on the street and sidewalks. My anger is once more focused on God, and again I silently curse him. Fuck you, God. I don't know what reason you had for doing this. I don't care what I said in there just now. You don't need a golf partner. You are selfish and cruel, and I want nothing to do with you ever again.

The pastor's words cease. I step forward and rest my right hand on the casket. I am so angry and heartbroken that this is the last time I will ever be in Todd's physical presence. This is the last time Brooke will be with her daddy. This is the last time we will all be together as a family. I rest my cheek on Brooke's fuzzy head, unable to hold back my tears. My hand is magnetized to the casket; only when the pallbearers step forward to slide it into the hearse do I reluctantly pull it away. The door shuts, and the hearse proceeds slowly down the street. I watch it go—driving away with my husband and my life.

* * *

More than anything, I want to sit in a dark room and cry. But the day isn't over; there is a luncheon at the armory, and I have to keep rallying. My parents and I arrive to a room that's as packed as the auditorium was. I am grateful that so many people have come to pay their respects to Todd, but I'm resentful too. Their presence means I have to socialize, and that means hugging. I try to hide at a table with some high school friends. I can be comfortable with them and just talk about normal things like our kids, our jobs, and celebrity gossip. But people still find me. They stop by to say they are sorry. To say how beautiful the service was. To say how much they will miss Todd. And as thankful and appreciative as I am that they all came, I just want to go home.

After a couple of hours, people finally start to trickle out. All I can do is breathe a sigh of relief as Troy gives me last-minute information about what will happen next.

"The flowers will go to local schools and churches, except the ones you want to take," he explains.

I look at the beautiful floral arrangements that span the length of the room. "Okay, I'll take the ones I want. The rest can go wherever you think is appropriate."

"The cards and gifts are all in boxes. I think it was your uncle who took them out to your car. And all of the other things from the funeral are in there—the candles, crosses, some extra programs, a copy of the obituary write-up, the guest book."

It occurs to me that these are the same things I already have at home from our wedding and Brooke's baptism—everything but the obituary. My eyes start to glaze over, and my mind starts shutting down. I am done. I can't take one more second of this, and I need to escape. I find my dad.

"Let's go," I demand, urgency breaking through the tightness in my throat.

"All right. Find your mom and Brooke, and we'll go." He takes the flower arrangement I'm holding—one of the few I have decided to keep.

"Brooke is going with the Browns, so let's just get Mom and get out of here."

I make it to the car with as few final hugs as I can get away with, and we drive in silence back to my grandpa's house. My aunts and uncles are already there, and they watch me sink into a chair.

"Can I get you anything?" someone asks. But there is nothing I want except to have Todd back. No offers of cake, soda, slippers, or child care can ever give me what I want. So I just sit, staring at nothing, letting my mind wander while my relatives' idle chatter floats around me.

"Kristen, do you want to go over to the Browns' and see Brooke?"

The question brings me back to my body, which immediately tenses. Please don't make me suffer through another social situation. But I know I have to go and pay my respects to Todd's family. I find my coat and purse and steady myself to walk the three blocks to Todd's parents' house.

When I arrive, my stomach flips over as I survey the scene in front of me. It is worse than I feared. The tiny house is overflowing with people, forcing me to make physical contact just by walking through the rooms. I clasp my purse close to me in an effort to avoid touching anyone, scanning the room for Brooke, my security blanket. I pick her up and manage to find a less crowded spot where she can play on the floor, but within moments we are surrounded. Although I know everyone means well and are just showing their support, I want to yell at them to back off and let us breathe. But I don't. Instead, I force myself to make small talk, playing with Brooke and trying to think up any reason to leave. Conversation drones in the background as I nod, smile, and pretend to listen. Finally, I've had enough.

"Do you want to keep Brooke here overnight?" I ask Mary and George, knowing they will say yes and knowing I won't have the energy to deal with an infant tonight.

"Oh, we would love it." She tenderly takes Brooke from my arms, and I am reminded of how important Brooke is to them and how she will now be their only link to their oldest son.

"Thanks. I'll be over sometime in the morning to get her before we head back to the cities." I'm hoping to make a hasty exit, but everyone hovers around me, and I am forced into a long, drawn-out goodbye that once again involves hugging. When I finally make my escape, it's dark. Glancing at my phone, I see it's blinking with several voice and text messages.

"We're at the bar. Come and meet us if you want."

"Everyone is here, the bar is crammed. Come down."

"You probably don't want to see people right now, but if you're up to it, we would love to see you down here."

Our friends have gathered at one of the local watering holes to drink away their sorrows and share stories about Todd. Part of me wants to go, but most of me just wants to lie in the dark. I walk back to my grandpa's house, and again my relatives ask if there is anything they can do for me.

"No," I reply, taking off my shoes. "All I want is to go to bed. See you in the morning." I can see the pity and concern in their eyes.

"Okay, goodnight," they respond as I slowly climb the narrow steps to my room. I pull off my clothes, tossing them into an untidy heap on the floor, slip on lounge pants and a T-shirt, and go into the bathroom. Looking into the mirror, I am shocked by my appearance. My normally bright, wide eyes are bloodshot and hooded with exhaustion, and my skin is pale. There is no trace of the makeup I applied this morning, and my hair hangs limp around my shoulders. Somehow I manage to brush my teeth and wash my face. I go back into the bedroom—the same room where Todd and I usually slept when we came to town. We were here just a month or two ago, and the sheets probably haven't been washed since then. I crawl under the covers and switch off the light, rolling over to face the side of the bed that was his. It's empty and now will always be empty. The grief and anxiety of this long day finally find their outlet, and I cry, long and deep and hard. I clutch the pillow that had been his and hug it close to me. I want Todd. But I am alone now.

ALONE

*"Where you used to be, there is a hole in the world,
which I find myself constantly walking around in the daytime,
and falling into at night. I miss you like hell."*
—Edna St. Vincent Millay

NINETEEN

The funeral was behind me, and I was supposed to get back to the everyday details of life. But my life as I knew it was over. My plans, dreams, and goals—all shattered. What I thought was my life's course was now an unobtainable fantasy. The second and third kids, the new house with a big yard, the vacations together, growing old with someone—all of that was gone. Now I was a lonely, bitter, angry widow who had lost my faith in everything.

For weeks after the funeral, I existed in a fog of tear-stained images, as if seeing everything through a camera lens shooting in the rain. My memories of those days are just fragments—broken impressions of a time I would rather forget, a time when my body and brain couldn't wrap themselves around what had happened to me. Todd was dead, and I was the living dead—a zombie. So many things affected my already fragile state of mind, internal and external forces that seemed to wage war within me. I barely ate, so my blood sugar would plummet, leaving me sweating, nauseated, and lightheaded. I barely slept, so I was always exhausted and unable to think clearly. I was lonely. I was angry. Nothing I did had any meaning. I just went through the motions, sinking deeper and deeper into a pit of despair and self-pity.

There were moments when I just wanted to die. While driving down the interstate after a particularly painful trip to Target, filled with memories of Todd's soap and toothpaste and the sound of his work shoes clicking on the store's tile floors, I felt an overwhelming compulsion to end my life. As I passed a large semi, I imagined how easy it would be to veer quickly into its path, and within seconds I would be gone. Maybe just a quick turn of the steering wheel into one of those heavy cement bridge supports, or a sharp turn off the on-ramp into the steep ditch below. At other times, I wondered if I could will myself into getting some fatal disease. The power of the mind is huge; I could make it happen if I just wished for it hard enough. I'd refuse treatment and just let myself die. That's what I wanted—to escape from the pain and be with Todd. I was so lonely without him.

It's crazy, but although his absence left a gaping hole in my world, I sometimes forgot that he was dead. For six years I would often call Todd's cell phone to tell him some bit of news or just to say hi. It had become second nature. One afternoon a couple of weeks after the funeral, I was driving home and instinctively called Todd to ask what he wanted for dinner. I listened to his entire voice mail message before remembering that he wasn't going to answer. Todd was gone, but his voice wasn't. After that, I would often call his number just to hear him, always ending up a mess of tears and memories.

But no one would have guessed how much of a mess I had become. I put on a happy face for my daughter. I went back to work. I went out with friends and family. I was externally strong, forcing myself to go about the business of life. I had checklists and to-do lists and grocery lists and Brooke lists and work lists—every kind of list imaginable to keep myself organized and on track. Those lists were the only way I would remember I needed to buy groceries to feed myself and Brooke. Thankfully, my mom and dad remained at my house those early months, helping with household chores, cooking, taking care of Brooke.

We have always been a close family, taking vacations and camping trips together when my siblings and I were younger and having family dinners almost weekly as adults. My family has always been supportive of me, even when I have been a cranky know-it-all (a tendency I have periodically had throughout my life). My parents were the ones who discovered Todd in bed that morning, not breathing, unresponsive. I can't imagine the images burned into their memories or the nightmares they have had over the events of that morning. How could you not suffer, knowing your oldest child and first grandchild have lost the key person in their lives?

My parents had moved to Minneapolis a few years earlier, after my dad retired. They were in their early fifties and excited about the opportunity for a new beginning. They had stayed with Todd and me while searching for a place to live. Now they were back in my home, but this new beginning didn't hold the promise of a new life and a new city. This new beginning was laden with stress and sadness as they were thrust into the roles of guardians, keeping me from giving up, from crawling into bed in my dark bedroom and staying there indefinitely. I am so grateful to them for taking care of Brooke and me, for helping me to find my way through the emotions that haunted me.

One of the few memories I have of that time occurred a week or two after the funeral. I made a trip to Todd's office to pick up his personal belongings and sign the paperwork for all of his benefits. I brought Brooke along, mostly as a security blanket and excuse to get out of there quickly. I had never been there before and felt awkward and out of place walking in, with everyone knowing who I was but me not knowing anyone. My face burned as all eyes stared at me while I waited for Todd's boss, Ed. I had met him a few times at company functions and again at the funeral, and Todd talked about him often, so I felt like I had known him for years. He led me into his office, where a box of Todd's things lay on the desk. I sat down in the chair with Brooke.

"We packed all of Todd's personal belongings up for you. How are you doing?" Ed asked.

"We're okay, doing as well as can be expected," I lied. I wasn't doing okay. I felt like shit. My husband had died with no warning. I couldn't sleep. I couldn't eat. I had to care for a ten-month-old infant by myself. But I didn't say that out loud. I kept my composure.

Maria from Human Resources entered, and we went about the business of signing paperwork and going through Todd's benefits.

"I did some investigating of the insurance policy, and unfortunately you are going to have to do a lot of that legwork yourself," she said, pulling out some paperwork for me to review. "They won't share information with me since I'm not his next of kin, and they need more specific details that I can't provide them. Are you the executor of his estate?"

"I don't know what that means," I responded, confused. We had a house with a mortgage, car payments, and student loans; we didn't have an estate—not one that I knew about, anyway.

"That just means you have legal rights to manage all of his financial matters. I have all the forms you need and have initiated the death benefit process, but you need to call to take the next steps."

"Okay, I can do that. Did it sound like it would be a quick turnaround?" I asked hopefully, shifting Brooke to the other side of my lap. I stared at the box of Todd's personal items. A notebook with his handwriting on the cover. A framed picture of Brooke and me. A stack of business cards. Perspiration rose on my upper lip, and I tried to focus on the details that Maria was launching at me.

"It looks like it should be pretty straightforward once they get the information they need, but I can't say for sure. Just let me know if you have questions or run into any trouble after you talk to them. I'll help you through the process. Insurance companies can be difficult to navigate." She smiled reassuringly, placing the paperwork and forms in an envelope and sliding them into the box of Todd's things.

"Thank you for your help. I really appreciate it," I said, standing and shaking her hand. I needed to escape that environment where Todd spent so many of his waking hours.

Ed scooped up the box in his arms. "Let me carry this out to your car for you." Again all eyes followed me as we exited the office. I pushed the door open and sucked in a deep breath of fresh air, relieved to get out of the stifling environment and to clear my head.

"Thanks, Ed. I know this must be tough for you," I said, knowing he was struggling to keep it together.

"Todd was such a great kid. I just can't believe he's gone," he replied with a tremble in his voice. He set the box in the back of my SUV and hugged me. "Hang in there and let me know if you need anything." He turned to go, trying to hide his emotion. I knew how close he and Todd had been and how awful it must be for his protégé and friend to be gone so unexpectedly.

I strapped Brooke into her car seat and climbed into the driver's seat. Exhaling a long, slow breath, I dropped my head to the steering wheel and sobbed—for the coworkers and friends who had lost Todd, for our families, but mostly for me. I was thirty-one years old and managing death benefit insurance claims. I was thirty-one years old and being asked if I was the executor of my husband's estate. I was thirty-one years old and a widow and all alone, trying to manage these details and be a parent. I cried because I wanted out of this situation—anything, just get me out! But there was nothing to save me from my despair and loneliness. I had to keep moving forward, whether I liked it or not.

It took me a few days before I could bring myself to start the task of investigating the accounts and paperwork Maria had given me. I knew I needed to get the insurance money, as awful as it felt to take it. We had bills that would be due in the next couple of weeks, and I couldn't pay them all on my own. So I dug out the insurance forms and called the number.

"Hi, this is Kristen Brown, and I am calling about an insurance policy that was opened by my husband a few months ago. He is now deceased, and I need to determine how to access the insurance money." I squirmed nervously, not knowing what red tape I would have to go through.

"Yes, Ms. Brown," replied the agent. "I'm so sorry for your loss. To look into this I just need to get some information from you. Let's start with your husband's name and Social Security number." She proceeded through a laundry list of questions, and I fumbled with the paperwork in front of me, looking for the required information.

"I'm sorry, ma'am, but it looks like this policy was just opened a few months ago. We are unable to process it at this time without going through some additional investigation to ensure that there is nothing questionable about the nature of your husband's death. I am very sorry to have to tell you that, but it's just procedure."

I held my breath and bit my lip, trying not to cry or blow up at her, trying to remain focused and calm. "Okay, what do you need from me to investigate it and prove it's not questionable?" I asked, hoping it would be a simple process but knowing it wouldn't be. I felt like a criminal.

"Well, we will need to have all of his medical records for the last five years, along with an in-depth interview with you to go over the details.

Once we've received all of that information, it will go through several steps of underwriting and investigation before we can actually release the funds to you."

I could feel a lump forming in my throat but managed to choke back the sob. "What kind of questionable nature could there be in a death that was from a heart attack, determined by an autopsy?" I asked. I struggled to direct my anger at the company and not at this poor woman who had answered my call.

"Ma'am, I understand you're upset, but it's just procedure because the insurance policy is so new. It does look like some of the money is not locked up because it was an employee-paid benefit, so you should be able to receive that within a few weeks without the extra paperwork. But the additional part that he just signed up for this spring is the amount in question. I apologize for the delay." She said this too matter-of-factly for me to believe she was really sorry.

I sat there, wondering what to do next. I had mortgage payments due. I had bills due. I had to wade through all of Todd's personal finances and figure out what money he had. I felt completely overwhelmed, staring at the mountain of paperwork in front of me. This woman was my only connection to the money I needed to be able to pay the bills, and she said I had to wait for some undetermined amount of time. I had always managed the bills every month, so I knew what we owed, but I had no idea exactly what financial position I was in now that my husband and our second income was gone. And now I had to sit and wait while Todd's death was investigated so that the life insurance company could decide if his life was worth the money they were supposed to pay me. And on top of that, I had to deal with checking account closures, 401k-to-IRA rollovers, and mutual fund rollovers. I knew nothing about personal finance, about which investments were the best for my situation. I just wanted to talk to Todd about it and get his advice; he knew all about this stuff.

Every day, I would get out of bed, see the stack of paperwork on the table, and cringe, knowing I had to do more research to figure out what to do next. I had to make call after call and write letter after letter to the companies where Todd had debt, telling them he had died and then having to prove it with a death certificate and a letter. And our joint accounts were just as complicated. I had to remove his name, which required paperwork and a death certificate for each one. I spent months figuring everything out. For years, we had talked about getting our wills done and making sure we knew every detail of each other's financial situation "just in case" something happened. But we never got around to it. And now something *had* happened, and I had to spend hours on the phone explaining the situation over and over again, feeling like I was on trial every time.

* * *

While I was dealing with all of the financial issues, I was also forced to go back to work, needing the income to support us. Unfortunately, my chosen career path is not exactly something I am passionate about. I ended up in the business world after spending my entire young life thinking I'd be a doctor. In high school I went to the International Science Fair, and I always loved the biology behind medicine. But my plan started to fall apart when I failed a chemistry class in college. I blamed it on being unable to understand the Russian professor, but that was just a poor excuse. Nevertheless, I became frustrated and started second-guessing my decision to go into the medical field. That led me on a scholarly journey through several schools and several majors, including English, interior design, and graphic design. I eventually graduated cum laude with a bachelor's degree in business.

My career path thus far had been one of continual movement up the corporate ladder, but while I ascended, my satisfaction and enjoyment plummeted. I am one who gets bored easily, and if I'm not motivated and empowered by my company and my superiors, I feel stifled. Micromanagement does not suit me well. When I moved into managerial roles, my main concern was to develop my employees into superstars. I let them do their job and stayed as uninvolved as possible because I believe that pride of ownership in a project, and ultimately in a job, is the best way to learn and grow, even if it takes a struggle to get to the end result. Unfortunately, the more promotions I got, the more I realized the business world is filled with snakes.

At the first company I worked for, I encountered the politics and games involved with getting ahead, but the firm was small and family-oriented, so it didn't feel too bad. At the second company, I always felt like I was teetering on the edge of what was morally and ethically incorrect; the ownership in Hong Kong spun stories of their factory "issues" to make them appear less serious than they were. That experience drained me, and my spirit for the business world officially disappeared. I felt uninspired and unsure of what my next step should be.

Fortunately, Todd was supportive of my desire to leave that company even without having another job in hand. He saw what it was doing to my mental and emotional state. It was just a month before our wedding, my grandmother was very sick with cancer, and I needed to get away from the negativity I continued to feel every day. During that time off, I should have been exploring a new career path or looking into going back to school. Instead, not long after we were married I got another corporate job as an account manager for a global market research company. I was responsible for one of the top retailers in the country and excited to move into a larger organization with a history of continual growth in its industry. But again, overwork, stress, and burnout were a constant force. Over a period of two years, I had five managers, each with a different approach. Regardless, I continued to keep the account on track and growing and received three promotions. Most people would be happy with that success, but my upward mobility at work was negated by my downward spiral at home.

A couple of weeks after Todd died, my manager changed yet again. I can deal with just about every type of personality and idiosyncrasy, and I have always believed in the mantra, "it's business, it's not personal." But this new boss made a specialty of micromanagement, degradation, and lack of empowerment—the three traits I find the most challenging and demoralizing. Every day I dreaded going into the office. My boss wasn't physically there, but her constant, negative phone calls and e-mails would send me into a panic, giving me anxiety, nausea, and every other stress-related symptom a person can get.

But I stayed. I knew a job change wasn't a good idea. Every book I read on grief said that you shouldn't make any big decisions until several months had passed because you're just not thinking clearly. So I decided to give her a chance, thinking that maybe my grief-stricken state had lowered my threshold for dealing with bad bosses. And I did feel some loyalty to my company. They had been good to me over the years with promotions and bonuses. After Todd died, they provided a cleaning service for a couple of months to relieve the burden of housekeeping— the best gift anyone could have given me. I was thankful to my company for this service, but it also made me feel indebted to them—a feeling I didn't like in this scenario with the new boss, who made my life hell on top of the hell I was already experiencing. I wasn't sure what I was going to do, but I knew I couldn't continue in that toxic environment indefinitely.

TWENTY

On top of all the crappy stuff I went through during the day, my nights were even worse. I've always been a light sleeper, but after Todd died I couldn't sleep at all. Any little sound would kick my adrenaline into high gear with the thought that it was a murderer sneaking through the house to kill us in our sleep. I was constantly on high alert, listening for Brooke, listening for a sign that Todd might be around. I tossed and turned and cried, and when I did doze off, I'd wake up and feel like I'd lost him all over again. I couldn't sleep on our pillows; I had to throw them all away and buy new ones. And yet, I still wished I had taken the pillow from the hotel where he died, where he slept for the last time. I can remember exactly how that hotel bed looked with and without him in it, and those images always put me in a crazy fantasy, wondering what it would have been like if Todd hadn't died that morning.

* * *

I Wish

Todd gasped, sucking oxygen into his starving lungs. The color rushed back to his face. He coughed and sputtered and managed to whisper, "What's happening?" I fell to my knees and scrambled to his side, aching for his touch, to feel that he was really alive and breathing. The paramedics lifted him onto the stretcher, still fighting to save him, to save the other half of me. We reached for each other, but the paramedics forcefully pushed me back. "We have to get him to the hospital ma'am." Knowing how I hate being called ma'am, Todd managed a smile. They raced him to the ambulance waiting outside in the damp, depressing drizzle, and I desperately followed. I held my breath for a moment while he balanced precariously as they angled him up and in, then leapt in after him. "I love you, hang on, just fight and stay with me, for us, for Brooke!" He looked up at me through bloodshot eyes and could only say, "I'll try, I love you."

* * *

What I would have given, what I would still give, if I'd been able to have that scenario—just a few more minutes to exchange last words. But that wasn't our fate. Instead, I had been launched into this new reality of life insurance, single parenthood, and no future. What the hell had happened to me?

Memories and images of him that morning haunted me, the whys and what-ifs. What could I have done to prevent it? Should he have gone to the doctor more often? If he had slept with me that last night, would I have known what was happening and been able to prevent it? Why didn't I realize he had a bad heart? Why didn't he? He had mentioned a week before that he was tired and had chest pain after a walk with the dog, and I'd told him to go to the doctor and get it checked out. Why didn't I make him go that week? Why was he always so stubborn? Why wasn't I a better wife? Why did I bug him about golfing too much or spending too much time with his friends? Why had he retreated? Why didn't we take that trip to the U.S. Open we'd almost taken the month before?

All of it stirred up emotions that had become so familiar, like my own personal demons: Sadness, Anger, Regret, Guilt. Sadness ebbed and flowed like a tide, barely discernible during its shift, yet violently powerful in its movement. It could take me down in moments from a regular day of working and parenting to one where I was sobbing on the bedroom floor alone, tears and snot running down my face as all energy and livelihood were zapped out of me by the loss I suffered. I always knew what Sadness would do—make me quiet, introspective, and lonely for days. I didn't always cry, but those times when Sadness visited me always reminded me of my broken heart, one that barely beat when I thought of Todd.

Anger would sneak up on me, surprising me at unexpected moments, stealing away my spirit. Anger flared—nothing like Sadness with its smooth corners and reliable outcome. Anger was like a right hook, a jab to the gut that knocked me off balance, messed with my vision, elicited in me the rage to punch back, to scream and curse and tell God I was pissed and ready to kick his ass for leaving me all alone.

Guilt and Regret were different animals altogether. While Todd and I usually lived a pretty charmed life, there were so many things I wished I had done differently. My regret over not staying at the wedding dance was eating me alive. I kept reliving that night, trying to remember every moment I saw or talked to Todd. The image of him walking away after I told him I was going back to the hotel was burned into my brain— the last moment I would ever see my husband alive. I lay in bed reliving every moment and every memory, good and bad, yearning for sleep but rarely finding it.

TWENTY ONE

At five o'clock every morning, I was always awake, reliving moments, replaying scenarios in my head. When the sun started to brighten the sky, I started to consider whether I should remain in bed or get up and get on with the day. It was a fifty/fifty chance which decision I would make. Some days I stayed there in bed and considered my options, thought about Todd, or planned my day with Brooke. Other days I just came to terms with the fact that I wouldn't get back to sleep and forced myself to get up, but not without at least fifteen minutes of mental preparation.

There is an excerpt from the poem "Pluto" by Diane Ackerman that sums up my early morning waking.

> I return to Earth now
> As if to a previous thought,
> Alien and out of place,
> Like a woman who,
> Waking too early each day,
> Finds it dark yet
> And all the world asleep.

That was me all right, alien and out of place, not knowing what else to do but just get out of bed and start my day despite the early hour and no one else up yet. But I felt alone all the time, so it was fitting that I was up that early, a lone soul drifting with no anchor and no direction.

Once I did get up, I spent hours feeling sorry for myself, not just because Todd was gone, but because I was now a single mother left alone to deal with all the crap that was being thrown at me. Single parenthood was not something I had ever planned or wanted at any point in my life, and now that fate had been thrust upon me without my having any say in the matter. I got so angry and embarrassed when I was out in public with Brooke and saw people looking at my naked left ring finger, judging. I saw it in their eyes, assuming I made bad choices. And I found myself still saying "we" about everything to counteract that single mom-ness. "We" had a birthday party for our daughter. "We" went to the mall. What, do I have a turd in my pocket, I'd ask myself every time I caught myself saying "we." Speaking in couples' terms is a tough habit to break after doing it for six years. Sometimes I'd catch myself before I said it, but depending on the audience, I would still say "we." When I'd talk to someone I knew, I'd correct myself to "me" or "my," but when talking to a stranger, I'd still say "we" or "our" so they wouldn't think I was a single mom. I hate that term *single* but equally hate *widow*. It has such a sad, foreboding tone of loneliness and hopelessness. I always envision an old lady dressed in black, in her formal sitting room with all of her cats, drinking a cup of tea, the world spinning on around her while she is locked in time and space—always alone and always waiting for someone who will never come.

When people compare widowhood to divorce, I just want to scream. They are *not* the same. The person you divorced is still alive, and you can still talk to and see them; you are apart by choice. When you're widowed, the person is gone. You can't talk to them. You can't see them continue their path in life. You can't see them raise the daughter they hardly got a chance to know.

At a writing class, I met a woman who has been both divorced and widowed in her lifetime.

"I just don't understand how people can compare widowhood and divorce," I complained to her, shaking my head. "They don't seem the same to me at all!"

She replied, matter-of-factly, "Let me tell you, there is a huge difference, and I would choose widowhood because when you're widowed, you're left with the love. When you're divorced, you're left with bitterness and anger."

I continued to shake my head. "But with divorce, at least the person is still alive. If I could have Todd back I would completely change my attitude toward him. He could golf as much as he wanted, he could be on ten softball teams, he could hang out with his buddies every night, and I would not bitch or complain about any of it. I wouldn't nag him about completely pointless things, like not helping more with Brooke, or driving erratically. None of that stuff really matters. It's the milestones and the little things that all add up to a life, shared experiences with your loved ones that create memories. I just wouldn't let any of it get in the way of our life together." My voice rose as I tried to get my point across.

"Maybe you would, or maybe you wouldn't," she said simply.

I was struck by her words. Maybe I wouldn't. If Todd were still here, would I give up my own happiness to let him do whatever he wanted? That wouldn't make me any happier than I was now without him, would it?

That day in class, our assignment was to write whatever we wanted. I chose to write to Todd, confused and angry about the conversation I had just had with my divorced/widowed classmate.

Damn you, Todd! Couldn't you have fought harder when death came for you? Weren't we enough? Did you want to go so badly that you couldn't fight the light to stay with us? Now I'm alone and have to be a single mom, and I hate it. I hate all of it! It's not fair, and I'm so pissed at you for leaving and pissed at both of us for not being more engaged in our relationship after Brooke was born. Maybe if I hadn't been so stressed and crabby I would have noticed that your heart wasn't right. Now I'll never know until I die and see you again. And when that happens, I'm coming to find you—to get some answers.

TWENTY TWO

A few weeks after Todd died, a friend asked me to a movie. I don't know why, but we decided to go to "Dan in Real Life," about a widower played by Steve Carrell. In one scene, he gets out of bed, but it takes a huge amount of effort to do this one simple task. It's as if every cell in his body needs to be mobilized in order to take that leap of faith off the edge of the bed and move forward. But he takes a deep breath and just does it. As I sat in the theatre, surrounded by people, I felt completely alone and completely identified with the scene playing out on the screen. That was exactly how it felt for me—it took everything I had to face the day, every single day.

Crushing loneliness is the closest I can get to describing it. I missed Todd so much when I woke up that it hurt to breathe some days, and the tears would come no matter how hard I tried to stop them. My days were always pretty much the same. When I finally convinced myself to get out of bed, I moved slowly, letting my memories of Todd linger for a few more seconds and then letting the morning cruelly overtake me. I tentatively rolled over, hoping my nighttime fantasies would overrule my daytime nightmare, but when I slid my hand under the sheets toward his space, the bed was cold beside me and the pillows lay undisturbed, the contours of his head no longer imprinted there. I breathed in and out for what felt like an eternity as I once again prepared to face another day in my new life that wasn't so new anymore—my new normal. I reluctantly eased my legs off the bed, and Cosmo immediately sprang to life, tail wagging, anticipating his breakfast.

Cosmo. When Todd and I decided to get a dog, it was at my instigation and not without much discussion. It was before we were married, so we decided that the dog would be at my house except when

I traveled for work. But would Todd mind watching the dog when I was gone? What would we do with him when we traveled together? Were we ready for that kind of commitment and responsibility? Little did Todd know I'd already decided I was getting a dog no matter what he thought.

I looked for a couple of weeks for the right dog ownership scenario. I didn't want one from a pet store or a puppy mill, and I didn't want just any breed. I wanted a Labrador retriever from someone who owned both parents. I finally found a family about half an hour away who owned both the mother and father, and they had a large litter from which to choose.

"Todd, I'm going to go look at the puppies now, but I'm just going to look. I'll call you later," I said to his voicemail as I pulled into the family's driveway. A very nice woman of about thirty came to the door with a baby on her hip—a good sign that the dogs were family- and kid-friendly.

"Hi, I'm Kristen. We talked earlier, and I'm here to look at the puppies," I said, trying not to sound too excited.

"Oh yes, they're in the garage. Let me go open the door." She shifted the baby to her other hip and retreated back into the house. I walked to the front of the garage, and a few seconds later the door sprang to life, rising to reveal the inner sanctum of puppy land. At the back of the garage was a large, fenced area with the most precious sight I'd ever seen. Nine tiny black puppies scurried to the eighteen-inch-high fence, tripping over each other as they tried to scale it. They panted and yipped at me as if trying to get my attention, saying "pick me, pick me." How could I choose just one of those adorable little creatures? I am a big dog lover, and if I hadn't brought only enough cash for one, I'm pretty sure I would have walked out of there with two dogs that night. I got teary-eyed as I ran toward them and started petting them and picking them up.

"Go ahead and take them out. Sit down and play with them. Take them out in the grass and see which one you like and which ones like you," the woman said.

I scooped up two dogs and brought them out into the yard while the woman opened the fence and let the rest out. They all came running to me, and I was overwhelmed again, wondering how I could pick just one.

I decided I needed to be smart and separate myself from the cuteness of the little buggers. I saw that a couple of the puppies had drifted off on their own. "Those two obviously don't like me," I said, and the owner picked them up and brought them back to the garage. That left seven. I tried picking up two others and petting them, but they squirmed out of my arms. We were clearly not a match, so they went back to the garage too. Down to five. They all sniffed around me and tried getting onto my lap, but eventually a few wandered off to do their own thing. Down to two. I cuddled and loved them up, and it became clear that one of them was my guy. He didn't want to leave my side and nuzzled in closer as I held him. Down to one!

"This is the puppy. He didn't leave my side the whole time," I announced, cuddling the ball of fur to my chest.

"He's a big boy, the biggest male in the bunch," the woman replied, smiling.

And he would become my big boy. At six years old and almost ninety pounds, he thought he was a lapdog. When I sat on the floor for any reason, he took it as his personal invitation to crawl into my lap like a puppy, even though only his head fit. And he would turn into a crazy doggie toddler, completely destroying most bones or dog toys in less than five minutes. After Todd died, he didn't leave my side unless I physically left him alone in the house.

He is the best dog. Although high maintenance in his neediness and cuddliness, that's why I got a dog, to be a companion and family member. I couldn't imagine life without him, despite the pain in the butt that he could be sometimes. He missed Todd, too. Every time Todd's scent wafted from anywhere, Cosmo was right there, bouncing around as if he just walked in the door, just as he used to do when Todd would get home from work or just come back into the house from the backyard.

About six weeks after Todd died, I decided to sell his car. I cleaned it out slowly, emptying it of Todd's things over the course of a couple weeks.

With every item I carried into the house, Cosmo would anxiously circle me, thinking maybe this time Todd was finally coming home. When the day finally came for the buyer to come pick up the car, I wasn't ready. I'd known this moment was coming and had been mentally preparing for it for weeks. But suddenly, that presence, that symbol of Todd, the car he was so proud of, that he kept immaculately clean and regularly serviced, was going to be taken away. I went to the garage, which was filled with Todd's things—golf clubs with divots still clinging to them, grass-stained softball gear, remnants of decorations from the surprise fiesta-themed thirtieth birthday party I'd thrown for him just a few months before, countless duffel bags and coolers, college paraphernalia. The garage had been his area, as it is for most men. But unlike most men, Todd had no system of organization whatsoever, so things were piled on shelves, tucked into drawers, crammed into boxes—a mess I couldn't tackle on top of the task I was now facing. I opened the car door. His scent poured over me, and the emotions and memories came flooding back.

He hadn't wanted to buy a new vehicle without my "approval," so when he finally found one he liked, we ventured out into the wintry, icy weather to look at it and take it for a test drive. I wouldn't drive it myself that night because of my irrational fear of driving during the winter and of the dreaded black ice, but he drove it and loved it. His characteristic months of research paid off, and he bought the silver Lincoln LS, decked out with all the bells and whistles he could ask for. He drove it home like a parade float for all to see, so proud of his new purchase. And now I felt like I was discarding his prized possession.

I started to clean out the last few things left in the car—his CDs; the latest Vince Flynn book he'd been reading, still dog-eared where he'd left off; and a surprising treasure—cards and photos I didn't know he'd saved from Brooke and me, tucked neatly in his side console and above the mirror. At that moment, I experienced the most intense pain I'd felt up to that point—a piercing, stabbing, crushing weight as I realized he was really, really, really not coming home. I sat in the driver's seat with tears burning my eyes and sobs choking my throat, unable to breathe. It was as if the presence of the car in the garage meant that Todd was just on vacation and was coming back for it. But when I backed it out and parked it in the driveway with the keys inside, stripped of everything that was Todd except its scent, the harsh reality set in, and I began to lose my footing. I dragged myself back into the house. The darkness obscured my tear-stained face, but my mom could tell I was distraught. All I could manage to say through my sobbing was, "I guess he's really not coming home." My mom put her arm around me as I cried, then I walked to my bedroom in a haze, all energy gone. And that was it. An hour later, the car was gone, and I felt like I'd lost him all over again.

The next day, when I carried the rest of Todd's things inside from the garage, Cosmo went crazy, sniffing his clothes and scampering around, wagging his tail. Those moments when Cosmo was missing Todd were so hard for me, knowing I wasn't loving the dog enough, or was loving him enough but not able to show it by taking him for enough walks or giving him enough attention. I was so distracted by work, Brooke, home projects, and just trying to cling to what remained of my life that, unfortunately, Cosmo sometimes got the dregs of my attention. He still slept with me every night, and I tried to walk him when I could, but during those early weeks it didn't happen very often. Todd had walked the nature trails with him so many times, and I felt so alone knowing that was a place he frequented but wasn't there now. When I did walk Cosmo, he would pull and sniff and basically walk me as I shuffled along the trails, lonely and wishing Todd were with us. But all we had left were the possessions, scents, and memories of the guy who once walked with us in life but was now gone.

Every time I cleaned out a closet or a drawer of Todd's things, Cosmo anxiously showed up, sniffing, confused, wondering where Todd was and why he could smell Todd but he wasn't there. I would get confused sometimes too, when the scent was still so strong, his clothes still smelled as if he had just worn them. When I cleaned out the last things from his closet to move Brooke into that bedroom, I ached for just one hug—to be able to smell his soapy clean skin, his Pantene-scented hair, his Trident peppermint gum breath one more time. But now those scents lingering in his old closet and the faint traces of cologne left in his clothes were all I had as I navigated my new world alone.

TWENTY THREE

After Todd died, I became extremely protective of Brooke, a mother bear fighting for her cub's survival in every way I knew how. I did everything short of monitoring her heart rate to be sure she was safe. In one of my many attempts to be a responsible parent, I enrolled Brooke in swimming lessons. Despite her not being able to stand on her own, let alone swim, we went to weekly forty-five-minute lessons with four other kids and their parents. The other children were a little older than Brooke but equally as unenthused about being in the water surrounded by onlookers. But I tried to be positive and enthusiastic to get Brooke excited about it.

Before our first lesson, I packed our bag—swimsuits, swimming diapers, shampoo, conditioner, soap, lotion—everything we would need to get in and out of the water, clean off the chlorine, and get dressed for the rest of our day. I loaded Brooke into the car.

"Here we go to swimming lessons. It's going to be so fun!" I exclaimed, too enthusiastically. She looked at me inquisitively, her vocabulary skills too undeveloped to express her confusion and apprehension. If she could speak, I imagined her asking, "What's swimming?" I gave her a peck on the cheek and drove the ten minutes to the swim center in a neighboring suburb.

We pulled into the parking lot, and I got out our giant bag of supplies, slung Brooke onto my hip, and walked into the center. Several other parents were there too, all with kids and towels. Towels? I hadn't brought towels. I just assumed they would provide those, like my old health club did.

"Do you have any spare towels I could borrow? It's our first time, and I forgot them," I explained to the receptionist, feeling stupid that I had forgotten such a key component of swimming lessons.

"Of course, let me grab a couple." She reached under the desk and handed me two of the rattiest, most threadbare towels I had ever seen. The edges were frayed, and I could see light penetrating the fabric as she handed them over the desk. I took them from her quickly, tucking them under my arm to hide my unpreparedness and shame. Bad parent move of the day #1.

"We're here for the baby class—Brooke Brown. I'm not sure where to go," I said, hoping no one would pass us and see the towels.

"Just head into the changing room over there and then follow the signs out to the pool. You'll be at station five on the far side of the pool.

We followed her directions and entered the changing room, where I expected to see rows of lockers and benches. Instead, we walked into a brightly lit, gigantic room lined with hooks and benches and filled with fully clothed women helping their independent kids change into swimsuits. Umm, where was the somewhat private, dimly lit, locker-filled area I'd been expecting? Where was I supposed to remove my clothing and don a swimsuit, something I wasn't thrilled about to begin with? I walked in the other direction, hoping to see another changing area, but the only things in that space were two bathroom stalls, both with large signs saying "No changing in the bathroom stalls!" Okay, that's fine. I can change in a room full of women and children. No big deal.

I returned to the room, and all eyes turned toward me. The moms stared me down as if I'd entered some exclusive club where I hadn't been invited. The kids looked at Brooke. I smiled weakly and slid our big bag of supplies off of my shoulder onto the nearest open bench seat. I somehow managed to get us both undressed and into our swimsuits without exposing too much.

"Okay, let's go out to the pool," I said to Brooke, relieved to get out of that uncomfortable situation.

I followed the signs and pushed open the door leading to the pool area. "Oh, crap!" I'm not sure if I said it aloud or if it was just in my head, but as I entered the humid, chorine-filled atmosphere, I was once again met by stares. The pool was encircled by chairs filled with parents, grandparents, and other kids watching the lessons in progress in the pool. As I looked for station five, the words of the receptionist came back to me: "You'll be at station five *on the far side of the pool.*" Spying a large number five hanging above the end of the pool, I realized that the only path to get there was between the pool edge and the chairs filled with onlookers. I strategically slid our bag around to cover my backside and placed Brooke on one hip with her legs covering my stomach and the thigh that would be facing the audience as I walked by.

"Brooke, this is going to be so fun," I lied, speed-walking past the spectators toward the promised land of station five, where four other parents with babies were gathered. The instructor, a woman in a Speedo one-piece and a rubber swimming cap, walked toward us. At her prompting, we all got into the water. Brooke was *not* happy and cried the whole time. At one point, her slippery body scooted right out of my hands as we did the back float. She went completely under water with no warning, sputtering and crying as I pulled her back into my shoulder. Bad parent move of the day #2.

After the lesson, I quickly got out of the pool and had no choice but to pull out the raggedy scraps of fabric to dry us off. I carried Brooke back toward the locker room, looking forward to rinsing off and getting cleaned up. But there was another surprise—the showers weren't in the locker room, they were in the pool area—open-air showers for all onlookers to see, filled with little kids who had just finished their lessons. I figured all the supplies I'd brought wouldn't get used that day, or any swimming lesson day for that matter. I inserted myself and Brooke into the middle of the kids in the shower area and tried to get at least a trickle of water over us to wash away the chlorine, rewrapped us in the towels, and went back into the locker room to dry and dress without giving a peep show.

Finally back in our street clothes, I happily handed the poor excuse for towels back to the attendant at the reception desk, and we headed back to the parking lot. I was relieved and glad to have that hour of my life over with and was ready to get back home. I opened the back car door, tossed in the unused bag of supplies, and leaned over to secure

Brooke into her car seat. I threw my purse in the front and slammed the back door, stepping toward the driver's side. I grabbed the front door handle and pulled. The door didn't budge. I pulled again, at least ten times. It still didn't budge. I grabbed the back door—locked. I ran to the passenger side—locked. I tried the back hatch—locked. I peered through the window, and there next to Brooke's car seat were my keys. They must have fallen out of my pocket when I leaned over to fasten her in. *Oh my God, I have locked my daughter in the car!* Bad parent move of the day #3. Or, more precisely, bad parent move of the year!

I started to panic. "I cannot believe I just did this; I am such an idiot," I scolded myself, continuing to pull on the door handle but knowing it wouldn't open. I told myself to remain calm. Brooke was happy and secure in her car seat. It wasn't too hot or too cold out, so she wouldn't cook or freeze in there. All I had to do was call someone to bring me my spare key. Oh crap, where is my phone? Is it in my purse? Did it fall out of my pocket too? I frantically checked my pockets, realizing I didn't know anyone's phone number by heart if I had to go in and use a pay phone. My hand closed upon the cool metal of my phone in my back pocket, and I couldn't get it to my ear fast enough. I pulled up my mom's phone number on speed dial and waited impatiently for it to ring. And waited and waited. No answer. I tried my sister's number and waited for an answer. And waited and waited. What the hell? Where is everyone? I glanced in the car at Brooke while I composed myself. She was looking at me strangely, and I imagined her wondering, "What are you doing out there? Let's get out of here and away from that awful swimming thing you just made me do."

I inhaled deeply and smiled at her so she wouldn't see my anxiety and fear. I then tried Matt. I was so glad my sister had married him. I felt like he was my real brother, and I knew if he answered, he would help. Luckily, after two rings he picked up.

"Hi, what are you doing right now?" I asked quickly.

"I'm just at a friend's house watching a game. What's going on?"

"Can you run to my house and get my spare car key out of the desk and bring it to Knollwood Mall? I just locked Brooke in the car accidentally," I explained, feeling I needed to clarify that it was an accident.

"Oh geez, is she okay?"

"She's fine, but can you go fast? I don't want her to start crying. The spare key is in the top drawer on the right side of the desk. Sorry for the hassle, but no one else answered." I started pacing in front of the car.

"No problem, I'll be there shortly."

Help was now on the way, but I felt worse. I had just locked my child in the car. What if it had been hot out? What if I didn't have a spare key? What if my phone had been in the car? To make matters worse, Brooke then started to cry.

In an effort to keep her happy, I did something I would never do under normal circumstances: I danced. Yes, right there in a busy mall parking lot filled with people coming and going, I danced outside the car to keep Brooke entertained for the twenty minutes it took Matt to get there. I danced, moved from window to window, played peek-a-boo, and jumped around— anything to keep Brooke from having a meltdown while I stood helpless and unable to comfort her. Several cars drove by and looked at me strangely, and I was surprised that no one called the cops. I looked like a crazy person out there, either unstable and on drugs or a carjacker trying to break into our car.

Finally, Matt showed up and tossed me my keys as he pulled into a parking spot. I frantically unlocked the door and scrambled into the backseat next to Brooke. I hugged and kissed her.

"I'm so, so sorry! Mommy didn't mean to lock you in. That will never happen again," I murmured into her ear, hugging her close.

I meant well by following my protective instincts, but that didn't mean I didn't fail sometimes. And every time I did, I felt like I failed Todd, too. I was a mom and a dad now and had to do the best job I could at both. Brooke was relying on me, and so was Todd.

One of the largest responsibilities that I felt was financial. I had to pay the mortgage, pay the bills, and pay for day care. How would I do it all on my own? I had been waiting for two months for some sort of answer from the insurance company about Todd's policy, but they continued to tell me that they were still investigating it. So I waited and paid for things with my credit card and hoped that they wouldn't reject his policy, leaving us with nothing. Finally, two months after he died, I got a call from the insurance company.

"Hi, Ms. Brown? I just wanted to let you know that we have released the funds for the standard employee-provided death benefit, but we are still working on the voluntary amount," the agent explained.

"Thanks. When can I expect the check?" I asked, hoping it would be a quick turnaround.

"We are overnighting it to you today, so you should get it tomorrow. Please let us know if you don't receive in the next two days." A wave of relief washed over my tense body. I could finally feel like a responsible parent again and not rack up credit card debt. But it still wasn't enough to help with the mortgage. My ability to pay that each month was contingent on the policy that was still being investigated. So I continued to wait for the answer that would determine what my plan would be to provide for Brooke. But for now, we were safe.

TWENTY FOUR

While I did my best to protect Brooke, my own health and well-being were at the bottom of my to-do list. I didn't think things through very well. I didn't exercise. I didn't eat. When I would eat, it was always crappy food. Whenever I worked from home, lunchtime meant processed meat time. I'm an early-lunch girl, so at eleven or eleven thirty I would go to the refrigerator to peruse my food options. Seeing ham, salami, bacon, hot dogs, and prosciutto in the meat drawer has always made me smile. Is it wrong that I could eat processed and cured meat products for every meal? I am well aware of their health pitfalls. And I know, I know—I should be more conscious of what I put in my body, considering my husband died of a ninety-nine percent blockage in one of his main arteries, but it's a hard habit to break. I think there is a chemical in the meat that turns it into a drug—one that's fully capable of causing addiction. Because I admit, when it comes to smoked meats, I need my fix. I could probably name fifteen or twenty that I love just off the top of my head, but here are my top three in no particular order:

1. Bacon. What other food is there that is so versatile it can be eaten at any time of the day, breakfast, lunch, snack, or dinner? What other food can enhance anything you put it on, from salad to burgers to peanut butter toast? (Try it, you'll see!) What other food can be incorporated into virtually any ethnic food so seamlessly? Italian pizza—just add bacon. Mexican quesadilla—just add bacon. Norwegian potato klub—just add bacon. I've never had Chinese with bacon—but Chinese food, good; bacon, good—so how can Chinese food with bacon be bad? I've even tried bacon chocolate bars (not good) and seen bacon martinis (probably good) advertised at more than one location. I know I won't

find matzo ball soup with bacon or vegetarian falafel with bacon, but the rest of the world is covered.

2. Chorizo sausage. Smoky, spicy goodness. Enough said.

3. The good old reliable hot dog. There is no food on the planet that is so easily consumed no matter where you are. Standing on a street corner while hailing a cab? Check. Stranded at an airport sitting on the floor? Check. Walking around a giant fairground on a one hundred degree day surrounded by thousands of sweaty tourists? Check. Aside from its extreme portability, the hot dog is also delicious. Why else would people stand in endless lines at famous hot dog stands for one? Why else would competitive eaters participate in a contest to see who can eat the most? Because they're good in so many ways, that's why. I have tried to seek out the world's best hot dog every time I visit new cities. One such hot dog nirvana experience occurred two and a half months after Todd died.

After the funeral and early months of emotional meltdown, I thought a trip would be good for me. It would give me time to reflect, relax, and unwind. So I booked a trip to Kauai, Hawaii, over Thanksgiving. I splurged and flew first class, made reservations at a nice resort, and rented a car for the week. Wow, was I wrong about thinking a solo vacation was what I needed. Rolling my suitcase through the lobby of the hotel to check in, I saw couples everywhere: bellying up to the bar, strolling hand in hand down to the beach, kissing and cuddling. What had I gotten myself into? The first day I went down to lie by the ocean, but everywhere I looked were couples—unpleasant reminders of my sad state of affairs. I decided that lying on my verandah was a better option, and it was more peaceful, but I felt guilty for just staying in my room when I was in one of the most beautiful places in the world. I went to a luau one evening, feeling anxious and embarrassed for being alone, and ended up breaking down when a woman asked me about my life. So in an effort to fully participate in my vacation while maintaining distance from couples and avoiding conversation with strangers, I ended up spending most of my time at the spa, pampering myself with massages, facials, and body treatments.

One afternoon I walked to the little shopping village near my hotel—here it is, the hot dog nirvana story—in search of a little stand called Puka Dogs. I had seen it on the Travel Channel. Of course I hadn't missed the "Top 10 Hot Dog Havens in America" special. As I approached the shopping village, I saw a slow procession of people snaking around the perimeter of the palm-tree-fringed pathway. As I got closer, I saw that it was a line for none other than my destination, Puka Dogs. I figured if all those people were patient enough to stand in line for that long, it must be worth the wait, so I joined the rest of the tourists and locals to await my own taste of processed meat byproduct goodness.

When I got up to the counter, I was intrigued. The bun was a giant sweet roll that they stuck onto the end of a big metal pole to make a hole in it for the hotdog. There were a variety of condiments. Not your standard ketchup, mustard and relish, but local flavors like passion fruit, mango, and pineapple sauces that they squirted into the bun prior to adding the hot dog. After the twenty minutes in line, I couldn't wait to get my hands on one. It sounds pornographic and it almost was, the way I devoured that dog. The whole concept of the sweet bread and fruit initially seemed a little weird, but it came together in a heavenly combination of tastes and textures that ranks in my top five favorite meals of all time (and I've had some pretty damn good meals). It was fantastic, and I had more than two while I was there, trying a different sauce each time. Mango was my favorite. I also discovered stands all across the island selling yummy snow-cone-like treats of shaved ice and fruit syrup with thick, creamy milk poured over the top. Scrumptious. I had more than one of those while I was there, too.

I did try to get out and do some things. I took a breathtaking helicopter tour of the island, seeing places where they filmed *Jurassic Park* and *Lost*. I explored some charming towns and shopping areas, went to a couple of movies, and of course spent some quality time at the spa. But I was still so depressed and operating under a thick fog that I didn't appreciate what I was doing. Only now in retrospect do I realize that it may have been just what I needed to get my head around what had happened to me. But as I lived it, all I kept wishing was that Todd was with me.

I Wish—Hawaii

We stepped off the plane into the bright Hawaiian sunshine, the brilliant hues of red and yellow flowers and green foliage greeting us even here at the tiny island airport. Todd hugged me tightly to him, and we made our way to the cramped luggage claim and then to our waiting rented convertible. We put the top down, letting the humid warmth surround us, and leisurely drove out of the airport to our seaside resort twenty minutes down the palm-tree-lined, single-lane highway. We held hands and talked excitedly about what we'd do first—full-body massages, a big fruity drink in a coconut, some nooky and a catnap before dinner, a dip in the pool, a leisurely stroll down the deserted beach—so much to do in just five days. But we accomplished all of it and more, cuddling in the curtained cabana by the pool, indulging in mass quantities of seafood oceanside at quaint, candlelit restaurants, relaxing in the luxurious spa, and just spending time together away from the chaos of our everyday lives back in Minnesota.

We decided we would make this an annual tradition and spend our Thanksgiving in a tropical location every year, giving thanks for each other and what we have and reconnecting as a couple. It would give us perspective to make us the best parents, kids, friends, siblings, and employees we could be by learning to appreciate ourselves and each other first.

If only that's what had happened. If only we'd taken that trip to paradise together—another locale to add to our long list of vacation destinations we'd been to through the years. Instead, I went alone and left Hawaii feeling more lonely and more sad and more angry than I had been before I left. Everywhere I went and everything I did reminded me of Todd. The gourmet meals I ate were sand in my mouth without him to share them with. The beautiful scenery was marred without him there to appreciate it with. The long, lingering naps we so loved were fraught with nightmares and sleeplessness without his arms around me. What should have been the trip of a lifetime was a misguided detour that left me crying and missing his companionship more than ever. I suffered through those endless days, staring at the ocean from my seaside suite built for two that instead housed just me and my broken heart. I was alone in the world.

Sad Trip

Push, pull -
    Endless time wraps and coils.

Breathe in, out -
    Embracing and fighting solitude all at once.

Shadowy figures hover -
    Unseen, guiding, revealing truths.

Straining to see them –
    Midnight darkness leaves deep wounds.

Salty tears, salty air and a salty rim -
    Poor bedfellows make.

Desperate for something to make me forget -
    I sip.
    I sob.
    I sleep.

Awakened by a memory -
    The smell of sea and sweat and sun on coconut-oiled bodies.

Alone now to revel in this paradise–
    Revelry in grief.

Alone with only the sea –
   And a bottle of Coppertone.

The bottle flies –
   Half the contents spill to the floor.

Perfect–
   Enough left for only me.

   —*Kristen Brown*

TWENTY FIVE

I was desperate for Todd to somehow come back to reassure me he was okay. I lay awake at night, hoping every creak of the floorboards and every leaf blowing against the window was him ready to show himself. And finally, late one night as I dozed in and out of sleep, those imagined visitations I had been fabricating became very, very real.

* * *

I open my eyes to impenetrable darkness. The air feels thick and heavy with electricity, and my body is soaked with perspiration. I strain to see through the shadows. My bedroom is filled with a suffocating heat that burns my skin; yet I shiver, chilled to the bone alone under the blankets, hoping this might finally be the night he shows up. The hot, oppressive air pins me to my pillow. As my vision adjusts to the night, my eyes see that the room is empty, but my instincts say otherwise. The hairs on my arms stand on end, and I stare into the blackness, sensing him and straining for a sign, some hint of his presence. My pulse pounds. I can feel my heart thumping and racing in my chest, anxious and confused, excited and hopeful. I am not breathing for fear that any exchange of air will disrupt the flow of energy in the room—Todd's energy. I am not afraid. I feel his particles vibrating around and through me, his spirit hovering over me, yet I still see nothing. But I feel it and know it's him. Finally, after months of waiting, he's showing himself.

"Todd, are you here?" I whisper, my eyes welling up with tears. I wait anxiously for a response, a shifting of light, a faint breeze, something to know he's acknowledging me. "Are you okay?" I whisper again, hoping I'll get an affirmation that he is happy on the other side. The heat in the room intensifies as I wait for him, missing him so badly. I scan the room.

Did I see the curtain move?

Was that a sound?

I listen and look, willing something to happen.

The air changes suddenly, an abrupt cooling and calming. The feeling of electricity relents, and I sense him leaving.

"That's not enough!" I sob, my heart breaking. But he's gone. Then, like a bittersweet kiss goodbye, Brooke babbles in her crib next door, and I know he's with her now. She's just a year old, awake and cooing as her daddy makes his presence known to her. Moments later she is quiet, and silence punctuates the fact that he is gone and I am alone again in my bed with only emptiness filling the space beside me.

Knowing I won't sleep again this night, I get up. I walk by his closet, and my heart leaps: the bi-fold doors are ajar. They were shut when I went to bed just two hours ago. As on most other nights, I had squeezed inside the tiny space to inhale his scent, letting the familiar, sweet musk of his body and cologne wash over me. I would curl up on the floor on top of the clothes stacked there—sometimes for a few minutes, sometimes for hours—and then pull the doors shut, not wanting to let any of his smells escape. But now the doors are open. Todd was here, trying to communicate with me, to let me know he's okay.

Todd, are you still here? I've spent so many nights waiting and longing for you to visit me somehow—as a ghost, in a dream—hoping for any sort of connection or sign to prove you're still with me. I wanted to apologize and make peace. To let you know of all my regrets about our relationship before you died. To express my frustrations with how you changed—and how I changed. And now you've finally shown that you were here, and I feel worse than ever. Like I've lost you all over again. The pain and regret I feel are eating me alive, and I don't know what to do.

But suddenly, I don't feel lonely any more. A feeling of peace settles over me. My husband, my best friend, Brooke's daddy—he isn't gone.

He really is here with us, and we're not alone anymore. And yet, I'm lonely. Yes, I'm lonely. Not the "I-need-a-night-out-with-the-girls" kind of lonely, but the kind of lonely where the tears and snot are indiscernible before they even hit the pillow. It's a black hole in the soul kind of lonely that I hope I won't experience more than once in a lifetime. It's the only kind of lonely you can feel when you're drifting directionless through a murky world with no light penetrating the fog no matter how hard you look in every direction. This wasn't a part of my plan. I am supposed to have 2.5 kids, 2.5 acres and $250K in the bank. I'm in my early 30s, supposed to be settled, supposed to be happy. Instead I'm alone with a lingering grief over a life I should have had that's now gone, a grief over the loss of my husband, my best friend and the father of a daughter who will never know him. And so I'm lonely in a way that no one can measure and only I can heal.

REALITY

"The past exists only in our memories,
the future only in our plans.
The present is our only reality."
—Robert M. Pirsig

TWENTY SIX

Although I had been a closet writer all my life—journaling, creating stories, expressing myself through letters and poems—I hardly wrote anything after Todd died. Finally, on December 10, 2007, three months and a day after his death, the words started to come again. They weren't coherent at first, just scrawled lines and the occasional sentence, but at least it was something. Once the first line came out—"I just want to live again, get away from this pain"—the pent-up emotions that had been troubling me for ninety-two days finally found their outlet. Soon, the sentences became paragraphs, and the paragraphs became pages. After that, it became an avalanche of emotions and thoughts puked onto paper. That's the only accurate description of what those early writings were—puking on paper. I would heave out everything from the very bottom of my soul until there was nothing left. And when I hit that wall, I would walk away, immerse myself in some other task to erase all the pain and hurt I had regurgitated. My type-A tendencies usually drove me to organize closets or clean something in the house to ground myself in routine and familiarity.

One such afternoon I was working in my home office, sorting and putting away junk, when I stumbled upon a packet of pictures from a vacation Todd and I had taken to Mexico early in our relationship. And I just lost it—tears, snot, blubbering, a real mess. As I sat in that space that didn't feel like Todd was a part of anymore, I so badly wanted him there. I looked at those pictures and couldn't bear the loneliness and sadness. It was as if he had been there just the previous day, and yet like he'd never been there at all, as if I dreamt him. My chest was crushing me as I tried to breathe this air that he wasn't breathing, and I felt helpless again, sinking into an ocean of sorrow that wouldn't release me from its current. All of those years that had been ahead of us were now a distant memory. More babies, more pets, a bigger yard, maybe even a farm—I couldn't stop thinking about them. All of that should have been happening instead of the nightmarish reality I was in and trying to overcome. I didn't know how I would ever get over him.

Looking through those Mexico pictures, I punished myself even further by opening the photo boxes and going through each one, picture by picture, my heart aching for all those times with the man I had lost. As I sat there on the floor surrounded by my memories, I found a note I'd written to Todd almost a year before, on our second wedding anniversary.

Todd,

Last Christmas, I got the best Christmas gift I could have gotten—you! Now, two years later, I'm still thankful every day for what has become the best thing that's ever happened to me.

I can't imagine spending Christmas or my life with anyone else! I'm proud to say that you're not only my significant other, but you've also become my best friend. Nothing and no one makes me smile and laugh more than you. Even when I'm stressed or crabby, you put up with me and always manage to cheer me up—and for that I want to say thank you! I can only hope to spend the rest of my life being half as happy as I am now. In return, I promise to do all I can to bring you as much joy as you've given me.

Never before have I been so excited about the future, and I'm looking forward to spending many more holidays together. Thank you for making me a better person. What we have is more than I could have ever wished for, and I love you more than you know!

Always yours,
Kristen

Now those words still felt one hundred percent true—despite our challenges after Brooke was born, despite all my regret and anger over his death. Todd had been gone for three months, and I missed him now more than ever.

A few days later, on the eve of what should have been our third wedding anniversary, I stayed up late and wrote to Todd. I wrote for hours, my mind jumping back and forth between emotions. I was not celebrating, although I knew I should have been joyful and thankful for the time we had. But I was so terribly angry that Todd wasn't there to share things with every day. He wasn't there to love or love me back. I wasn't alone, but I felt so lonely, even in a room full of people. Sadness permeated my being, and even when I smiled, laughed, or talked, I was crying and crushed inside, always thinking of him and wishing he were somehow there again. We hadn't been sappy in our relationship, but then all I could think were sappy thoughts. I wished he were here so we could dance and I could tell him how much I loved him and appreciated what he did for me. I knew he felt he was sacrificing a lot of his time with friends after Brooke was born, but I also knew he loved it, too. One of the things I wrote to Todd the night of our anniversary got to the heart of how I was feeling.

Todd, three years ago tonight we were so happy and had our future in front of us. Who could have known it would end so tragically? I wish you'd come around more often, just so I'd know you're okay. I haven't felt you very often—your presence—and I'm wondering why. I miss you so much and love you more now than ever. It's not fair how you don't appreciate what you have until it's gone, and now it's too late. We may not have had a grand romance or a timeless love story, but it was our story—a short story, one with a tragic ending. I knew you for just six years, but really I knew you my whole life. I dreamt about you when I was a little girl, I just didn't know then it would be you who would make all those dreams come true when I grew up. There isn't an hour that goes by when I don't regret not loving you better and not doing more to make us a priority. I let myself get sucked into the routine of everyday life and in the process forgot to really "live." I forgot that my soul mate needed his best friend just as I needed you, and I was too stubborn to reach out. We got so overwhelmed by parenthood and our jobs and everything else that could and would consume our time that we forgot to value and love each other the way we should have. I've been living with this guilt and regret of not being the best wife I could have been and not motivating you to be the best husband back. We had such a complementary love, one that forced us to both grow as people, to become better and wiser and happier. Why didn't we continue doing that? Did we both feel ourselves shifting so far away from our former selves that we dug in our heels and just stopped caring or trying? I never stopped caring, but I think our complementary yet opposing personalities caused us to forget each other. Now, all I want to do is remember you and love you and be the best wife I can be to you, but you're gone. The only thing I can do is carry on and give you in death what I didn't give fully in life—the respect, love, and true faith that our relationship could and will get us through anything, including helping me get over your death to start to live again.

I missed Todd and loved him more each day as I uncovered deeper layers of myself and related to him and our relationship in new and different ways. It was Todd who got me through that mess, Todd who silently guided me on the right path, Todd who kept my head above water. So many people turn to God and their faith to get them through rough patches in their life, but that wasn't me. I turned to Todd and let him be my strength while I struggled with my place in the world. Even in my loneliness and his absence, I wanted our connection back. And a few days later, I got it.

On Christmas Eve, my immediate family and I were in Florida at a relative's house to avoid the group festivities of that first holiday without Todd. We decided to take my uncle's boat on a cruise just before sunset. We were cruising along slowly in the bay off Fort Myers Beach, when a pod of dolphins suddenly appeared just feet from us. It was surreal and almost unbelievable that something I'd only seen in movies was happening right in front of me. They swam together, weaving in and out, as we coasted along behind them. I was amazed at the true beauty and significance of this experience—this once-in-a-lifetime commune with nature. That night, I lay in bed and wrote about it.

Todd, I felt as if you were here tonight. I finally felt a connection to you again. I didn't tell anyone that, but I really felt as if it was you leading those dolphins to us, giving us something to be awed by on that first Christmas Eve without you. You weren't just my significant other, you were a part of my family, and they loved you as a son and brother. You left a void in their lives, too—one that will always be there. You'll always be missed and remembered, not just during these significant moments like being surrounded by dolphins in the ocean on Christmas Eve, but also during quiet times when you'll creep into our thoughts to say hello and remind us of the imprint you left on our lives. You were a fun, happy guy who valued your friendships above all else, and you weren't willing to let anything compromise your relationships. You lived your life like poker. You relaxed, played your chips right, took some risks, and hoped your hand would fall into place in the end. And while in my mind we were both dealt a shitty hand, I can only hope that you'll get a better hand the next time around, and I will too.

I laugh as I use a poker analogy. I had never understood Todd's love, or should I say obsession, with it. How could a simple card game really be that fun and exciting—even with betting involved? It's just ten bucks! I could not fathom why he'd stay up until two or three in the morning playing cards at a buddy's house. One night I finally asked him to explain the game to me, to let me in on that magical world of straights, flushes, and poker chips. I'd watched it on television with him—quite possibly the most boring thing to watch on television ever, except for maybe auto racing. We got out his poker set, and he explained the rules and the object of the game and how to win. I still didn't get the allure, but I gave him the benefit of the doubt and agreed to play a few hands. Within minutes, I was hooked. I loved it—the betting, trying to maintain a poker face (which I am horrible at), trying to outwit the other players (namely him, since it was just us playing). For once, his athletic prowess couldn't be used against me, and it was a battle of wits and tricks—and I was pretty good.

After that night, we'd occasionally play together, and eventually I decided to join one of his boys' games at a party a couple of our friends hosted. The girls couldn't believe I was agreeing to play. One by one, I picked the guys off, much to their anger and frustration. Finally, it was down to me and another guy. He did not like to lose, much less lose to a first-timer and a girl at that. Slowly, I eroded his chip count and finally emerged the winner. Todd was pretty impressed with me, and proud that his wife finally shared one of his interests. After that I continued to play at family gatherings or whenever the opportunity presented itself. I finally understood the game and Todd's addiction to it.

And sometimes I felt like I was betting it all in real life. Todd's death raised the stakes for me, and every move I made had to be much more thought-out and strategized because it wasn't just me I was living for, but Brooke and Cosmo, my new little family. The three of us were like a little team—playing together in the house that was our stadium, cheering each other on, picking each other up when we fell, slapping each other on the butt with every win. I knew Todd was there, too. He was our unseen defensive line, keeping all the opposing forces at bay in order for us to have our breathing room and space to heal. He was there as we developed our new family ties and our new home without him.

Webster's defines home as "one's place of residence ... the social unit formed by a family living together ... a familiar, relaxed, comfortable setting." In our home, I was the most comfortable and happy, surrounded by memories and our things—things that now held so much more significance. Even the house itself was like a friend, welcoming me with open arms as I pulled into the driveway and reassuring me that things were okay. I had molded and shaped the house and its landscape to fit Todd and me. Now I was shaping it to fit Brooke and Cosmo and me. As a team we rallied together to survive that crushing blow of defeat we suffered, but we wouldn't let it win. We were fighters—a team in the truest sense of the word, fighting an uphill battle together until we came out victorious in the end. I'm sure Todd loves that analogy, and that's really how it felt. I only hoped I could defy the odds stacked against me and be a good mom and dad to Brooke. I wrote to Todd often about that, hoping I was doing an okay job despite everything I was feeling.

Todd, after you died, the remaining three months of 2007 were a blur. I tried to find some happiness. I went to Hawaii alone for Thanksgiving to escape the pain. Mistake. I went to Florida with my family for Christmas to escape the first holiday without you. Mistake. I could have been in our house, in Hawaii, or on Mars and it wouldn't have changed anything—I still would have been lost, alone, and lonely missing you and trying to be a mother—and now a father—to Brooke. I hope I am not failing at the job that should have been yours.

TWENTY SEVEN

I stared at the ceiling. The same twelve inches burned into my brain as I memorized the features of the air conditioning vent. Sleep still eluded me. I dreaded those hours between midnight and six a.m. when it seemed that all the world was resting except me. I slept fitfully, tossing and turning, in and out of good and bad dreams, always listening for another sign of Todd's presence.

After that nighttime encounter when he first visited me, he started showing up in my dreams. I welcomed, yet also dreaded, those dreams. When I met Todd in slumber I wanted to go on sleeping forever, just to stay with him. Sometimes he'd talk to me; nothing meaningful or enlightening that I can remember, just everyday conversation about whatever was happening in the dream. Regular, mundane things like playing in the yard with Brooke, meeting at home after work, going out to eat—things from our normal life. But most often, my dreams of Todd were bittersweet fantasies about him coming back from the dead but not wanting to be with the living. Many times I dreamed I was hosting a welcome-home party for him, but he didn't want to be there. He was distant and melancholy; he wasn't the same fun-loving guy that I knew and loved, with sparkling eyes and a sarcastic laugh. Instead, he was silent and sad with dead eyes and no vitality. Those dreams were disturbing, but comforting too, because as much as I wanted to believe that he would come back to us if he could, I also wanted to believe that wherever he was, it was so wonderful that he wouldn't want to leave.

Because I was always in and out of dreams, I was always tired, forced to go to work with very little mental clarity. And trying to focus on anything beyond what was happening right in front of me, trying to regain my grip on reality, became exhausting. To make matters worse, it was wintertime, when I typically feel tired and depressed. Now cold, snow, and sadness were my constant companions. My parents had moved back home, and I was overwhelmed with the responsibilities of both being a full-time single mom and working a full-time job.

All other winters, no matter how cold the weather or depressing my circumstances, there was always one bright spot, a glimmer of joy that took away my depression—movie awards season. I know, it sounds ridiculous, but year after year, I have always looked forward to it. For me, it's like the playoffs and the Super Bowl. My friends and I always try to see as many of the nominated films as possible, and we have movie parties where we watch the awards shows together. That year, anticipating the movie awards was what helped me keep my sanity. Among all the craziness of dealing with emotions, finances, and single parenting, it remained in the back of my mind that soon, very soon, I would be able to start crossing movies off of my printed lists of nominees for the Golden Globes, the SAG Awards, the Spirit Awards, and the granddaddy of them all, the Oscars. But it started to look like even that bit of happiness was at risk.

It began with the writer's strike early that winter. The buzz was that the new television season could be canceled, shows were at risk, and no new movies were being made. But the worst news was that the Golden Globes might be canceled. No—it couldn't be; they had to happen, it was the best show of the year. The stars could eat and drink (although you never really saw anyone eating), and it was less formal than the Oscars, so there was more of a chance to see some really crazy fashions, both good and bad. And of course the movies—I can't forget the movies. This was the first year I'd seen almost all of the big films. In my free time away from Brooke, I went to movies by myself, which I had done before, but now it just felt like the right thing to do to fill my time. I was alone, so why not go to the movies alone and try to escape my loneliness?

I've always been able to escape reality when sitting in the theater, and now I had an awful reality to escape. I could sit in the dark and forget that I was a widow and instead let myself become completely immersed in the story unfolding on-screen. I could pretend I was a damsel in distress being rescued by a hero in a tuxedo. I could pretend I was a villainous sorceress controlling the world around me. I could pretend I was a happy mother of three with a career as a writer, a home on a lake, a loving husband, and a couple of dogs. Oh, how I loved going to the movies!

And then the writers' strike officially shut down the Golden Globes. I sat on my couch with what should have been a celebratory glass of champagne or two while watching the show and instead saw a ridiculous press event where television announcers from various entertainment news shows read the awards on camera. No red carpet, no stars, no fashion police, nothing. The cancellation of the Golden Globes only exacerbated my anger and frustration. Why was I letting a little thing like a Hollywood writers' strike affect me so much? Because awards season was the one thing I'd been anticipating to get me through the winter. It was the one thing that made me feel connected to the outside world. It was the one simple pleasure I had left. It was one of few bright spots I could find after Todd's death.

My love of celebrity goings-on is not just an external appreciation of the art of filmmaking and acting. I had acted throughout junior high and high school and was even an extra in a couple of scenes in the movie *Joe Somebody* with Tim Allen. I loved acting, but career and family took priority, and I hadn't done it in years. I decided to try it again, to get back in touch with that old part of myself that I had lost so long ago and to get myself back out into the world.

On a frigid January morning, I pulled into the parking lot of the local zoo for my first audition. (Why it was held at the zoo I have no idea.) I entered a very old building and found myself in a room full of middle-aged men in coveralls, drinking coffee. As I opened the heavy, squeaky door, camouflage-clad bodies and bright orange-hatted heads turned toward me.

"Umm, is this where the play auditions are?" I mumbled, knowing it wasn't but needing to augment my awkward presence with something besides a blank stare.

"No missy, this is the fishing expo. I think you need to head downstairs," one of the men said, winking at me and pointing toward another doorway.

"Unless of course you want to come over here and talk about fishing with us. We could use a cute one like you in the group," another guy teased, patting his knee with his hand. That was my cue to move on.

"Okay, thanks," I blurted and darted through the doorway away from the leering fishermen.

I descended the steep steps in the back of the building and entered a dark hallway lined with tables and chairs. At the end of the hall was a table with a sign for the auditions. It looked like I was the first one there. I peered into the room next to the table, and a huge, red-haired, red-bearded man peered back.

"You here for the auditions already?" he asked in a condescending tone.

"Don't they start at nine?" I asked, pulling out the info sheet I had printed off the Internet and hoping I had the right time.

"Yeah, but actors never show up until eleven." He sneered, clearly annoyed that I was there on time. I shifted uncomfortably, not sure what do next.

"Well, sign in and I'll call you in after a while. She'll give you the sides." He motioned toward a woman coming down the hall behind me. The sides? What the hell are those, I wondered. I signed in, and the woman handed me an excerpt from the play. Aha, the sides are the parts of the play I had to read for the audition. Apparently, my junior high and high school auditions didn't use the same terminology as grown-up theatre. I took the sheets and sat down to wait on the folding chairs that lined the wall opposite the table. It was ice cold, and I could still see my breath, even indoors.

About ten minutes later, the burly guy came out and motioned me into the room. Wondering what he'd been doing in there all that time, I entered his realm. To say I was nervous would be an understatement. Adding yet another layer of anxiety, this gigantic beast of a man had a terrible, hacking, phlegmy cough that just wouldn't stop. At one point I thought he might vomit, but he finally cleared his lungs and explained the setup.

"It's a takeoff on "Mary Had a Little Lamb" and is about two shepherds who are battling over territory, so really get into it. I want to see over the top." I took a deep breath and began to read. I knew it was awful from the first word that came out of my mouth. It was supposed to be funny, and I sounded serious. It was supposed to be dramatic, and I sounded sick.

"Stop, stop, stop," he interrupted, looking me up and down and glancing at my resume. I stood awkwardly in the middle of the room.

"You haven't done this in awhile?"

"No, not since high school, but I really miss it and want to get back into acting again," I blurted out too fast.

He sighed, humoring me. "Okay, try it again, but this time really get into the action of the scene. When you get to the end, the character dies, so show me you die."

Oh crap, I thought. Do I really have to pretend to die? But I tried it again.

The second time was better, but when the death scene came, not only did I make myself laugh, but the director laughed, out loud and not in a good way. Instead of dying by cleverly easing myself onto the ground in a slow, tortured manner, I opted for a comical trip over a chair in the corner and a bounce off the table on the far wall, rolling to a halt just below the director's table, clearly dead. Or at least my chances of getting the part in that play were.

"Well, not exactly what I had in mind, but I admire your spirit. Thanks for coming." He dismissed me with a flick of his hand. I got up and gathered my things, feeling defeated but also a bit amused by my awful audition. I had really bombed. I guess I was a little out of practice.

So practice is what I did. I practiced monologues and watched myself in the mirror. I auditioned two more times, and on the third try, I got a part. It was a small theatre company and just a short ten-minute show so I thought it would be manageable with my schedule and not take too much time away from Brooke. I loved the whole process—rehearsals, costuming, researching the character—yet I was torn because it became more time consuming than I had anticipated requiring at least four nights a week of babysitters and two full days away from her for the weekend of the performances. Once the play's run ended, I decided I just couldn't trade my time with Brooke for a hobby, no matter how much I loved the art and craft of it. So I moved on, hoping to find new ways to ground myself in my new reality.

TWENTY EIGHT

While I tried to come to grips with my new reality, while I tried to be a good mom and be functional, I was struggling with my health. The digestive issues I typically suffered when stressed or nervous (remember the pre-wedding energy drink?) became the worst they had ever been. I had a stomachache or diarrhea most of the time, and my weight plummeted from a hundred and thirty-five pounds to one fourteen. I would later learn that my heart and gut were extremely unbalanced, which made sense since my heart was broken and my stomach was constantly in knots. I'm a Virgo, and we are predisposed to digestive health problems, so I had a double whammy working inside me. Eventually, I was advised to get a colonoscopy. If you've had one of those, you know it's not a pleasant experience. But despite the two days in the bathroom beforehand and the discomfort of the procedure, I was glad to learn that it ruled out any type of lower GI tract issues. But that didn't stop the constant rocking and rolling of my stomach and intestines.

My doctor suggested I was experiencing a physical response to my emotional and mental stress. Well, duh, I could have told her that. She recommended I go to a therapist to talk about my situation and see if that would relieve some of my tension.

"If you want, I can prescribe you an antidepressant," she offered sympathetically.

"Thanks, but I think I'd rather try to get through it on my own first before going down that road," I replied, knowing that antidepressants weren't something I wanted to do before I even knew what I would feel.

So I started with the therapist. But I found that therapy was the exact opposite of what I needed. I would leave the therapist's office and feel even worse than I had going in—almost always crying the entire session and again when I got into my car afterward. I tried it for a couple of months and finally had enough. I was willing to suffer with the digestive issues if I didn't have to cry for two hours twice a week during those sessions and then feel bad for at least a day after each appointment. So I suffered.

As I lived with my gut issues and struggled with what food to make for myself that would also satisfy Brooke, mealtime became a not-so-amusing game. Every night I tried to cook, feed the dog, and keep Brooke happy, and some sort of minor accident would usually occur during the chaos, like a spilled water glass, a bumped head, or an untimely phone call, adding another layer of confusion to the turmoil. Luckily, Cosmo was around to help clean up all the spilled food and drink—one of the reasons he ballooned up to almost a hundred pounds that winter, not to mention my total sloth and his lack of walks for months. Cosmo turned into a blimp while I turned into a waif. I figured my weight would be one less thing to worry about when swimsuit season rolled around in a few months. But an opportunity to wear a swimsuit arose sooner than I had expected.

TWENTY NINE

A friend invited me to go to surf camp in Costa Rica. Yes, surf camp. You'd think that after two failed attempts to alleviate my sadness and anger through travel, I would have learned my lesson. But I was on the fence about this trip. I knew I hadn't enjoyed Hawaii or Florida like I should have, so why would this be any different? Why should I spend money on a trip I didn't think I'd enjoy? Plus, going with people I didn't know and doing something like surfing (remember my poor sense of balance?) were negatives, too. But I was tempted to get away from my daily routine and put some adventure back into my life. So I decided to sleep on it (or toss and turn on it, as my nights tended to be) and see how I felt the next day. Miraculously, I actually fell asleep that night. I was wakened the next morning by my phone ringing. I jumped out of bed disoriented, not used to sleeping through the night.

"Hello?" I answered, trying to disguise the sleepy tone of my voice.

"Hello, Mrs. Brown?" the woman on the phone asked in a too-businesslike tone. It had to be a telemarketer.

"Yes, this is?" I responded, irritated that a telemarketer had woken me before Brooke had, pacing across the floor of my bedroom anxiously.

"Hi, Mrs. Brown. This is Jessica calling about Mr. Brown's life insurance benefit." I stopped abruptly, my back tightening, preparing for another heated exchange over the "investigation" into Todd's death. I had talked to the insurance company numerous times over the last six months. I had received the initial company-sponsored payout but was still waiting to hear on the larger amount that would determine if Brooke and I could stay in our house.

"Hello. Do you have an update?" I asked, hoping for a positive response, but feeling anxiety tighten my insides.

"Yes. We finished the investigation, and it has been found that Mr. Brown did indeed die of a heart attack and didn't have any preexisting conditions or risk factors."

I still didn't know what that meant. I started pacing again. "So what's the next step?" I asked quickly, wanting resolution.

"We are overnighting a check to you today, so you should have it by tomorrow. Thank you very much for your patience in this matter."

I stared at the phone. Had I just heard her correctly? The life insurance was approved? I wouldn't have to move? We wouldn't have to eat ramen? "Great. Thank you." I couldn't believe the long wait for that money was finally over. It was the last piece of the financial puzzle I had put together over the last few months—figuring out investments, closing accounts, opening accounts, transferring money. Now I would have the means to keep us afloat without having to tap into Todd's or my 401k funds. I hung up the phone and sat on the corner of my bed. I still felt like it was cursed money, but it was cursed money that we needed. Todd had been right all along about that life insurance. He had saved us. So now it was time to save myself by taking a leap of faith and getting out of my comfort zone. And if surf camp was that first step, okay! Destiny puts opportunities in front of us for a reason, doesn't it?

THIRTY

I arrived in Costa Rica on a Monday afternoon in February. After gathering my bags I found my driver, one of the courtesies of the resort where we were staying. I had dropped Brooke off with my parents the previous day, when the other girls in my group arrived, so I was alone with the driver during the two-hour ride from the airport. He spoke some English, and I spoke just enough Spanish to get by. While we conversed I tried to keep my motion sickness at bay (yet another example of my bad stomach). We drove the unpaved roads through villages and jungle, but I saw no sign of the ocean. Finally, the driver told me we would soon be turning on the road that followed the coast for the final leg of our trip. He rounded a sharp curve, and we were met by a turquoise expanse of clear water, the waves gently hugged by a swath of powdery, white sand beach.

"Oh wow, el mar es muy bonito," I exclaimed, mixing my English and Spanish grammar and not one hundred percent sure I had the words right.

"Si, it is very beautiful," he said, humoring me. We drove along, the ocean coming in and out of view as the road meandered through the jungle. Forty-five minutes later, we pulled into a little village of newer homes nestled into the jungle. I stepped outside, the air-conditioned interior of the vehicle giving way to a wall of heat and humidity that penetrated my capri jeans and T-shirt. I immediately felt the need to don a swimsuit to soak up the fresh air and sunshine and let the soul soothing begin. The driver pulled my bags from the back of the van, and I looked around, overwhelmed by the beauty of my surroundings. Everything, even the buildings, was in harmony with nature. I instantly felt a sense of slowing in my body.

I turned to the driver, handing him a big tip for his time and his patience with my limited Spanish language skills. "Adios. Muchas gracias," I waved, bidding him farewell as he pulled away. I dragged my suitcase down the gravel path through the palm tree shade of the resort that would be my home for the next five days. Everything was outdoors except for the six sleeping cabanas. In the center of things were a swimming pool and hammocks underneath a palapa. The three girls I was meeting were lounging in the pool along with a few guys. I immediately got nervous. What had I gotten myself into? Was I supposed to socialize with these guys? What do I say? That my husband died? I felt that was the only thing that defined me now. When I emerged from the path, they saw me and waved.

"Hey, you made it! Get your suit on and grab a beer."

Erin, who had invited me, was a mutual friend of Todd's and mine from high school and the daughter of Todd's parents' best friends. She hopped out of the pool and gave me a hug. "I am so glad you came. This is going to be a great trip," she said reassuringly, sensing my anxiety. "This is Jane and Jen and our surf instructors." She introduced everyone, and I nodded hello.

"I'm glad I'm here, and I really need a swim and a beer after all that traveling," I said, my shoulders relaxing slightly.

"No problem. The kitchen and bar are over there. The chefs make the meals, but we can grab beverages and snacks whenever we want. You and I are sharing that cabana there. It's open. Jane and Jen are in the one across the pool. Go get your suit on, and I'll show you around."

I rolled my suitcase the fifteen feet to our cabana, stepped inside, and closed the door behind me. Through the slats of the wooden door, I could still hear the pool party outside, everyone laughing and relaxing. I took a deep breath and looked around. "I can do this. I can be with people again and have fun like I used to. Just relax," I repeated to myself over and over as I hefted my suitcase onto the empty bed and started unpacking. I pulled out my bikini and put it on. For the first time ever, my appearance wasn't an issue. I had lost so much weight after Todd died, I was borderline too skinny—and I had never thought that about myself before. I pulled my hair into a ponytail, grabbed my towel and sunscreen, and walked back out to the pool, faking confidence and a smile as everyone turned to greet me.

Erin handed me a beer. I quickly cracked it open and drank about half of it in one gulp. If I was going to do this, I figured I needed some liquid confidence. I set my towel down and slid into the water next to Erin, Jane, and Jen. We talked and got to know each other while the surf instructors played catch in the water. Less than an hour later, the guys all got out.

"Come on, girls, time for open surf," they announced, walking down the path to the kitchens. I looked around and realized I didn't see a beach anywhere.

"What's the story? How does this work?" I asked the girls.

"Our surfboards are in front of our cabanas. We can leave them there when we're not using them. We just take the carrier things and haul them down to the beach. There's a path just out there behind the resort." They pointed through the jungle. A few minutes later, I was carrying a long, heavy surfboard down to the ocean through a rocky jungle path in tender bare feet—and I was terrified. A key component of surfing is balance, which is not my strongest suit. As we emerged from the jungle onto the beach, I got my first glimpse of our surfing locale and almost turned around and sprinted back to the safety of the pool. The waves were enormous, giant cliffs of water rising and falling, crashing and retreating. My heart raced and my adrenaline kicked into gear. How was I going to do this?

My instructor that first afternoon was Jake, a nineteen-year-old, dreadlocked surfer dude from Huntington Beach, California. First he had me practice all of the elements of surfing on the beach. He explained how waves work and how to position my body on the surfboard. He taught me paddling techniques and the moves I would need to get "up and over" the waves. Eventually, it was time to get into the water and practice what I had learned. I waded out slowly with my surfboard floating next to me, the leash attached to my ankle. When I reached the whitewater, the place where the waves were gentle and breaking up before hitting the shoreline, it became much more difficult to walk;

the currents swirled around my ankles, pushing and pulling me as the waves moved.

"Okay, get on your board now and paddle out. Just get comfortable out there and practice getting up and over the waves you don't want to take," Jake yelled from behind me.

I slid onto the board on my stomach, rocking slightly, but regaining control and positioning myself the way I had been taught. So far so good. I started paddling, but it felt like for every paddle I made, a wave would sweep me back toward the shore—and I was only in the tiny waves, not the giant ones farther out.

"You have to paddle harder," Jake yelled again. Harder? I was paddling as hard as my out-of-shape body could go. I had been housebound and horizontal for most of the last six months, for God's sake. And now I had committed to a sport that required cardiovascular endurance. Seriously, what had I been thinking? But I gave it another go. I paddled as fast as my emaciated arms and burning lungs could take me. I floated around for a while, taking in the power of the ocean. I felt a super-connection with the universe. I looked around me at the waves, the sand, the jungle, and the sky and knew at that moment I was a part of something bigger than my own little bubble of a world. And I felt like Todd was right there with me, perched on my shoulder or hovering over my head somewhere, silently encouraging me to enjoy this crazy vacation I had decided to take.

I looked back at Jake.

"You're in a good spot," he said. "Now keep paddling out until you see a wave coming that looks good, then turn your board around and paddle hard until you feel the wave at your back. And then paddle even harder and stand up, just like we practiced on shore. Now go!" he yelled, putting me into a panic.

I paddled hard and finally saw a nice, small wave coming at me. I maneuvered the nine-foot board around while still on my belly and looked back at the wave closing in on me. Panic set in, and my heart raced. I thought through the steps that Jake had taught me. Paddle. Push up. Lunge. Turn. Stand. It couldn't be that hard. I paddled harder and harder and felt the wave start to lift the back of my surfboard. Oh crap. Oh crap. Oh crap. Oh crap. (Except I wasn't using the word crap.) Push up. I raised myself into a push-up position. Oh crap. Oh crap. Lunge. I thrust my knee forward so I was in a lunge, the wave propelling me, still miraculously on my board, through the water faster and faster. Oh crap. Oh crap. Oh crap. Turn. I slowly lifted my arms off the board, relying on my feet to keep me balanced. (I didn't have much faith at that point.) I turned to face the side of the board, my legs burning from the squatting position they were in. Oh crap. Oh crap. Stand. Just as I was about to stand upright, the wave broke up below me. The sudden change in momentum catapulted me ass over teakettle off the board and face first into the churning saltwater. I immediately covered my head with my hands, afraid the giant board would knock me out, but the water was only three or four feet deep, so I was submerged only for a second or two, although it felt like minutes. I found my footing, figured out which way was up, and struggled to stand in the swirling current and waves, sputtering to get the water out of my lungs, nose, and eyes. *Oh crap!*

I turned to look at Jake on the shore. He was laughing and gave me the thumbs-up sign. I had done it! Sort of. I spent the rest of the trip practicing and never got much beyond that same point, always either picking a bad wave or wussing out and falling off before I got to the standing part. But it was an amazing and empowering experience, feeling how mighty the forces of nature can be and learning how to master them in some way through surfing. I loved it, despite the comical nature of my attempts.

As I surfed (or attempted to), I got to know the girls in my group and the others staying at our resort. There were only six bungalows, occupied by a young Yale grad from New York City, a middle-aged entrepreneur from Texas, a mother and daughter from Connecticut, and my group of four. We spent most of our time together, sharing meals, taking afternoon siestas between our morning and afternoon lessons, and spending evenings out on the town with the instructors and Rick, the owner of the surf school.

During the course of this "getting to know you" time, I talked with Kris, the mother of the mother/daughter duo. She was a therapist and former jack-of-all-trades who truly changed my life. Early in the week, she told us about her animal spirit guide, her sea turtle that she called her tortuga. She told us how she often turned to her power animal for guidance and that we too could have a spirit guide who would choose us. I was intrigued and felt that having a kindred spirit, whether it was animal, vegetable, human, or whatever, would be a great comfort to me as I tried to navigate my new life as a single mother. Kris had us gather some things from around the beach—shells, driftwood, and rocks. We sat in a circle, and she guided us through a short meditation through which we'd hopefully connect with an animal. I was a bit apprehensive when the meditation started, but then I let my mind go, and immediately a vision came to me. It was of a large bear jumping to get a fish in a river. I couldn't get the image out of my head. After Kris guided us out of the meditation, we shared what we'd seen and talked about why we felt our animal truly fit ourselves. That night, I dreamed that a bear was sitting in one of the trees on the path down to where we surfed, which confirmed to me that I was indeed the bear and not the fish in my vision.

After I found my power animal, I wanted to learn all about bears and their spiritual meaning. I was shocked by all of the parallels and commonalities I found between their habits and powers and my own. Bears are tough. They are survivors who can weather obstacles and changes. They hibernate in winter much like I do, using this quiet time to recharge and reflect. They love spending time in their cave, like I prefer to be in my home instead of out in public. They're independent, as I have always been. I don't like to ask for help if I can handle a situation on my own. Bears are fiercely protective of their offspring, just like I will do anything to protect Brooke. I was amazed how these descriptions of bears' strengths matched my own. Even if this spiritual idea of a power animal is complete nonsense, it's intriguing to think that animals can help guide me when I need support.

An even more mind-altering conversation with Kris took place as we sat on the beach one afternoon. She told me that a few years before, she had been hit by a car while out walking and had crossed over—had been dead and seen the other side. Kris was not a weirdo or strange medicine woman, so I completely believe that her recollection and experience was true and factual. She said that after getting hit, she felt herself detach from her body almost as if she were floating outside of herself. She saw a bright light and at first was sad because she was going to miss her family, but then felt as if she'd turned into particles and was everywhere and always would be. And she then felt pure happiness and pure love as she realized she would always be able to be there with her family in that particle state. She was revived and somehow brought back to the world. She said for the first year after that happened she felt detached from everything, like she didn't belong or fit. But as time went on, she realized that everyone who has gone before us is still with us as particles, and they surround us all the time. When I think about that, it makes sense. We are all made up of particles—atoms, molecules, solids, liquids, gases—so why wouldn't we continue on as particles, just transformed?

As I thought about Todd and where he now was, I couldn't help but think what this trip would be like if we had taken it together. Over and over, I thought about what we would be doing if he were here.

I Wish—Costa Rica

I hauled the heavy yellow surfboard through the dense jungle, my bare feet and ankles screaming as the sharp undergrowth and rocky footpath pierced my flesh. I turned to see Todd hefting his equally long board over his wet, curly-haired head like a macho guy would. He winced as our virgin feet trod the jungle trail for the first of many treks to and from our quaint hacienda to the beach. "You ready to tackle the water?" he asked, betting me he'd be up and riding waves within an hour. I chuckled under my laboring breath, knowing it would probably happen, given the multitalented athlete that he was (it's true; just ask him!), but I didn't want to encourage him. I just shook my head and replied, "Okay, whatever. Good luck with that."

We emerged from the lush jungle path to a breathtaking view. Stretches of pristine white beach arched for miles backed by towering stands of palm trees and low masses of thick, verdant jungle. Ferocious waves pounded the shoreline, carving out level upon level of shell-strewn dunes. My heart pounded as loudly as the surf. The last dregs of courage I'd mustered had quickly dissipated, and I was terrified.

Todd saw the panicked look on my face, set down the board that he had tethered to his ankle, and came over for a quick, reassuring hug. "That little beaner toe of yours will give you lots of extra leverage and balance on the board. You'll do fine." He was always giving me crap about my crazy pinkie toes, which I swear have their own brain but no nerve endings. I smiled, trying to make myself feel more confident, but Todd knew me better than anyone and saw my fear. "I'll come in with you, and we'll just get used to the waves."

We tentatively waded into the churning sea, letting the swirling currents drag us out. We bobbed around for a while, splashing as we lurched, hugging as we were thrown into each other, and just being silly as we prepared to brave our boards once again. As he predicted, Todd was up and surfing the giant waves within the hour while I continued to struggle just paddling out against the waters that didn't want to let me pass. But we laughed and joked, enjoying this once-in-a-lifetime adventure together in those volatile waters that moved violently in one moment and lay as still as time the next.

In reality, of course, I was in a strange country with people I'd never met before, doing something that was completely out of my element and missing Todd every moment. But I also felt something changing inside my formerly empty shell of a self. I don't know if it was the power of the ocean or being out of my comfort zone, but I sensed something rising within me, and I knew that I would survive this. In the early weeks and months after Todd's death, I wasn't so sure I would make it as I lay awake in the suffocating dark of my bedroom. But now I felt hopeful again.

Todd, although I still miss you, I knew after going to Costa Rica that I would survive losing you. The words of a poem I read haunt me as I think of you out there watching over me.

Sir, if you love me, teach me to thrive
Without you,
To be my own genesis.
—Diane Ackerman, Entreaty

SEEKING

"There is in every true woman's heart a spark of heavenly fire, which lies dormant in the broad daylight of prosperity, but which kindles up and beams and blazes in the dark hour of adversity."
—Washington Irving

THIRTY ONE

After that crazy, amazing, transformational trip to Costa Rica, the fog that had been clouding my brain for six months began to lift. Before the trip I had practically denounced God, lost all motivation to work because the business world felt so meaningless, and became a total cynic, feeling as if I had nothing to live for anymore besides my daughter. I definitely didn't have anything driving me to become personally fulfilled or happy. But after being pummeled by the ocean while attempting to surf, hearing about Kris's near-death experience, and finding my animal spirit guide, I wasn't completely numb anymore. I began to feel again.

The anger was still there, though; anger at that entity that I'd been raised to believe was a loving God. But if he is loving, how could he do something like this—take a father away from his infant daughter, take a husband away from his wife, take a healthy son away from his parents? It just didn't make sense, and all the anger I had was directed at this entity of God—yet I wasn't convinced he even existed. Thus began my search for the truth, or at least my version of the truth—something that would help me make sense of what had happened and help me move on with my life. Once I started my research, I began to emerge from the darkness, to feel glimmers of hope. I had been putting on a happy face around my daughter but felt dead inside. Now I felt like I was coming back to life and that my life could and would be good again—maybe even happy.

I had existed in shadows for months before going to Costa Rica, and the experiences I had there forced me to reevaluate life, happiness, and peace. I knew after that trip that I couldn't exist as I had been, and I needed to find something to soothe my soul and make me feel free again. I needed to be released from the prison of grief I had been living in for six months. So I started my search by reading and learning everything I could about religion, spirituality, and most every self-help topic out there. I have always been one who has to know everything I can about the things that happen to me, and this was a *big* thing that required some really big research. The idea of God was not foreign to me. I'd been raised Lutheran, went to church and Sunday school, got confirmed, did all that was expected of me by my Lutheran parents and relatives. But I wasn't a devout practitioner. I had always struggled with religion and didn't feel as if it moved me as it moved and guided some. I was never ready to give up on the idea of being religious and had always planned on raising my kids Lutheran and giving them that moral compass. But Todd's death was like a slap in the face. Instead of feeling comforted by the presence of the God I grew up with, I was driven in the opposite direction. I did not believe a God like I'd been raised to believe in could have any reason for doing something like that. Every experience I had with church from the time of Todd's funeral only led to me saying "Fuck you, God" under my breath throughout the whole service. Harsh, yes, but that's how I felt listening to the words of the pastor and all the hope and saving; it just made me angry.

I needed to figure it out. I started with some books on world religions that gave an overview of belief systems, history, and customs. It was eye-opening. I learned so much I didn't know, not just about other religions, but about my own. I thought thirty years of church and Sunday school had taught me everything I needed to know, but that was not the case. I found so many commonalities among seemingly disparate religions. Hindu and Catholicism have common elements. Shinto and Judaism carry some similar themes. And as I dove into my research, I found myself looking at Todd's death from those different religious viewpoints. How could one man's death be perceived in so many different ways? Why was my religious upbringing forcing me into a specific belief about his death? So began my quest for answers and anything to help me make sense of this unfair, tragic, sudden loss that had been eating me alive.

First and foremost, I wanted to understand the universe. How does it work? How big is it really? What links us all? I was amazed by the volume of research and the number of theories out there—some proven, some truly just theories about the origins of the universe and human beings. And while there were some contradictory facts and assumptions, when I started to look at the wealth of information available I realized that, like religion, there are many common themes. I started to feel comforted by the fact that I wasn't the only seeker out there trying to find some seeds of wisdom about my place in the universe and the meaning of life and death.

I became a zealot for information. At least six or seven books on physics, the afterlife, religion, finding your true purpose, and the idea of soul and spirit were always on my bedside table and scattered around the house. I couldn't get enough, and I'm sure the sales clerks at barnesandnoble.com had a field day looking at my orders. (And I probably paid for someone's kid's braces or a nice trip to Tahiti!)

One afternoon, while I was tooling around on the Internet, looking at sites on life, psychology, stress relief, and other mind-expanding topics, I stumbled upon a page with a graphic that immediately got my attention. It was a four-quadrant grid with the heading "Integral Model"; the quadrants were labeled I, We, It, and Its. What was this? Something inside me wanted to know more about this simple but somehow powerful image. I clicked on the accompanying link, and it brought me to an article by Ken Wilber, the creator of the model and founder of the theory it represents.

Before I knew it, I was sucked into a vortex of fascinating research, unfamiliar terminology, and philosophical ideas that made my mind want to burst; at the same time, I felt an immediate and powerful connection to the goals that Integral Vision, as Wilber described it, was trying to reach. In simplest terms, it is a framework for looking at myself, others, situations, problems, entities—anything really—and making sure that they are focusing on all of the areas that are most important. It reinforces the interior mind, the exterior body, relationships, and the bigger world and has an entire spectrum of research and manpower behind it. It isn't a cult. It isn't a niche idea only known by a small group of academics. It's a frontier of thought that is being used by leaders across industries around the world. I was on to something big. I could feel it. This was calling out to me to be a part of it.

My old ways of thinking and the beliefs I was taught as a child in the Lutheran faith no longer held any realism or meaning for me. They felt like a fairytale, completely inane and fictitious. I held no judgments, and still don't, about people's beliefs, both in Christianity and in organized religion in general. People are free to use whatever ideas they need to feel connected to the world and those around them. But I needed to know more.

While continuing my research, I had an "aha" moment as I read more about Christianity, the roots of my upbringing. I knew that within the Christian belief system there are many subdivisions—Catholic, Lutheran, Methodist, Baptist, and so on—but the overarching theme remains the same. All Christian denominations believe that Jesus was the son of God and that we are meant to live by his words and teachings and abide by the Ten Commandments. But I did not know until I started my research that Jesus was a real person. I had always thought he was just a fictional character that someone made up to personify the stories that shaped Christianity. Not that this discovery gave me any comfort or moved me to some huge sigh of relief, but it proved to me that everyone has his or her own viewpoint, and those viewpoints are often ill-informed and uneducated—or maybe I should say, "miseducated," as in my case.

From the Christianity point of view, Todd's death was a common occurrence in the circle of life, and now he's in heaven with God and in a better place. His good deeds on earth led him to this eternal resting place with his creator. But that view doesn't sit right with me. When I think of the "heaven" I learned about in Sunday school, it sounds like a place we all go after we die, a big party where the streets are paved with gold and we experience eternal happiness. Sounds fun, but where *is* this place? I don't want heaven to be separate from us; I want it to be in and around us. And how do we get there? Do our beliefs and criteria for "entrance" into heaven manifest themselves in our mind just before our bodies die? Do our souls really ascend to another place, or do we just continue to exist as memories in others' minds? Or do we just die and that's it, we're done?

I have read theories about heaven, and the one I connect with the most is the idea of heaven as a state where we are everywhere after we die and that comes from inside of us. We don't cease to exist just because our body dies. Our energy continues on, contributing to this heaven we're surrounded by and living within all the time. This theory helps my mind wrap around the idea that we are all linked, not just in space through this powerful network of ether, spirit, and energy, but through time as well. All things, living and dead, since the beginning of time, fill up the spaces around me. I am connected to this energy field and life force, and I can derive wisdom and guidance from this crazy, unfathomable existence by knowing we are all just particles—vibrating masses of energy connected to each other and everything for eternity.

I find so much more joy and connection to the true science behind our lives than any individual religion brings me. It makes me feel much more at peace, knowing that our bodies are continuously being born and dying, that twenty million cells die every second in our bodies while another twenty million are formed. It is much more comforting for me to know that everything in the universe—animate or inanimate, solid, liquid, or gas, alive or dead—is made up of energy that's constantly on the move and being transferred at alarming speeds within us and between and everything else. I know there is a higher power that energizes everything, and that power will always be here for us to tap into, now and after we die.

Paradise, heaven, the afterlife, the other side. Regardless of what it's called, it's clear that most people believe there is something after we die, that we don't just cease to exist. I don't like the idea of severing our connections with our living family and friends, just as I don't like the idea that we cease to exist completely. I also don't like the idea that if we're not believers in every monotheistic "teaching" that we won't "get into" heaven, if it does indeed exist.

When I was in high school I wrote an essay on death. I had limited experience with the subject then, and reading the essay today, I am amazed at how much truth I find in it from my new-found perspective.

As we grow older and wiser, our views of death begin to take on a new and different meaning. We begin to realize that death is not merely an ending,

153

but it is also a beginning. Not a beginning in terms of the afterlife, but a beginning in terms of renewal, rejuvenation, and rediscovery of life itself.

Everyone at some point in their life reaches an age when death becomes more than just something that happens to others. As we begin to understand not death as a whole, but death as a concept, our entire life experience begins to change. Our lives are renewed with an energy for experience. We enjoy and savor things as though we'll never have the chance again. Our relationships are rejuvenated as we begin to see others as precious and needed. We, as individuals, go through a period of rediscovery of ourselves as we realize that life is beyond our control and will imminently end someday. We begin, as the old phrase states, to "carpe diem" or "seize the day," realizing that it may be our last or that it may be a friend's last or that it may be a family member's last.

As death approaches we also take on a new character that may go through periods of ups and downs, but this new character is still enlivened and energized with a zest for life. Although we may not consciously realize it, we are trying to make our lives worth something and to make ourselves worth something. As death nears, we also want not only something tangible to show for ourselves, but also intangible things like dreams, goals, mementos, and memories to show that our lives had meaning.

Death in itself is a sad thing, but when you look at the big picture it can be positive. If there wasn't death, there wouldn't be cherished relationships. If there wasn't death, there wouldn't be treasured memories. If there wasn't death, there wouldn't be life. Life can be whatever you make of it.

How could I have thought that way as an adolescent without ever experiencing death, yet it took me this long to realize it after Todd died? I guess it just takes an actual loss to make the words I wrote as a teenager meaningful in real life.

THIRTY TWO

As I started working on my beliefs, thoughts and emotions, and as the world began to make sense again, I decided it was time to work on other parts of my life that I had been neglecting. I started with something that seemed simple—organizing my house. If I could get my emotions and mind under control, I could surely do that with my house. But I am a pack rat, so it was a bigger undertaking than I expected it to be. I spent days purging closets and drawers, sorting stuff to donate to charity, and reorganizing the spaces left behind after removing so many things.

During one of those junk-purging sessions, I found a story about reincarnation that I wrote in 1986 when I was just ten years old. It was the first of many stories I would write about death, religion, and the meaning of life, and reading it again really got me thinking.

Me the Mosquito

One day as I was sitting on a log in the woods, a mosquito bit me. I went into the house to put some ointment on it. I put the ointment on and went to sit on the couch.

While I was watching Happy Days, I started feeling sick. My head started to hurt, my throat was dry, I had a stomach ache, and ooh it was terrible. I looked at my mosquito bite; it was all swollen with white creamy pus coming out of it. I went to show my mom. She said she was going to take me to the doctor.

We got to the hospital. We went into the room the nurse told us to go to. The doctor came in and looked at my mosquito bite (which was on my arm). He said he had to test it. When the doctor left the room, my mom said she hoped it wasn't something serious. The doctor said the mosquito had a disease, because he said I had a fatal illness called zopoleenano and that it was a matter of weeks before I would, well, before I would, before I would lose it.

My mother cried and my father was out of town so he didn't know yet. When my father did come home, he said he was sad, very, very, very sad. He wished he had the illness instead of me. I had to stay in the hospital and it seemed like my mom was sitting by the side of the bed every second of the day. I have to get four shots every day. I also have to take three kinds of medicines every 1-2 hours.

One day as I was getting my shot and medicine, I started breathing really hard, my heart and my body stopped working. Then, that is when I LOST IT!

When it seemed like I had been asleep for years (which I really wasn't), I awoke and found myself sitting on a big puffy white cloud. I looked down. I was about 30-40 feet above the ground. I guess I was invisible though because I was at a graveyard and there were crying people everywhere and they didn't notice me. Then I found out it was my funeral because I flew down from my cloud with a pair of plastic and cement wings I found on my cloud.

I flew back up to my cloud, took the wings off and pushed a little purple and green button. It made the cloud go up. After I had gone up for awhile, I hit a gold tube with little olive colored, pinstriped lines. I followed the tube until I got to the end. At the end there was a sign. It said "Person to Animal within Minutes. Push the animal button you want and presto, mali, kazubo!"

I don't know what happened but suddenly I found myself on the bottom, moving part of the tube. I was studying my legs; they were long, brown and skinny. They looked like mosquito legs. Then I looked at my arms, they looked like mosquito's legs too. Then I looked at my body. I screamed!! I looked like a mosquito. But the most shocking thing about me, I had an extra set of legs.

Finally I got to the end of the tube. There was another sign that said, "Bow at the silver St. Bernard." I got to the silver St. Bernard and bowed, but when I tried to leave, a hand sprung out from behind the statue and seized me. Before I knew it, I was sitting on a stick in the middle of the woods I had gotten bitten by the diseased mosquito that gave me my Zopoleenano disease. Then I got what was going on. I was turning into a mosquito so that I could bite somebody and give them a disease.

Next I went to the house I used to live in and snuck in through an open window. My whole family, even my friends and relatives, were sitting around mourning. Then I went over to my mother's head and tried to give her a kiss but instead I bit her. I just gave her disease. She slapped me with a flyswatter.

When I opened my eyes, I wasn't a mosquito anymore. I was an orange and white flyswatter just like the one my mother hit me with.

Then I was burned up in a fire. When it seemed I had awoken from a dream (which it wasn't) I wasn't a flyswatter. I was a flame.

This time I wasn't on earth or for that matter anywhere else I had ever been. I was in a land where all kinds of things lived in cloud houses. Paperclips, safety pins, ice cream, boxes, etc. were running all over. A garden hose came up to me and said, "This is your final stop, no more things to turn into!" Then it took me to King Clip. King Clip said he had a house ready for me and I could move in anytime. I moved in and got acquainted with everything and lived happily ever after. THE END

It's such a silly little story, and I have no idea where I heard about reincarnation; but clearly, even as a child I found the concept intriguing. Was my interest in theories of death when I was just ten years old a foreshadowing of my life to come? Had fate known I would have to deal with untimely death, and I started working it out even back then?

For weeks after I found this story, I researched reincarnation. According to both Hinduism and Buddhism, Todd has been reincarnated and will continue to be reincarnated until he's freed from this cycle by doing good deeds in each subsequent life. Good deeds are encouraged and reinforced, while bad deeds lead to punishment and a life of entrapment in the cycle of reincarnation. Hindus believe that when a person dies, the soul leaves the body through a chakra or spiritual channel. Which chakra the soul leaves through depends on the person's level of spirituality. I was fascinated by the chakra concept, so I went to a class on chakras, auras, and energy fields to learn more about them and find out if I was "balanced." As it turned out, I wasn't.

The class was taught at the local community education building just a couple of miles from my house. I had no idea what to expect.

I didn't know if I would walk into a room full of hippies, Hindus, or people like me—curious, intrigued, and open to possibility. I was pleasantly surprised to see a room packed with women of various ages and appearances, all hoping to learn something new about themselves. I found a seat and got out my notebook and pen as the instructor stood to introduce herself. She was a regular woman, just like me, who had found the concept of charkas, auras, and energy fields to be intriguing and so took it a step further and got her certificate in order to teach them to others.

The first thing we did was to have a photo taken of our energy fields with a special device that measures the vibrational frequencies coming off of our hands. These vibration levels correspond to the different energy vibrations that colors give off. For example, the color yellow has a different set of vibrations than the color red. Since energy is emitted in different ways through our bodies, the camera can measure how it translates into color. I was skeptical to say the least, but also very interested in finding out what my energy had to say about me.

When it was time for my photo, I laid my hands on the device's cool metal platform while the instructor directed me to relax. A few seconds later, I walked back to my seat with my aura and chakra report. I saw a photo of a body silhouette that was colored in glowing shades of mostly blue and indigo with little circles down the middle from the head to the tailbone in various colors. I learned that the colors within and surrounding the body were my aura. Mine were mostly blue. And the colors down the middle were my chakras. Mine were all different. I wondered if everyone's looked the same and tried to sneak a peak at my neighbor's photo. She caught me looking.

"What does yours look like?" she asked curiously. We held our photos out for each other to see.

"Wow, ours are way different," I commented, seeing her predominantly red and violet colors.

As each of the thirty women in the class got their photo, we saw that we all had different colorations, and the instructor reviewed what the colors and patterns meant. My mostly blue aura signified that I am communicative, loving, loyal, sensitive, and helpful—pretty accurate a lot of the time, I think. Above my head, the color was white, which showed I was imaginative, quiet, spiritual, and going through a transformation. If that didn't describe me perfectly, I don't know what else would. The report also revealed that I was going through a stressful time and that I was not very energized. Again, a perfect description for the previous months of grief and sadness I'd been feeling. And amusingly, it's also common for people with blue auras to dislike physical activity or work. I am not a sloth, but I hate exercise just for the sake of exercise. And even though I know how important it is, especially since Todd died, it still takes a whole lot of inner motivation to get me moving beyond a brisk walk with the dog.

Next we looked at our chakras. Mine were all different sizes and shapes. In almost every one of the seven chakras I had low energy, and overall I was very unbalanced. One thing that jumped out at me was a blazing blob of yellow right on my stomach. This was my navel chakra, which corresponds to creative, productive, and emotional expressions of life energy and relates to the intestines, spleen, and digestive tract. This was the only area that showed my energy to be above average. The instructor said that when this area is overenergized compared with the other six chakras, there is a chance for digestive tract issues. Right on the money!

It was incredibly interesting to see this alternative view of my well being. Even more intriguing was that it was so accurate. The other women in the class were also amazed at how well their own reports described them. We were a diverse mix of people with completely different colors on our photos, and the science underlying it all gave us unique yet accurate readings. The fact that the energy around us can be photographed is yet another reason it seems to me that science is the thing that connects us all.

After all of my research, I realized that I feel most connected to these more spiritual, as opposed to religious, ways of thinking. It's comical, really, that a small-town girl from rural Minnesota raised Lutheran who makes lefse and bread from scratch should have such an existential, spiritual view of life—one where Buddha, Dr. Seuss, and a big flat-screen television coexist within twelve inches of each other. I couldn't help but feel that Todd was happy I had found interests, regardless of how foreign they might have been to him if he were here.

Another new endeavor I tried was painting. I thought it would be a good way to access my long-dormant creativity and to continue to draw on my new-found spirituality. I took a painting class and was so amused by my efforts (lack of talent) that I had to tell Todd about it.

Todd, you would laugh at me, but I have started painting. I took a class through the school district community education office and loved it, and I am now painting while Brooke finger paints. I am terrible. Most of my work looks like Brooke painted it, but it's a great creative outlet to make up for the lack of creativity in my data- and spreadsheet-driven job. I think you'd be proud of me for doing it, though. You'd be glad I have my own hobby and things I enjoy doing on my own now. I'd always gripe about your golf and poker and sports and the time you spent away from me doing your favorite pastimes, but now I know it wasn't because you didn't love me or want to be with me. You were simply exercising your own identity and interests. I understand that now and realize it's important to know yourself and be comfortable in your own skin. I never was before. I'd flex to fit my significant others—and really did that with you. But now I see the value in loving myself first and making time for my own interests just like you did with poker, golf, and watching every sporting event that was televised. Thank you for helping me see what I was missing.

THIRTY THREE

So many times I have felt like I was destined for something more—something better—something great. (Besides going to the Oscars someday.) All of my readings about spirituality and religion have led me to question my own fate and what I should do with my life. I've always struggled with feeling satisfied and happy with what I have and have felt like my fate was to do something great with my life, something that would impact the world and help people in some way, while bringing me fulfillment and satisfaction. I used to think maybe that greatness was fame in some way, but now I think it's something else, something like being a good person and influencing the world by perpetuating this goodness in others. Could my story, this heartbreaking, awful story, be that greatness I am seeking? Could it help me touch others' lives in a meaningful way?

My search for answers continued. I read everything I could get my hands on, watched every mind-expanding television show or movie I could find, and spent hours online combing through research. I'd never been a big magazine reader, and had never considered reading more than my old reliable teenage wizard or vampire series, fiction bestsellers, the occasional Oprah book club memoir, and maybe a self-help book once a year for good measure. But now I was poring over every magazine article and book on spirituality, religion, power, astrology, death, the afterlife, and self-help I could get my hands on and was seduced by any magazine in the grocery store checkout lane with articles on living green, connecting with others, or finding peace and serenity. I subscribed to five or six magazines on spirituality, health, politics, and culture. I became a voracious seeker of knowledge and continued to fill my mind with bits of information that helped me formulate my ideas of what I wanted my life to be like.

No one was more surprised by my newfound feelings, interests, and beliefs than I was. I have always been one to think I'm always right—it's my way or the highway. I've been self-absorbed and extremely egocentric. But after seeing how life can change in a heartbeat, or loss of a heartbeat, I gained a completely new perspective on how to behave and act and began to realize that the world does not revolve around me.

I was surprised by a visceral reaction I had to a situation I witnessed on an airplane. I sat in my window seat, listening to those around me complaining about a group of Muslim travelers who were struggling to get their luggage into the overhead compartments and holding up the line behind them.

"What are they doing? Sit down already," a man a couple of rows ahead complained.

The woman next to me leaned toward her husband on her other side. "They shouldn't even be allowed to bring carry-ons onto airplanes. It'll be 9/11 all over again," she whispered too loudly.

My shoulders tensed up, and I felt my jaw clench. I had to physically grasp my armrests to refrain from yelling at her. *Who do you think you are to judge them? They are women and children from another part of the world with different customs. They aren't frequent travelers who know the "rules" of an airplane. They are simply trying to get from point A to point B as quickly, easily, and safely as possible just like everyone else on the plane, and just because they don't know to put their bag in the overhead compartment the way* you *think they should doesn't mean they should be abused and belittled, especially when some of the members of the group are children. You judgmental, stereotypical b....* But I remained silent. My Minnesota-Nice attitude came out, and I passively sat there, cringing in my seat.

So here it is—my preachy moment: I believe everyone should read a book on religion so that we understand the different belief systems and the people who practice them. Everyone should read books on cultures and history so that we understand why different groups are driven to certain actions. Everyone should read a book on physics and the origin of the universe so that we have a full perspective of how and where we came from, why we exist, and where we're going. Everyone should open their minds to other possibilities. No one person or group is right about everything. We all need to let go of aggression toward and judgments of each other to start taking the steps toward understanding. That is just one way that we can bring about a measurable change in society, and it will take the combined efforts of all of the different religions, ethnicities, and cultures in the world.

And so I have been trying my best to be a good person. In this new reality in which I'm living, I'm feeling good about things. I feel like those negative emotions aren't sneaking up on me so often anymore, and I'm able to maintain control of myself most of the time. And when I don't, it's in the safety of my own home where I won't make a spectacle of myself. I spend so many hours just sitting and thinking, usually at night in bed when I can't sleep, and I'm finally starting to wrap my mind around this life I am now living as a widowed working mom. Through the craziness that surrounds me all the time, I'm starting to feel moments of quiet when my brain is able to rest and take in what has happened to me. And in those quiet moments, I feel Todd, guiding me and supporting my decisions, sending energy my way to keep me going through the long and difficult days, and laughing with me through the happy ones.

TRANSITION

*"The interval between the decay of the old and the formation
and establishment of the new constitutes a period of transition,
which must always necessarily be one of uncertainty,
confusion, error and wild and fierce fanaticism."*
—John C. Calhoun

THIRTY FOUR

The first summer we were dating, Todd and I were invited to twelve—yes, twelve—weddings. We made it to nine of them. I have such happy memories from that summer—we took road trips to wherever the festivities were held, danced (even me), and really got to know each other. I have been to a couple of weddings since Todd died, and each time it rips my heart out when I remember those I attended with him and, inevitably, think about our own. That day, we were so happy and felt that we had our whole lives in front of us. Little did I know that we wouldn't have sixty years together, like I had hoped and planned.

If I had known then how things would turn out, I would have spent what precious time I had with Todd so much differently. I wouldn't have complained when he wanted to golf all day with his friends. I wouldn't have nagged him when he drove too fast during heavy traffic. I wouldn't have taken my work frustrations out on him. I would have let all the little things go and just enjoyed the ride. I would have appreciated all of the sweet and selfless things he did, like walking the dog almost every day, shoveling the driveway when it snowed, indulging me when I wanted to fantasize about a new travel destination, cooking me dinner, taking care of me when I was sick.

If I had known how things would work out, I would have loved Todd better. I would have taken myself out of the details and stress of everyday living to see the bigger picture of our life together as an ever-evolving entity to be appreciated, nurtured, respected, and enjoyed. I would have reminded myself every day how lucky I was to have found him. Now I am thanking him every day for wanting me in the first place and for all the things he's done for me since. He is my sounding board, my mentor, my inspiration, and still my best friend. He has been with me this whole time, helping me to get over his death and guiding me to my life's purpose. And I so hope that my story and experience will open people's eyes to their own lives so they appreciate what they have now before it's too late.

In all of my crazy research I found a poem that I read to myself every once in a while when I'm feeling lonely. It reminds me of how I felt about Todd even at our lowest points, and how I feel now.

I Want You

I want you when the shades of eve are falling
And purpling shadows drift across the land;
When sleepy birds to loving mates are calling—
I want the soothing softness of your hand.

I want you when the stars shine up above me,
And Heaven's flooded with the bright moonlight;
I want you with your arms and lips to love me
Throughout the wonder watches of the night.

I want you when in dreams I still remember
The ling'ring of your kiss—for old times' sake—
With all your gentle ways, so sweetly tender,
I want you in the morning when I wake.

I want you when the day is at its noontime,
Sun-steeped and quiet, or drenched with sheets of rain;
I want you when the roses bloom in June-time;
I want you when the violets come again.

I want you when my soul is thrilled with passion;
I want you when I'm weary and depressed;
I want you when in lazy, slumbrous fashion
My senses need the haven of your breast.

THE BEST WORST THING

I want you when through field and wood I'm roaming,
I want you when I'm standing on the shore;
I want you when the summer birds are homing—
And when they've flown—I want you more and more.

I want you, dear, through every changing season;
I want you with a tear or with a smile;
I want you more than any rhyme or reason—
I want you, want you, want you—all the while.

—Arthur L. Gillom

THIRTY FIVE

Out of peer pressure and guilt, I apathetically went to my computer and logged in to match.com. It was summer 2008. Widowhood had been my life for almost a year, and most of my time was spent caring for Brooke, traveling, and getting out of my comfort zone while seeking out answers to life's big questions. I was plenty busy. But at the prompting of my family, trying out an online dating service was now on my to-do list—just to get my feet wet and see how it felt to date. Initially, it was a mini-rush because, although I thought no one would want to date a widow with a young child, I got a lot of responses from some very nice men. After a couple of months of scouting, I finally decided to dive in and go on a date with one of those men. I didn't want to. I was terrified. I didn't know what to wear. I didn't know what I'd say. I didn't think I'd be interesting to this guy who was a successful world traveler with no kids. What in the world would we talk about? I fretted over my hair, my makeup, the locale for our meeting.

Sitting on my couch, trying to kill the half hour before I had to leave, I was transported back twelve years. I was in the lobby of my former workplace, my head between my knees, a paper bag to my lips, and a garbage can at my side. My lungs screamed for air, but my clenching stomach and pounding heart had taken over all my energy and senses, rendering me a gasping, nauseated, nervous mess. I was about to go on a first date—not just a first date with someone new, but my first date ever with someone I hadn't met before or someone I wasn't set up with by a friend. I'd always hated dating, thus the reason I have always been in long-term relationships. But now here I was, a widow about to go on a first date with a stranger. I forced myself to get up and walk out to my car, trembling with nerves, my stomach on the verge of rejecting the contents of my earlier lunch.

I drove downtown to the rendezvous point, a feeling of regret starting to creep into my consciousness. What am I doing? I'm married! How can I betray that by going on a date with another man? But wait, was I still married? We vowed to be together "until death parts us"—but did that mean the death of both of us? Did Todd's death qualify as a deal breaker, making our marriage contract null and void? I couldn't get my arms around the concept of not being married anymore. And at that moment, it became crystal clear to me that I was absolutely, positively, not ready to date yet.

You want to know when I'll know I'm ready to date? When I don't bawl my eyes out afterwards, like I did after that date, that's when. I left feeling empty and sad, like I was cheating on Todd. It was clear that I didn't have the facilities to be in a relationship. I was completely unsuitable for being someone's significant other. I was still too invested in my relationship with Todd, with whom I thought I'd spend my entire life—until we both died in our eighties or nineties. Instead, I was in my early thirties, supposedly the prime of my life, lonely and feeling completely helpless to the powers of fate controlling me. Obviously it wasn't time to date yet. I didn't know who I was yet without Todd. He defined me for so long. I had to get comfortable in my own skin and get to know myself—by myself—before I could move on.

In a dream, Todd told me to "let an arrow aim straight and true," which I could only understand to mean I should fall in love again. It's the corniest line, but those were his words exactly. I hope I will find someone again someday. No one will ever be able to replace Todd, but there is a special person out there who will respect that about me and honor his memory for the sake of Brooke and for me. I don't know when I will find him, but when I do, he is in for one heck of a ride. This terrible loss has helped me realize how to treat a spouse and how I want to be treated and how to operate within a marriage. And wherever Todd is, I know he is rooting for me to find someone again someday, when I'm ready. But until then, I have to keep on going, despite the emotions that sometimes take me down.

THIRTY SIX

I don't know who was louder at night, Brooke or the dog. They both snored, but I didn't mind. Their snoring let me know they were alive and well beside me. I barely slept the nights Brooke slept with me; I was so busy listening for her breath that I'd forget to close my own eyes. It's because of this that I slept so much better when she wasn't around. I let my worries and concerns go and allowed myself the permission to shut down.

I got two much-needed nights of sleep without her one early spring weekend when we visited Montevideo. Brooke stayed at Todd's parents' house, and I stayed with my grandpa. On one of those evenings, I went out with friends. It was the first time since Todd died that I went to our old familiar hangouts, and every moment reminded me of the times we spent in those bars together. I would always get there early (like my normal self), and he would show up with his friends an hour or two later. Yet we always had that radar—we knew when the other walked in the door.

I heard a character in a movie say that she didn't feel as if she was really in a room until her husband walked in. That's how I felt during my entire time with Todd. If we were meeting somewhere, we'd both look for that familiar face and light up upon finding each other in the crowd. I felt proud and happy knowing he was mine and I was his. He validated my presence and made me feel attractive and funny and smart.

That night out in our hometown, I kept looking around for someone I knew, but realize now I wasn't looking for just anyone; I was looking for him. Instinctively my radar was still set to "Todd" and kept searching for him, even though he was nowhere to be found. One of the places I went was the Hunt Bar and Grill. It was there that we met, we courted, we attended friends' wedding receptions, and we had our own reception and spent our first night as a married couple in the honeymoon suite upstairs. I'll never again be able to enter that building without remembering all the good times we shared there.

I walked the ten blocks back to my grandpa's house that night, taking the same route Todd and I had taken home so many times together, only this time I was alone, crying and shivering in the dark. I felt as if my soul's purpose had been lost. I was struggling to find my way but kept running into setbacks. I didn't know what I was here for anymore or where to go next. I just knew I needed to move forward, to get off the tightrope I'd been balancing on and get back to a life that made me feel happy and fulfilled. One where I wasn't constantly bombarded by memories, guilt, and loneliness. One where I wasn't just going through the motions of every day, but controlling my life's course and doing something I'm passionate about. I was knocking on the universe's door, begging to be let in on the plan, but instead was shut out, left to find my own way—obviously part of the plan for me, but not a part I was enjoying.

THIRTY SEVEN

Because my company was located in New York and I was in Minneapolis, I had the luxury of working from home. But most mornings after dropping Brooke off at day care, instead of going home to work I would go to the mall or Target. Throughout my mourning process, I felt that I deserved to just be nice to myself. I wanted life to be easy and didn't want to have to think about anything. That's where "retail therapy" came in. A lot of women do it—something bad happens, and they buy themselves an overpriced purse or impractical shoes to make themselves feel better. Well, I was a case study in retail therapy. Not only did I buy the purses and shoes, I remodeled my kitchen, re-landscaped my backyard, and basically bought anything and everything I wanted with no regard to price or practicality. I didn't have a lot of money, but Todd's life insurance covered the house, and my salary covered the bills and Brooke's day care. Anything left over went to my shopping habit.

I knew I shouldn't do it, that it wasn't a good idea to spend money and make decisions when grieving. But I couldn't help myself. It was a drug for me, the high of a new purchase. I was purging closets, drawers, and entire rooms, ridding my house of junk, only to replenish my newly found space with my freshly purchased treasures. And staying home wasn't a safe haven either; online shopping became a favorite pastime. I even had a folder in my e-mail box for online order confirmations to keep track of everything. I would see items in magazines, tear them out, and then investigate them online, making the purchase if I liked what I saw.

It was a pair of incredibly impractical shoes that started it all— purple, croc-embossed, oxford-style, peep-toe pumps with four-inch, suede-covered platform heels. Seriously unnecessary, but I had been carrying around a photo of those shoes for months. If I liked them that much, I should just get them, right? Well, I did, opting for the more practical brown version, and every time I saw them in the closet I smiled and felt happy—one more thing to throw into the gaping hole that I tried to fill with something, anything to make me feel better.

I also decided that my cleaning lady was a necessary indulgence. I sound so snooty saying "my cleaning lady." After my company offered to get me the cleaning lady for a couple of months, I realized how much of a burden it really did lift off of my shoulders. By the time my two months of prepaid services expired, I was hooked and decided to build biweekly cleanings into my budget. This service was now the number one thing I spent my money on for self-indulgence. You can't imagine how much easier life is when you don't have to worry about keeping your house clean. And with a dog and a toddler, mine needed it, probably more often than it actually got cleaned. But even every other week helped me manage everything else I had to deal with—walking the dog, raising a smart, respectful daughter, working full time, and just coping with the grief I still felt.

THIRTY EIGHT

I was up early most days, opening curtains, stirring up the energy in the house. In those moments of silence right before the world sprang to life, I felt the same eerie stillness I felt the morning Todd died—as if the universe was frozen in time and etched permanently into my brain. I would look out the window, and whether it was sunny or cloudy, warm or cold, that lingering sadness and confusion would swell as I remembered that morning of September 9, 2007, which seemed so long ago yet just like yesterday.

I could still feel the mist in the air and the way the parking lot looked that morning when I went out to the car for Brooke's bottles. In hindsight, I believe that was when Todd left us. After hearing and reading stories about near-death experiences and people who had crossed over, this is what I imagined it would be like—thick air filled with particles and mist as a person's soul transitions from their body to the universe; initially thick and near to us, slowly dispersing as the particles move outward and surround us. I think that morning I was walking through Todd's particles and just didn't know it at the time. That morning at breakfast, just an hour or two before we discovered Todd had died, my mom told me it was about that same time earlier in the morning when she heard what she thought was Todd snoring strangely, but what I now believe were his last breaths. What is that saying, "Life is not measured in breaths, but by the number of moments that take our breath away"? All I can think of is that right before we die, it will be the last moment that takes our breath away—forever.

How fortunate for Todd that it happened in his sleep and he was free from pain, but how sad for us that no one got to say goodbye or had a chance to save him, that he was all alone in bed that night. I wonder constantly if, had he been sleeping with me that night, I would have known at the moment it happened that something was wrong and gotten help. Why of all nights did he choose to sleep in another room and not with me? Was it fate's way of sparing me the anguish and memory of waking up next to a dead man? I know it's morbid. I don't know what is worse, the idea of sleeping with a corpse or the images I have of walking into the room where he had slept and seeing him there in that bed lifeless and alone.

It had been nearly a year since Todd died. For almost three hundred and sixty-five days I had lived this new normal. Someone told me that the good days eventually start to outweigh the bad ones, but I felt a long way from that. I had so many terrible days, feeling sad, missing Todd. I needed to spend as much time as I could at home, nurturing myself back to life. Instead, I'd accepted invitations to social events out of a sense of duty. I had always been a "yes" person, agreeing to help out when asked, happy to listen and offer wise words to help friends put problems into perspective, willing to socialize and go out. But I couldn't be that person now. I didn't have the energy for it. I felt so much growth happening when I was alone, doing what I needed to do to heal myself, even if that was hiding. Yet people were used to me being that "yes" person, and when I preferred to spend the day gardening or going to a movie alone, they viewed that as being selfish. They didn't understand that I needed to be alone at home doing something productive like cleaning, writing, or even catching up on television, instead of being in a group of people looking at me with pity, not knowing what to say. They would chatter with each other about everything except what felt to me was the elephant in the room, but to them was probably nothing more than an afterthought. Keeping busy and productive at home was my "happy place" where I could just be me and not "that poor young widow."

But it was rarely just me at home with uninterrupted time to get things done outside of work. When I was able to have someone watch Brooke overnight, I would take advantage of it and have the "me-time" I so badly needed to center myself. When I was home alone without her, the tension in my body relented. The protective instincts that kept me up at night listening for her breath shut down, and I could breathe. I would take out a bottle of luscious Pinot Noir or crisp Riesling, a fresh French baguette, good cheese, and salami, spread it out buffet-style in the kitchen, and just relax—savoring the flavors and feeling my brain slow down, all of that thinking finally quieted once I was alone in my space.

And I only had me now to get things done. I had to mow and change light bulbs and call repairmen. I had to put away Barbies and color crayons and laundry. I had to kill spiders and dispose of dead chipmunks, and do all the errands. There was no one but me to do everything, so I took advantage of opportunities for me-time when they arose. I didn't think that was such a terrible thing, considering my situation. If I needed to be gentle with myself and indulge myself whenever I wanted, what was the harm in that? So what if I didn't want to be a joiner and a chipper, rah-rah person quite yet?

But while trying to find my own path again, I was so frustrated. I felt like everyone had all of these expectations of how I should be and what I should do. Why couldn't they just let me be? Just let me exist and relax in my own space and in my own way. If I wanted to lie on my couch with my dog for a day, just let me. If I wanted to go to a movie by myself or work on my yard or work on my house—just let me. What was wrong with some self-indulgence when I'd been dealt such a crappy hand?

Being alone has always been like a vacation for me. I am an introvert, although most people would never guess it, and I find so much inner peace and enjoyment on my own. I didn't have hobbies or other activities to fill my time. I was always defined by my significant others and then by Todd; but now I was finding things I enjoyed doing and in the process, finding myself. No one understood this, and it was frustrating for me to slowly start feeling so much better inside but not have it translate to others externally. And while I tried to make people understand my newfound ideas and respect my me-time, I was still evolving. Every day I learned something else about myself, and my persona to the outside world was ever-changing, too. I guess that's what it means when they say grief is a journey or a process. Because every minute I discovered something new on the twisting, turning path I was on—one minute good, one minute bad, but all culminating in a bigger understanding of myself. And that's what I needed now—to know myself without Todd. To know myself as a single parent. To know myself as a woman trying to find her career path in life. I needed to know all of those things, but I hadn't figured any of it out yet. The only way I could was to be left alone to work things out on my own.

THIRTY NINE

The night of September 9, 2008, on the first anniversary of Todd's death, I was stranded in a hotel room in Indianapolis due to a cancelled flight to New York for a business trip. I had been dreading this milestone day, when I would no longer be able to say that a year ago we did this, or a year ago we did that. Now it was a year ago that we had exchanged our last words. All I could do to commemorate that day was to write an e-mail to the family and friends who helped me survive this. They were always there when I needed someone to watch Brooke, when I needed to escape the house, when I needed anything. They were there even in their own grief.

Last year, this day started off like any other—a crisp, cool fall day. It was the first day of Sunday football, a first wedding anniversary for John and Kara and the first day of a new marriage for Matt and Audrey. Little could anyone have known that it would also be the first day of a new world and a new life for me—a world that was without its center. I thought my life had ended that day too, but because of all of your support—your words, letters and cards, emails and phone calls—I made it through those very dark days that I thought would never end. Thank you so much for everything, and even though I may not have asked for help—and I put on a strong show—you have no idea how your encouragement kept me going when my heart was broken and I just wanted to curl up in the dark and not get up. Luckily, Brooke helped heal me and is a thriving, energetic ball of sass and sweetness. Every day I wake up now and instead of being barely able to breathe as I face the day, my first thoughts are of her and what new discoveries and developments she'll have that day.

I know Todd is here all around us. I feel him all the time and believe that his spirit and energy is always around. I often ask myself "what would

Todd do?" and find myself asking his advice or just pointing out things that we'd discussed in the past. And sometimes I still want to pick up the phone and call him when something funny happens or Brooke does something new. He will always be with us, and he would not want us to mark this day with sadness or anger, but instead to enjoy it and celebrate his life and the impact he had on us all—and to celebrate our own lives and the good things we all have to be thankful for that we may take for granted sometimes.

So tonight when you get home, I want everyone to raise a glass and toast with me to Todd and the bright light that he was and continues to be in our lives. And live each day like it may be your last because you never know what will happen. Spend time with your family and reprioritize those things and those people that should come first in your lives and love them like there's no tomorrow. And thank you again for everything over the last year. You are all so very, very much appreciated and words will never do justice or be able to express the gratitude I have for you all! You are loved! Enjoy your day! Kristen

A couple of hours later, Todd's best friend, Derek, whom we had both known since elementary school, sent out a note too.

For most of us that have known Todd for a long time, there is something that reminds us of him EVERY DAY. In the last year, I have been thinking back, and I can't remember ONE single day that I haven't thought of Todd. Although that is very sad at times, I still try to focus on all the amazing things I remember about him! He was so fun, so easy going, he enjoyed life, he loved his family and friends so much, and what I miss most of all, is just being around him. Even if you weren't doing anything exciting, you still had fun being together! Even though it pains me to think that we can't go golfing together, or play poker, or just hang out, I still think of him every day and how his life has impacted me, and all of the memories we have together. Sometimes I just smile when I know he is looking down on me. I know he has made me think of how lucky I am to be here with the great family and friends that I have. I hope everyone will keep carrying on his wonderful memories, sayings, actions, and just keep reminding each other what a great friend that we had and will miss forever. Since we all can't be together tonight, here is a TOAST FOR BROWNER: "To the best friend anyone could ever ask for, a loving father and husband, the guy that always brought a smile to the room, the man who could carry a small bucket of golf balls in his pocket, who could get a base hit anytime at bat, who could catch any pass and was always open (just ask him), who thought he would win every fantasy football game and would let you know it, a brother, a son, a superstar, a friend to many and an enemy of none, to the ONE we call 'Browner,' 'T.J.,' 'Poker Face,' 'Small Bucket,' 'Brownie,' and to all the great phrases and names that we ever came up with together.... Here is to you 'Todd Brown,' the one we will miss forever but never forget! Your memory will stay in our hearts forever and may your spirit live around us and enrich our lives forever! We love you and miss you!!!" Your Best Friend forever!

I finished reading the note on the computer screen, lowered my head to my hands, and cried. I cried for the man that so many people loved, for the man I lost, and for the father he wouldn't get to be to Brooke. That's all I could do that day—the anniversary of Todd's death, the anniversary of the worst day in my life.

FORTY

In the middle of the night when I lie awake, I have some crazy talks with the powers that be—God, Buddha, the All-Knowing, the universe, whoever or whatever it is, we have become pretty tight. I call them the spirits, and they included Todd, my grandma, and everyone who has gone before me. I can tap into the wisdom of all of them. One such conversation took place a year after Todd died. I had been struggling all day at work, feeling burnt out and frustrated while the emotional weight of the anniversary of Todd's death crushed down on me.

"Spirits, I need you to help me figure this thing out," I pleaded silently from under my covers. "I'm not in my right mind and can't muddle through this on my own anymore. You need to help me get through this." I was met by silence. But then, I heard a voice that was not my own in my head.

"What is your muse? What heals you?" it asked.

"My muse? That's so corny," I thought, not sure what the answer was or even what I wanted it to be. But after a few seconds I had an answer.

"Everything I do heals me. It's all part of my journey."

"Who is helping you?" the voice questioned. Again I was stumped.

"No one, it's just me." But then I paused. It wasn't just me. Everyone I encountered every single day was helping me, whether they or I knew it or not.

"Wait, it's not just me, it's everyone. They're all part of my process," I exclaimed, sitting up in my bed.

"What do they ask of you? When do you feel most connected to them?" the voice challenged.

"I don't know. Why are you asking me all these hard questions?" I groaned, leaning back onto my pillow.

"You need to think about the impact you want to make on the world with your life. What is it that makes you feel most connected to yourself and those around you? You need to know that before you can take the next step in your journey."

And then it was gone. The voice disappeared and left me alone to sort out the garbage in my head. I was wide awake now, but I continued to lie there for another hour. I was on the verge of a breakthrough and didn't want to disrupt it.

The next night at almost exactly the same time, the voice spoke to me without my initiating the conversation.

"So what did you come up with after we talked last night?" it asked.

"I want to do something that helps people and makes the world a better place," I explained, having no idea what that meant.

"Okay, how will you do that? What is that thing you can do for hours and not realize time has gone by?"

"I don't know. There isn't anything these days that I do that doesn't feel like it takes forever and a huge effort."

"You're not thinking broadly enough. Keep thinking about it, and we'll talk again." Then the voice was gone, and I was alone again with even more garbage in my head than the night before. I pulled out my notebook, hoping I could work it out on paper.

Todd, what should I do? I am so lost, and nothing seems to make sense in my life anymore without you here. I am confused, and all my decisions, even the minor ones, take all the brain power I have to process. I don't know what I'm doing, and I have no business being in the real world right now. Isn't there a place I can go and hide for a few months to figure it all out?

The writing that night didn't work. My brain was overloaded, and all I could do was let it spin.

FORTY ONE

Most mornings after getting out of bed, I checked the couch and the basement, just to make sure Todd wasn't sleeping there. I can't count how many times I hoped he would call or show up, telling me he had faked his own death because he'd stolen ten million dollars and was coming to take Brooke and me away with him. It was a crazy fantasy, but one I thought of every time I saw a car like his or a guy with curly blonde hair or I got mail addressed to him—which was almost every day. I don't know what I would have done if he'd shown up—if he'd walked in the front door just like he always did after work.

Before searching for Todd, I would check on Brooke to make sure she was still breathing. I held my own breath until I saw the steady rise and fall of her chest, reassuring me that she was alive and well. I was so afraid that, like her father, she would end up with a bum heart, one that wouldn't be able to sustain her for a long and healthy life. I was even more afraid that, despite my most vigilant efforts to feed her well, keep her active, and maintain her health, again like her father, there would be no forewarning of the attack that would take her from me. But for now, all I could do was keep her safe and do my best to provide her a healthy and happy life—and if that meant I had to keep constant vigil at her side to watch for breath, I would do it.

After confirming that indeed I was still a widow and Brooke was still alive in the next room, I entered the kitchen and opened the cupboard, pulling out the latest vitamin and herb supplements I was trying. I counted out a few, opened a can of Diet Coke, and washed them down with a long pull of fizzy sweetness. I felt guilty, knowing that artificial sweetener can cause cell damage and carbonation just causes bloat and a puffy stomach—and since somehow I'd maintained my vanity through this whole thing, a stomach pooch was not my goal. But instead of opting for water, I drank the soda—and added insult to injury by slicing myself a giant slab of homemade bread, slathering it with a thick layer of real buttery goodness, and throwing it in the microwave for twenty seconds until it was just like fresh from the oven. My sister once told me my homemade bread was addictive, like taking crack, so I guess this was my drug of choice to kick off the day. Some people need coffee or a cigarette—I needed bread and butter.

One of my earliest memories was at age three or four, when I got my first taste of homemade bread. My Grandma Vivian would make it almost weekly, and it was such a treat to be there when she was baking. There was nothing like walking into her and Grandpa Orice's house in Montevideo and being knocked over by the mouthwatering aroma of freshly baked bread. I attempted to capture these feelings when I was in high school.

Bread

As I walk into the house, the molecules stimulate my olfactory nerve.
Odors waft through the air like silk.
The golden warmth is evident.
I can almost taste the moist, fluffy sweetness in my mouth.
I rip off a huge chunk.
The steam burns my fingers
And leaves condensation like dew on my face.
The taste is heaven; sensuous, sweet, moist—
Like a kiss.

When my appetite finally returned months after Todd's death, all I craved was homemade bread and butter. My best friend Rachel and I had started making homemade lefse a few years before. Every year before the holidays, we'd mix up the potato-y dough and roll and flip it until we had piles of the traditional Scandinavian delicacy, which everyone ate rolled up with butter and sometimes sugar. But now I also wanted to start making the homemade bread I had grown up with, to carry on the tradition my Grandma Vivian had taught me. Growing up, I had spent hours in the kitchen with her, first watching, then helping her make bread. Yet after all of those years of her guidance and teaching in the kitchen, something was missing in my own cooking. Bread, sour cream raisin bars, lefse—my favorite recipes from her never came out with quite the same result that she got. I experimented with her bread recipe for two years in hopes that I could recapture the essence of the homemade bread she used to make, but the perfect loaf eluded me. No matter how closely I followed her directions, my attempts at the golden-domed loaves of tender, yeasty goodness always fell short.

One afternoon, the spirits were with me in the kitchen—or they must have been because of what happened when I pulled that day's loaves from the oven and took a bite. Mist burned my closed eyes. Tiny drops clung to my lashes. And the flavors intermingling in my mouth jolted me back twenty-five years to what is still one of my fondest memories.

* * *

I was again in the warm and welcoming kitchen. The aroma of baking filled the air. A sink full of garden-fresh vegetables, herbs, and fruit—strawberries, tomatoes, cabbage, cucumbers, dill, and peas—awaited attention, soon to be canned, frozen, or eaten right from the sink. The air, warm from the oven and the late summer sun, raised a glisten of perspiration above the sweet and cheerful smile of my Grandma Vivian, bustling around the small kitchen with an air of combined authority and gentleness. Her short, soft frame covered by an apron, a line of white flour dusting her cheek, her curly brown hair disheveled, she was making bread.

"Grandma, can I help?" I asked.

"Okay, come on up," she replied. She never shooed me away, even when I was pestering her and getting in the way of her magic making. She brought over the stool with the gray, red, and white speckled plastic seat that flipped up to fit every size kid. Over the years, all of us who were fortunate enough to spend time in that kitchen used it, infants to adults. I excitedly climbed up, getting into position. I loved to watch her arthritic, but never compromised, hands knead and turn the dough into a smooth, elastic ball. She tore off a chunk, and I mimicked her, rolling and folding it until my hands and wrists throbbed, ending up with my own little mound. She then took it and worked it into her own, placed it into the big yellow Tupperware bowl, and covered it with a white flour sack dish towel to sit on the stovetop to rise.

"Stop peeking, it won't rise if you poke at it," she laughed when I walked by again and again, looking under the towel to monitor the status during the rising, waiting for the next step in the process. I always knew when it was ready. The dough looked like it was about to burst, the top brimming over the bowl in a perfectly domed puff of yeast and flour. I loved to punch my fists into the risen dough, watch it deflate, hear and smell the "poof" of yeasty air fill the kitchen, and then sneak a piece of the dough into my mouth.

"Now don't eat too much of that Kris," she said, chuckling a little, but never telling me I couldn't have it. I grabbed an extra dough wad when she wasn't looking. When the two risings in the bowl were done, Grandma pulled out the bread pans. "Here you go. Grease them up." She handed me butter wrappers or wax paper and a tub of Crisco shortening. I diligently covered every surface with the Crisco, not wanting to compromise the loaves by a potential sticking-to-the-pan situation. She brought the yellow bowl full of dough to the table and artistically shaped each loaf into a perfect oval while I struggled to make my mini loaves as perfectly shaped as hers. The loaves went into the oven and, just as I did during the risings, I paced back and forth, monitoring the progress, peeking inside the oven.

"Kris, you're letting the heat out. And don't slam the oven door, or the loaves will sink." I might have been annoying her a little at that point, but she never let on if I was. When the timer sounded, I was right there next to her, anxious to get the first slice of steaming bread slathered with real butter.

She always let me have the first taste, never telling me no or that we had to let it cool. She knew this was a little slice of heaven, and so did everyone else. Within minutes of the bread coming out of the oven, people would show up. Grandpa Orice came in from the back garage, home from work, or up from the basement, smelling of grease, dirt, and spicy cologne. Whoever was picking me up always seemed to show up right when the bread was coming out of the oven, my mom or dad scoring a piece or two before stealing an entire loaf to take home with us. And when Grandma packed up the tiny, misshapen loaves I had created into little baggies for me to bring home, I stuck close by her side, having just spent the day with my favorite person in the world—a woman who would come to define me in so many ways.

* * *

Now I wanted to recapture the happy times I spent in that kitchen and share a part of Grandma Vivian with Brooke, who never knew her but knows about her through the stories I tell. My Grandpa Orice was in the hospital, making me moody and nostalgic, and I hoped that finally my bread would turn out like Grandma's.

As the baking commenced, I was in the zone. I knew it from the moment the ingredients came together in the bowl and I saw the perfect texture of the dough. My heart beat fast and hard while I monitored the progress of the first rising, knowing this might finally be the breakthrough I had been waiting for. I watched Brooke punch down the balloon of dough, and the familiar feel and smell of the air electrified me. And when she popped a piece of the dough into her mouth and grabbed another, hiding it behind her back, a familiar laugh erupted from my chest—Grandma's laugh. I looked up at the Norwegian Rosemaled angel that sat on the shelf overlooking my work. It was a wedding gift from a friend who said it symbolized my grandma. Was she here witnessing and even guiding me? The second rising was perfection, the "poof" filling me with an impending sense of success. I shaped the dough into loaves and eased them into their pans, and for a moment almost thought I saw the gnarled and bent fingers of Grandma doing the shaping for me. As the loaves baked, the aroma penetrating the house was like nothing I had ever smelled before—except in Grandma's kitchen.

"Mommy, it smells good in here," Brooke announced when we went into the kitchen to check the progress.

"You're right, it does smell good. This is just how Grandma Vivian's bread used to smell," I said, hoping it was a good sign. The timer went off, and I pulled the golden loaves from the oven, their crusty tops exact replicas of what I had pulled from Grandma's oven so many times before.

But the real test was in the tasting. I immediately rubbed the tops and sides of each loaf with butter, just like she used to do. I grabbed the bread knife, sliding it into the crusty exterior through to the tender crumb of the inside. The steaming slice fell into my hand, and a lump rose in my throat. The texture of the bread was impeccable—moist, even, and soft, but not too dense or heavy. I spread a layer of butter on, the heat of the bread melting it on contact. But instead of taking the first bite myself, I handed it to Brooke, whose eyes lit up as she tasted it.

"Mmm, yummy!" she announced, smiling. I sliced off another slab, covering it in a generous layer of butter. Lifting it to my mouth, I took a bite, wondering if I had finally baked the elusive loaf of Grandma Vivian's bread.

As the warmth of the bread and the salt of the butter hit my tongue, I knew it was perfection. Tears welled up in my eyes, and memories of Grandma flooded my brain. For twenty-seven years I knew her, and she knew me. She was gone now. She died just a few weeks before my wedding, but her spirit was still with me as proven by the perfect loaves I finally baked that day with Brooke.

As we ate the delicious slices of bread, I looked up at that symbol of Grandma Vivian, the Rosemaled angel I turned to so often, and swear I saw her wink at me as if to say, "Now you know what your previous attempts were missing—love and family to share in it with you." A piece of her bread was a piece of herself, and she shared that with everyone who came through her kitchen—and now I was passing it on.

When I'm baking, I feel so close to my grandma. I know she's imparting her cooking wisdom to me as I experiment with different types of flour and ratios of ingredients. It's therapeutic, and who would think that something so simple would make me feel so good? I love the whole process—finding a recipe, getting out the ingredients, mixing it up, and sampling the raw dough. I've always loved bread dough and swear I eat about three slices worth during the kneading and shaping steps—always resulting in a stomachache, but one that's well worth it. Making bread has given me a new appreciation for the simple things in life. I even enjoy the cleanup while it bakes, knowing that once the kitchen and dishes are all clean again, the bread will be done and I can devour a steaming slice.

I have experimented with various recipes and methods, from standard white bread to honey whole wheat to a traditional French baguette (which turns out marvelously, I must admit). But it is my grandma's recipe that I always come back to; it never disappoints. Just like Grandma Vivian didn't ever disappoint. Whenever I was feeling low, she had words of wisdom to cheer me up. Somehow she could always put things into perspective for me, even when I knew she thought I was being a crazy teenager. When she died three weeks before my wedding after an up and down battle with cancer, I never thought I would feel grief like that again. But that grief was different than the grief of losing my husband. I didn't see my grandma every day, so that grief felt more like a dark shadow I looked down at, an outline that resembled the shape of grief, but not an everyday, every moment, all-consuming pain. I woke up to Todd every morning and fell asleep with him inches away every night. My grief for him wasn't a shadow, but a looming giant, blocking all of the light and stealing all of the air from my world. I got to have my last moments and talks with Grandma. I was able to let go on my own terms. But when Todd died, it was so unexpected that I was shocked not just by the actual death but by the sudden destruction of my entire existence and future. In ten seconds I went from the sweet serenity of a morning nap with my infant daughter to the horrific moment of seeing Todd's dead body—and every dream I'd ever had for the future erased.

No amount of homemade bread could bring my grandma back, but it did make me feel closer to her, like she wasn't so far away. I wished I could find something like that to make me feel like Todd was nearby. Shortly after the one-year anniversary of his death, that something came.

I walked to the mailbox, turning my face to the sky to feel the cool fall air and warm sun. Pulling out the mail, I flipped through it and walked back to the house, Cosmo running circles around me, thinking we were going for a walk. Bills, magazine renewal notices, yet another bank statement for Todd. I didn't know how many times I had to call his old bank to get that account closed; apparently more than three. When I got to the last letter in the stack, I saw an envelope from LifeSource, the organ and tissue donation agency I had spoken to the day Todd died. I received mail from them periodically, invitations to picnics or dinners for families of organ donors or informational newsletters. But this one looked different. It was handwritten instead of printed. Curiously, I opened the letter, walking up the steps to the kitchen. There was another envelope inside and a typed note that read,

Dear Mrs. Brown,
This is a letter from one of the recipients of Todd's tissues.
Sincerely, Jill

I tore open the enclosed envelope. I had been hoping for something like this, but after months of waiting, I assumed I wouldn't get one. The letter was from Carlos, a man in San Salvador who had received some of Todd's tissues as a result of a spinal cord injury. He told me he now had a chance to play his beloved sport of tennis again because of Todd and thanked me for the gift. I sat heavily onto a barstool, staring down at the letter. This man was living a better life thanks to Todd. Tears welled up in my eyes, and I smiled and folded the letter back up, tucking it gently into the envelope. I felt an amazing sense of peace—and a connection to Todd I hadn't felt until that moment. He was living on in a tangible, real way. Like a smiley face at the bottom of an unhappy letter, Todd was living on and making someone else's life better.

FORTY TWO

It was late afternoon, the sun just starting to set and the air still warm with lingering Indian summer heat. Brooke and I were playing with blocks and reading books in her bedroom. I took down a framed photo of Todd that I kept on her changing table, one of him in a baseball cap, looking like he most often did with a big grin and his blue eyes crinkling at the corners. She wasn't even two years old and her daddy had been gone over a year now, but still she took the photograph gently into her tiny hands and kissed it—a big old smooch right on the picture. My breath caught in my throat. I didn't teach her that, I don't know who did. Suddenly tears were stinging my eyes. I turned into a complete wreck as she looked at the photo and kissed it again, then turned to keep on playing like it was no big deal—as if she knew exactly what she was doing, just giving Daddy a kiss. But to me it was a *huge* deal—a sign that Todd might be here after all, giving Brooke kisses and getting them from her in return.

They say kids and dogs can sense ghosts and otherworldly presences. Many times Brooke has said, "Guy coming." I'll ask her where, and she'll reply, "Right there," pointing to a specific spot by the bedroom door. Instead of being scared, it comforts me, thinking and hoping that it's Todd watching over us.

"Brooke, is Daddy here?" I asked her once.

"Yes, right there," she replied as if I were an idiot, pointing to the same spot by the door. I don't know if she really understood what I was asking, but if she does sometimes see him, I'm so glad he's here and that Brooke senses that and recognizes him.

Brooke is my salvation. Just her presence can always make me smile, even when I feel awful or afraid or lonely. And when we're not together, when I'm traveling for work or vacation, I'm always anxious to hear her voice. She usually stays with my parents when I'm away. Once when I called to see how she was doing, my mom replied in an exasperated, defeated voice, "Oh she's great, but she is a load."

"Why? What's wrong? Is she sick?"

"No, she's healthy, but she just wants to be held and is so demanding." Welcome to my world, I thought, but didn't say it aloud. That conversation and similar ones I've had with other parents about their children remind me how hard I worked and why I felt so exhausted all the time. I hear others complain about how much work their kids are or how their spouse doesn't help out enough, and I am envious because at least they have a spouse to share the responsibilities of raising and disciplining a child. I see some children of single mothers who turn into terrors. They rebel in their teens and have no respect for their family, teachers, or friends. I'm scared that I won't be a good enough parent on my own despite my best intentions and love.

Maybe I'm setting myself up to fit into all the single-mom stereotypes by breaking the rules of child rearing. The baby and toddler "rule books" say you shouldn't rock your child to sleep at night or sleep with them because it causes them to always need that to fall asleep, and they won't learn to self-soothe. But bedtime is one of my favorite times of the day. I love to rock Brooke to sleep or let her sleep in my bed or lie with her while she falls asleep in hers. She nestles in so tightly and cuddles her face into my chest. I love the smell of her curls; even when they've gotten a good dose of maple syrup, sunscreen (to protect her still-visible scalp), or pizza sauce, they still have her fresh, baby scent of skin and sweetness. She clings to me tightly, not wanting me to lay her down, doing everything she can to stay awake—singing, counting, talking, humming, asking for snacks. She's a manipulator already, and it's my own fault—because she's my favorite person in the world. She's not just my daughter, she's my best friend—along with Todd—and my driving life force, the closest and only connection to Todd that I have. I'll do anything to make her life easier and more fun, even if the rule books tell me otherwise.

Todd, I wish you were here to help me with all of these parenting duties. It is so hard to be a friend and a disciplinarian to Brooke. Sometimes I just wish you were here to support me as I'm fighting or negotiating with a two-year-old. It's exhausting. You would have so much fun with her now. I'm trying to do what you'd do, teaching her to throw a ball, encouraging her left-handedness, and talking to her like an adult as opposed to that baby talk that drove you crazy. She's so polite and loving. You would melt if you were here to get all her hugs and "I love you's." And she looks just like you, but unfortunately has my temperament most days. But you put up with me, so I have no doubt she'll find her place in the world too, despite her temper. I hope you can see us from wherever you are and that you're enjoying the show!

Before bed, Brooke and I read books and sing songs. Like dancing, my singing ability is good only in my own mind, and often not even there. But when Brooke asks me to sing, I belt it out and she thinks I'm good—most of the time. Other times, I'll start singing something I think she'll like and she obviously disagrees. "Mommy, no singing!" she'll yell at me. I like to think it's because she just doesn't care for a particular song, but I'm pretty sure it's the irritating, nasally crackle of my off-key voice.

I purchased the Nintendo Wii video game system with great intentions of doing yoga every day with WiiFit. (I failed miserably.) I also picked up the American Idol game, knowing my family's love of karaoke. As I hooked up the system I showed Brooke the microphone that came with it.

"Mommy, Brookie Brown singing," she announced, holding it up to her mouth.

"Yep. Do you want to hear mommy sing to some real music?" I asked, inserting the American Idol disk into the game console.

"Yay, singing," she answered.

I took the microphone and followed the prompts on the screen, selecting my character and stage setting and finally getting to the song list. There wasn't a large selection to choose from, but they did have one of my family's favorites, "Sweet Dreams" by the Eurythmics. My mom always wants to sing it at karaoke events (yes, we have had many a karaoke event in my family), but she'll never go up alone so my sister and I always have to sing backup. But by the middle of the song, my mom is in full force, dancing and belting it out like she's Annie Lennox. And depending on how many drinks we've all had, we always sing "Love Potion Number 9," my dad (reluctantly dragged on stage) and brother included.

I wish I had the same gusto and guts as Todd did to get up in front of an audience alone and sing. He did "Runaround Sue," "Bad, Bad Leroy Brown", pretty much any oldie but goodie. I can do it in groups or even as a duet, but to have the sole responsibility of entertaining an audience for three to five minutes with my singing voice and dance moves is just too much pressure for me. I've tried to brave it, going so far as to pick specific songs and write them on the sign-up slips. But I've never gotten to the point of actually submitting them to the deejay. One of these days I'll just do it; it's not like my family and friends won't like me if I screw up.

I think it goes back to my vanity and not wanting to show weakness in myself. Historically, I have been very aware of the way people perceive me. I have always known I'm a little bitchy when it comes to certain subjects—my job, annoying people, salespeople who bother me, bad drivers. But I've let most of that go. As I've learned over the last couple of years, those little things just don't matter and shouldn't take up all that energy of frowning and exerting brainpower on negative thoughts. If all the negative thoughts about minor things were turned into positive thoughts, can you imagine what a change in perspective and lifestyle that would bring about in a person? And if everyone changed even half of their negative thoughts, how much change could occur in the world? I'm not saying we shouldn't think negatively at all. Without the bad thoughts and things that happen to us, we wouldn't appreciate the good, but if we're going to have those bad thoughts, it should be about something that really matters, something really big that deserves the self-serving self-pity we all need to have sometimes.

After Todd died, I had months of living in a pit of despair and feeling sorry for myself, but I needed those months. They gave me the perspective I needed to pick myself back up and find that inner strength I didn't even know I had. It is still unbelievable to me that I survived at all. But I had to for Brooke. I want to be a role model for her and not someone who is negative, bitter, and sad all the time.

So every night, despite my lack of talent, I sing to her to make her laugh so that she sees I am happy. After we say goodnight to every person she knows and to every item in her bedroom and give hugs, kisses, and cuddles to all her stuffed animals who've had to join us in bed, she falls soundly asleep while I lie there and listen to her breathe. Some nights she'll want to hold my hand as she drifts off to sleep, just like Todd used to do.

He was always a big hand-holder, but I was never one for public displays of affection, even something as simple as clasping a hand. The day Brooke was born was different, though. I held Todd's hand for support from morning til night as we prepared for and then welcomed our baby into the world. It was a week after my due date, and I was being induced. We drove to the hospital that morning with a bag packed for me and a bag packed for someone we hadn't even met yet. I had the nursery set up, brown and turquoise to suit either a boy or a girl. I had a six-month supply of diapers, wipes, baby shampoo, butt paste, and every item I could possible need to take care of a baby. I had assembled the crib, bookshelf, and changing table myself, Todd having no skill or inclination to partake in mechanical efforts. I had a closetful of unisex clothes just waiting for someone to wear them. Now we were finally about to meet the little being who had morphed my body into a misshapen vessel of safety and nutrients. I pulled out the video camera and flipped open the lens cap.

"Here we go, on the way to the hospital for the birth of child number one," I said, panning around the car to Todd in the driver's seat, my heart pounding with excitement and a little bit of fear.

He was wearing sunglasses that sunny December 1 morning. He looked at me and smiled nervously. "Yep, here we go," he replied overconfidently, but he couldn't fool me. I knew he was terrified. He was a guy's guy, the epitome of a sports fanatic, golf geek, and lazy man who could spend hours on the couch watching sports. I even caught him watching a jai alai match on some random sports channel once because "nothing else was on." So this baby coming into his world was really going to shake things up for him. But he was excited, too. When I screamed and pushed to get Brooke out of me, I held his hand in a vise grip and he clenched mine as if to say that we were in this parenting adventure together for the long haul.

Two years later, I was driving home with Brooke after picking her up from day care. Despite promising myself when she was born to always make her birthday a day just for her, job responsibilities were trumping my personal life as usual. I looked up in the sky and saw a perfect crescent moon, and next to it two bright stars. Just the moon and two stars were shining, like our family on the day Brooke was born. Todd and I were the two stars and Brooke our shining moon whose light we'd always look to for laughs and love. Now it's just me and my moon, the other star gone, but its light still shining to help me navigate life and the raising of our daughter.

His light shines through her bedroom window whenever I sneak quietly out of her room and breathe a sigh of relief that I survived another day, and it is then that I feel lost. I try to find something to give me comfort or occupy my time so I don't feel so alone and lonely. I've learned that those are different feelings completely. I can feel lonely even when surrounded by a room full of people. I prepare for bed, reflecting on the day. Often I get into my pajamas and then can't decide what to do with myself. When Todd was alive, we'd watch a movie with popcorn, play a board game, or just talk while lying in bed. Without him, I struggle with what my nighttime activities should be in the house alone after Brooke goes to bed. While I know I need sleep, I dread the tossing and turning that goes with it, so I usually distract myself with *US Weekly* or a self-help book. Or I catch up on television, feeling somewhat resentful of all the backlogged shows recorded on my TiVo, yet not wanting to ignore them either. Other nights I shut the light off and just think, sometimes drifting off to sleep eventually, but usually lying awake until the sunrise brightens the room and I am forced to get up and start another day.

FORTY THREE

In the morning after my breakfast of homemade bread, I try to squeeze in a quick shower. If I don't do it before Brooke wakes up, her two-year-old energy won't give me a moment to myself, so I take advantage of the solace and head into the bathroom. Disrobing, I catch a glimpse of myself in the mirror and immediately see my "ink." I'm still not used to it.

After Todd died, I wanted to get a tattoo, a physical sign that he really was a part of my life. Of course I have the emotional evidence, the broken heart, the mental scarring that have left a permanent mark on my soul, but I needed tangible proof that he was really here and was a part of me.

I'd always been anti-tattoo. I didn't feel that an indelible ink drawing on my skin that would be there forever was necessary. But I thought that if I were ever drunk in Mexico and a tattoo seemed like a good idea, it would be the infinity symbol. It was always a conundrum to me, infinity, too much to comprehend but so intriguing. Now though, the infinity symbol didn't seem meaningful enough. I'd had that idea since high school and wanted something more symbolic of my life with Todd.

I thought about it for over a year, but nothing seemed right until one morning in the early, still-dark hours when I lay awake thinking of him. We were opposites in almost every way, yet complemented each other perfectly. Our interests, attitudes, and personalities were so different, yet together we balanced out our positive and negative traits. Astrologically, we were exact opposites, a Virgo and Pisces born six months apart, and our daughter was born exactly in between, connecting us. What better represents complementary oppositeness better than the yin-yang symbol? It tied to my appreciation for Eastern religions and spirituality. It could be small and discreet, not too obnoxious. And it would be living proof that Todd existed and left a mark on me that I could touch and feel every day. It would be that burden of proof that might release some of the inner pain I was feeling with his leaving me so suddenly.

But the next decision was where to place it. I didn't want it to be front and center for everyone to see. I wanted it for me, a secret badge of honor I could proudly wear for myself every day. I didn't want it anywhere that might sag, expand, or droop as I aged, so the stomach, butt, and boobs were out. I didn't want it on my arms or legs, which are always bare in the summer. I was leaning toward a toe or back area.

I'd heard the actual process of getting a tattoo is painful, but I wasn't concerned about that. Physical pain is temporary, while the emotional pain I've suffered is ongoing and constant and will always outweigh any bodily suffering I may experience. After thinking about it for a few days, I decided the lower back was a good option—not in the middle, I didn't want a "tramp stamp," but off to the side. I'd get a small yin-yang symbol permanently inscribed there to represent the relationship I'd had with the man who was my best friend and my other half.

There was a tattoo parlor right up the street from my house. I drove by it almost every day and had always been tempted to stop in but didn't want to be swayed by the artist into getting certain symbols. I wanted to pick the image. Now that I had, that tattoo parlor was calling my name. I drove by for weeks after I decided to do it. I was excited but nervous. Did I really want to deface my body? Maybe in ten years if I married again I'd regret doing it, but I knew in my heart that I wouldn't. One afternoon more than a year after Todd died, while going to pick Brooke up from day care, I slowed as I drove past the tattoo parlor, and something made me turn my car into that parking lot. It was time.

I stepped out of the car, half expecting to see some long-haired, freaky guy fully tattooed from head to foot smoking a joint—stereotypical of me to think, right? But walking up the steps, the winter wind cutting through my clothing, I knew this was the right thing to do, and a wave of excitement rushed through me. I didn't want to seem too anxious or too much of an amateur, so I tried to look cool as I opened the door and stepped inside as if I'd been getting tattoos for years. I didn't stop to peruse the designs or the piercing ideas, but walked straight up to the pierced guy behind the counter who was staring me down. I clearly was not the normal tattoo client, but he seemed friendly enough.

"Hi, I'd like to get a tattoo," I announced.

"What kind of design are you thinking?" he asked.

I nervously pulled the yin-yang picture from my purse, printed out in three sizes because I still wasn't sure how much I could or would commit to when it actually came time to do it. "I want to do this yin-yang symbol to commemorate my husband who passed away a little over a year ago—we were complete opposites yet fit each other perfectly, so this is the perfect thing to show that." I'm pretty sure he only caught about half of what I said because I was speaking so fast.

"Okay, where and how big do you want it?"

"Well, I'm not sure how big because I've never done this before, but I know I want it on my lower back—not a tramp stamp but on the side, lower down where it won't show—but not sure how big, like I said, never done one before so not sure I want anything too big." I was overtalking again, and he probably sensed my nervousness.

"It'll be about sixty dollars. Randy will tell you for sure. Do you want to do it today?"

"Yes, but it's cash only, right? I need to run downstairs to get some cash. I'll be right back." I bolted out the door, mentally slapping myself for acting so totally uncool. Little did I know that was only the beginning.

I went to the adjoining convenience store that conveniently also sold "smoking paraphernalia" for all those smokers who like to use a bong instead of a regular cigarette. I grabbed my cash and then momentarily panicked. Do I tip a tattoo artist? If so, what's the standard percentage? If not and I do anyway, is that considered rude, or will I walk out the door with a tattoo and a dime bag of pot for the extra cash? I immediately texted Rachel, despite the fact that she is probably the last person who would know the current tattoo-tipping policies. But she has an ill-advised permanent inking on her ankle from college and she prosecuted drug dealers for a living, so I figured she might have the inside track. While awaiting a response, I walked confidently back into the tattoo parlor where the counter guy was ready with my paperwork, a one-page sheet basically asking if I had any health issues and stating that if I had any problems they had no responsibility.

A large man of about fifty emerged from the back, wearing gray sweatpants, a T-shirt, and the demeanor of an obviously former bad ass. He had many tattoos visible on his arms and legs and probably had a giant cross, naked lady, or dragon emblazoned on his chest and back. There were also several empty piercings through his nose and in both ears, so I figured his interests must lie beyond just tattoos. But he seemed to be a regular guy, like one of my dad's buddies or one of my fun uncles on my mom's side. He shook my hand.

"Hi, I'm Randy, and I'll be doing your tattoo today. Are you sure you don't want to do it bigger?" he chuckled sarcastically. My three example pictures maxed out at about the size of a quarter.

"Sorry, I'm sure you were hoping for a more exciting tattoo customer today, but I'm a first-timer," I responded, almost embarrassed by the smallness of my chosen design.

"Well, next time we'll get you a bigger one. This will take me a few minutes to set up, so if you want to go out and have a cigarette or light up the ganj, feel free," he offered.

I should have said something cool like "thanks but just hit the pipe at home" or "I have a drug test tomorrow for work so can't tonight," despite not having smoked a joint in fourteen years. Instead, I blurted out one of the lamest things I have ever said: "I'm a mom now, so those days are behind me." I'm laughing even now as I think about it.

"You're a *what* now?"

"A mom. I'm a mom now, so I don't do that stuff anymore." As if I smoked pot and cigarettes up until the day I became a mother. I'm such a geek, or at least I felt like one, standing there out of place, waiting for my mini-tattoo to be permanently inked onto my skin. Fortunately, Randy turned out to be very nice and very smart and made me feel extremely comfortable, even while I was sprawled over a chair with my pants unbuttoned, my shirt pulled up, and my butt crack hanging out so he could have access to my lower left flank.

We talked while he set up the equipment and, of course, I again flaunted my utter unhipness. "So, has the recent economic downturn affected the tattoo and piercing industry?"

Surprisingly, he answered me in all seriousness. "Yes, this time of year is always slow, but it's even worse now. Everyone is spending their money on the holidays."

"What kind of training did you have to have to become a tattoo artist?" I think he was a little annoyed but humored me nonetheless.

"Well, you have to have been in at least two bar fights, have been married and divorced at least four times, been an alcoholic, and take a yearly class on bloodborne pathogens." I chuckled, knowing he was ninety-nine percent serious. He was a funny guy.

Finally he got the equipment and needles all ready to go, and it was time for the actual tattooing to begin. I leaned over a tall leather chair, and the machine came to life.

"It sounds like really small and fast electrical shocks," I said.

"Well, that has happened," he replied.

"That's reassuring."

"It's rare. Here we go, it might sting, but if you think it's going to hurt, it probably won't." The first licks of the needle were painless, just a little "zingy." It felt like little rubber bands snapping really fast on my skin. I've had bikini waxes that hurt worse than that did.

"This doesn't hurt at all," I sighed with relief.

"Really? Good. You're doing great." He continued working on what he said was the outline of the tattoo. "I'm going to start making some longer strokes now. It might hurt a little."

"Okay, sounds good." I said expecting nothing more than a bit more of a snapping sensation. Randy started the longer strokes. "Sonofabitch, motherfucker" was all I could think. It was a scraping sensation like a knife grating my skin. I knew that wasn't happening, but that image in my brain made it seem more violent and painful that it really was.

"Okay, the black outline is done. Take a look while I change the needle to a bigger size." He dug into his drawer of supplies.

"*What*, a bigger size?" My heart beat faster, and I turned my head to see what he was doing.

"Yep, it's bigger, but it makes the filling in go faster and look better," he explained. "See, the first one was round, and this one is three needles like this." He held up the device.

Holy crap, I thought. But I just said, "okay, you're the expert," trying to sound cool but feeling my muscles tense as the buzz of the needle started back up. He worked for another ten minutes while I cringed and gritted my teeth against the pain but thankful to be feeling something other than sadness.

"Voila, it's done. I am a master of the yin-yang symbol."

I stood up from my awkward pose and turned to look at his handiwork—and I loved it. A perfect, quarter-sized yin-yang in black and white was etched onto my lower left back. At that moment, I felt like something in me had been released. I had spent months trying to find a way to keep Todd a part of me, and now this itty-bitty tattoo that only I would see was somehow giving me that. I knew it was ridiculous; the tattoo wasn't Todd, but it symbolized him—and us—and now I was proving it to myself. Upon seeing that perfect, finished tattoo that took a fifteen-month decision to get emblazoned on my unperfect upper ass, I felt that a piece of my broken heart grew back in just the twenty minutes it took to get it. Driving to day care to pick up Brooke, I talked to Todd, smiling and feeling a little bit sad.

"I know you're jealous of this crazy thing I just did, you always said you wanted a tattoo. Now I have one, and it's because of you—and for you."

FORTY FOUR

Not long after getting my ink, I got the question I had been dreading for over a year. She had just turned two, and we were driving by Todd's former work building on the way home from seeing her pediatrician about yet another ear infection. I pointed to the tall glass building.

"There's where Daddy used to work."

"Where Daddy go?" Brooks asked in her sweet, innocent voice. I knew the day was coming when the questions would start, but in that moment my heart broke again for the man I lost and the father he would never get to be to Brooke.

Choking back the tears, I knew exactly what I wanted to say because I had rehearsed it many times in my head. I didn't want to sugarcoat it and vowed I would always be honest with her.

"Daddy's body stopped working, and he died. So he had to go away to a very special place where we can't go right now, but we'll see him again someday." She sat in silence, and I could see her toddler brain churning, trying to process something that made so little sense to her. How do I explain the concept of death to a child when I can't even explain it to myself?

After she processed what I'd said, she yelled, "Daddy, wait for me!" My stomach rose into my throat, and my breath caught. Her innocent little mind really thought he'd gone somewhere without her, and she thought it was somewhere she could go, too. The rest of the drive home, I had to maintain my composure while she chattered, "Daddy, wait for me. Daddy, wait for me." It took every bit of strength I had not to break down crying and have to pull over on the freeway. My heart broke, my lungs burned from holding down the sobs, and my eyes stung with tears, listening to Brooke pleading for her daddy to wait for her. I know there are more tough questions like that coming, and I don't know how I'm going to explain where her daddy is, when even I don't know. Is he in heaven? Is he all around us? Is he in the box that holds his ashes? Is he just gone? Even after all my research, I still don't know.

By then I had known Brooke more than three times as long as Todd knew her. It's hard to comprehend that he never got to witness and have a hand in her little personality as she's developed or hear her talk or see her run and swim. I know he's here all around us and we breathe him in every day, but I feel so sad that he didn't get to experience fatherhood. He didn't get to develop that father/daughter bond that I know Brooke will miss so much as she grows older.

That night, I pulled the box of Todd's ashes from its shelf and held it to my chest. I needed him now. I needed him close by, even if all that I had was dust.

FORTY FIVE

Shortly after Brooke turned two, we went with my family on a second trip to Florida to once again try to mask the pain of another Christmas without Todd. On one of our first nights there, I lay awake listening to Brooke breathing next to me, the room silent except for her and the gentle chirping of insects and frogs outside. She'd just drifted off to sleep after a long night and day of being sick and cranky. I was exhausted, but my eyes wouldn't shut. Suddenly, the hair on my arms stood on end and I felt a buzz surround me. I knew it was Todd.

"Todd, I feel you, where have you been?" I said out loud, my eyes searching the room for him. Of course, he didn't answer, but I knew he was there. Tears came to my eyes, but I didn't want to wake Brooke so I gulped down my sobs, my chest feeling as if it might explode.

"Where have you been?" I pleaded again.

Then something happened, I don't know what or how, but I felt the warmth of his fingertips on my palm and his hand curled around my shaking fingers. It was so real that by reflex I grasped it. And for a moment, the vibration of his hand in mine was all I felt and all I needed. I lay there, gripping his hand tightly, not wanting to let him go. A moment later, his grasp released, and I grabbed hold of the blanket. Tears streamed from my eyes.

"Todd if you're really here, prove it. Send me a sign," I whispered. The very next moment, I heard the honking and backfiring of a car on the main street up the block. The chirping outside the window was silenced for a moment. It was just coincidence … wasn't it? My mind said it was just a coincidence, but my heart was pleading for him to be there. I had been missing him for months and I so wanted Todd around us.

"Show me again that you're really here," I said. A second later, a boy on a skateboard broke the silence, yelling as he careened down the street outside the window. And I knew Todd really was there.

"Todd, I wish you were here for real, to share all of Brooke's growing and learning, to be here for all of this," I said, looking over at Brooke sleeping next to me. The vibration I had felt in my hand now brushed my cheek and through my hair.

"Please, please stay." But the energy in the room shifted, and he was gone. I lay there for hours, hoping he would come back, pleading for him to return. Clinging to Brooke, I cried quietly, "Todd, please, please come back, just for a second."

FORTY SIX

"Mommy," Brooke called to me.

She's up—finally! I raced upstairs and did what I did every morning—sneaked down the hall, poked my head into her room, and tried to make her laugh. "Boo!" I shouted.

She giggled. "Hi, Mommy, hi, Cosmo." The dog, of course, was right on my heels. Brooke reached for me and I crossed the room to her bed, hardly able to wait the two seconds for our morning hug. She isn't a morning person, just like Todd wasn't, both taking a while to shake the sleep from their brains and get into the full swing of the day. She always wants to get into my bed if she isn't already there.

"Brookie Brown wanna watch a moo-gie," she exclaimed in her still-developing two-year-old-speak. We shuffled to my room, and she perused her movie selection, no different than the day before, but she scrutinized the options as if they were all brand-new titles she'd never seen before and not the same twenty she'd watched over and over for months.

"Wanna watch *Diamond Castle*," she decided. Barbie again.

I had every one of her movies memorized, including most of the songs, and to keep myself from getting too bored watching them, I tried to entertain her and myself with a little song-and-dance number. "There's a diamond castle in my mind, and someday soon, we're gonna find it, we're gonna find it...." I sang, spinning her around, flying her onto the bed, and breaking into my '90s dance moves. She smiled, wanting to laugh, but her morning surliness kept her from fully admitting her amusement. (Or maybe I'm really not as entertaining as I think I am; but those running man and MC Hammer moves are hilarious.)

Sometimes Brooke humored me and let me attempt to get her out of her morning funk by breaking into dance. Usually though, she frowned and pointed to the television. "Movie!" she demanded and settled in for a half hour of mind-numbing cartoons.

"What would you like for breakfast today?" I asked, although I knew the answer.

"Pancakes," she replied. It's always pancakes.

"Syrup or honey?"

"How about syrup *aaand* honey?"

Shocker—same breakfast every day since she turned two. I went to the kitchen, pulled out the mini pancakes from the freezer, and arranged her very specific breakfast setup—tiny little pink bowl, little tiny pink cup, really, really small spoon—her descriptors of her favorite eating utensils. I poured her juice, put the pancakes in the bowl with syrup and honey, and carried them to her royal highness. Yes, I allow my daughter to eat breakfast in my bed every single day, a bad habit that will come back to bite me someday. But it's easy, fun, and keeps her happy as she wakes up and comes out of her morning grouchiness.

I handed her the bowl, and she looked suspiciously at the pancakes. I sensed her dissatisfaction and backed up, anticipating what was to come.

"*More honey!*" she screamed.

"But look, there is a lot of honey on here already. It's just soaked in," I explained, feeling my neck muscles tightening.

"*Nooo, more,*" she demanded, her face turning red, her tiny fists clenching. She started to shake. I knew what was coming next—a terrible-twos tantrum. Once she starts she can't be stopped, and the only thing to do is let her get it out of her system. I took the pancakes before she could fling them off the bed and slid the juice to the other side of the bedside table out of her reach. Sure enough, she exploded.

"*Nooo! No pancakes! No juice!*" I wondered if it hurts her throat to screech like that. I tried to remain calm, but when she took her spoon and launched it directly at me, my pulse started to race. Time to leave the room before I had a terrible-thirty-twos tantrum. My departure set off yet another tirade.

"*Mommy, more honey!*" After about ten minutes of her head spinning around and green vomit spewing out of her mouth with the devil speaking through her in tongues, I returned to the demon child and started to talk her down.

"Okay, Brooke, let's take a deep breath and talk about why you're so upset. I understand something is frustrating you," I said in the calmest voice I could muster, using the tactics I'd learned on TV's *SuperNanny*. "What can I do for you to make you feel happy?"

Finally she started to quiet down, her tears slowing and the blood in her face retreating as she returned to the color of a normal child. It's hard not to chuckle when she has these tantrums. She gets so upset over such silly things—pancake syrup, scarves on her head that she calls "long hair," movie selections. But I have to remember she's only two. Sometimes I forget that because she is so smart.

I know all parents think their child is smart, but I have actually been told by doctors and her day care that she is way ahead of the curve. She has known her colors since she was eighteen months old. She can identify all of the letters of the alphabet. She can count to thirteen in English and ten in Spanish and knows her right from her left. She's a lefty, and I've heard that people who are left-handed have high intelligence—or maybe it's that they're more creative. Either way, she often shows flashes of brilliance that astound me.

After settling down, she finally ate her pancakes with the added cup of honey I'd given her for dipping. Then I said the dreaded words.

"Time to go to school."

"No! No!" she begged. It broke my heart the days we had to make that six-minute drive to day care. Once buckled in she calmed down, but when I turned onto the street and the yellow and blue awning of the school came into view, she started again. "*No! Nooo!* I wanna stay home. I wanna play with you." She wailed a most heart-wrenching sound, stuck out her lip, and big fat tears welled up in her eyes and slid down her cheeks. She clamped onto me as we went inside. The teachers immediately came over and diverted her attention so that I could make a quick getaway. They would tell me she loved being at day care and would do great after I left, but it always broke my heart that I had no choice but to work full time. Todd and I had always talked about me eventually being a stay-at-home mom. Not anymore. Now I was forced into a stress-filled life of constant worry about Brooke's health, my work anxiety, our financial future, and everything in between.

FORTY SEVEN

For months, I had been suffering from unbearable, debilitating stress—the kind of anxiety that would take me down just when I thought I was making progress. I tried to figure it out. I wrote out my thoughts. I reviewed the various aspects of my life, trying to pinpoint where the disconnects were. It all came back to the same thing—my job. Well, not exactly the job itself, but the situation I had been in with my new boss since she came on board a couple of weeks after Todd died. Yes, chances are high that Todd's death lowered my tolerance for difficult people. But after months of contemplation, reflection, and discussion with others about it, it all kept circling back to the same kernel of discontent. I knew I needed to make a change.

Believing another corporate America gig was my only option since I needed a decent paycheck and insurance, I started interviewing with other companies. I was being selective. I didn't want just any old job, because I knew that different didn't mean better; if I was going to stay in the business world, it had to be the right fit. I finally found the perfect job for me, the exact description of what I envisioned myself doing if I had to stay in the business world, and was thrilled when they offered me the position. But I wanted to give my company a chance to make things right. They had been great to me over the years, and after I told them of my job offer it was no different; they offered me a promotion. Unfortunately, it was in a newly formed group that would be led by none other than my current boss, who was the reason I wanted out in the first place. I don't know what veil I had over my eyes, but I thought that in this new role she might be different, and I wanted to give her the benefit of the doubt. So I turned down the new job opportunity out of loyalty to my company and the hope that things would change.

But they didn't. The micromanaging, the constant one-upping, the long hours—all of that was carried over to the new group, and after a few weeks it started to affect me physically. I got panic attacks and stomachaches constantly and gained back the twenty pounds I had lost after Todd died. Every time I felt my heart lurch just before panic set in, I thought I was having a heart attack and panicked even more, afraid that Brooke would be left with no parents. Just seeing my boss's constant e-mails in my inbox made me cringe with apprehension and anxiety. The panic attacks increased in frequency and severity.

Working for a micromanaging workaholic is not pleasant when you're trying to balance single parenthood, a job, and some sort of me-time. Late-night and weekend e-mails from her were the norm. I was supposed to be a director but was directing nothing. I was still doing my old job because the company hadn't hired anyone to replace me. I was running on empty. I was a puppet just going through the motions, waiting for the next criticism or go-fer task. I so badly wanted a mentor like I had before her, someone who knew my talents and let me do my job.

I felt trapped. The need for health insurance and some sort of income forced me to keep working. Yet I hated my current position, which was taking a huge physical and emotional toll. And I didn't want to look for another corporate position because I had lost faith in the business world, with all its games and politics. Even if I did want to make a move, the economy was tanking, limiting my options. I should have taken my dream job when I had the chance.

When I was in college working on my business degree, I had an idealistic view of life. I had a planned trajectory for my career and thought I would be in the corporate world until I retired. Now I was amazed that I ever felt so passionate about my career choice and struggled to find even one or two things that I enjoyed about it. I found an essay I wrote when I was younger, in which I mapped out my life. In it, I made myself out to be a sparkly and happy person—but when it comes right down to it, I've never been a very joyful person. I've always harbored anxiety and been overly concerned with the details of life instead of just enjoying the ride.

I had a moment of revelation on a flight about eighteen months after Todd died. A guy sitting in front of me was wearing a hat that said, "Fun is Good." I chuckled to myself, thinking "how true," but then realized that I wanted to be having fun and be happy, but I wasn't. While I was searching so hard for meaning in my life and answers to the big questions, while I was trying to heal myself and find happiness, I was again getting so bogged down by minutiae that I was forgetting to enjoy the act of living. Fun *is* good, and I knew I needed to start reflecting that in my actions, not just in my beliefs.

But that was easier said than done. There were moments when I felt enlightened and in touch with the universe, when I was writing or gardening or walking the dog. It was as if I could see and feel my interconnectedness with everyone and everything, as if my true purpose were clear. But there were other moments when I found myself trapped in my own body, focused on the turmoil and chaos in my brain and heart with absolutely no direction and no plan for my life. Both extremes presented challenges. The enlightened state offered hope and fulfillment at the prospect of a new, more meaningful career, but I felt unable to make anything a reality because I needed the financial security for my daughter. The state of inner turmoil drove me to the edge of insanity because I knew I needed to make changes for my own health and well being but again felt imprisoned by my work situation and need for financial security.

I was scared to make a move and scared not to.

I found myself wishing I would get laid off. I felt guilty thinking that, knowing that so many people would love to be in my shoes with a secure, well-paying job, but I honestly needed to rest. I was exhausted and just needed some peace to get my head on straight and start to really live again. I'd just been going through the motions, and those motions were starting to wear me down to a thin sliver of self. I didn't even know who I was sometimes. I felt like a rat in one of those experimental labyrinths—every direction I turned was the wrong way, every time I thought I was on the right path I hit a dead end, over and over and over again.

I thought a vacation might help clear my mind. It was winter, and I was craving warm weather anyway. That year there wasn't a writer's strike to disrupt movie awards season, and two girlfriends and I decided it was time to truly celebrate our love of movies and hit the big city where they were made. So we booked a trip to Los Angeles for Oscar weekend. We would finally bear witness to and participate in the annual event that we had been celebrating from our own homes for the last ten years. It was a great trip. We were next to the red carpet and participated in the preshow excitement. We ate fantastic meals every night and discovered a hole-in-the-wall bakery with the best doughnuts I have ever had (and I've eaten a lot of doughnuts in my day). After the Oscars, we even managed to score seats across the pool from where *Access Hollywood* was filming. We were actually living our dream and reveling in the annual movie festivities.

I came home from that trip feeling inspired, knowing life had more to offer me than the stress I was living with every day. I was determined to figure out my next move.

FORTY EIGHT

Every day I wonder how Brooke will feel when she gets older—how she'll perceive the father she never knew. Will she want to know more about him, what he was like, how he died? Or will she want to distance herself from that stranger, letting the past be the past? If it's up to me, she will see him as her best friend like I do, a man she can always talk to about anything. He'll be the one who will always listen, no matter what, and will be silently guiding her on the right path in life.

I was trying my best to guide her, but it was proving to be a difficult task—not because of how or what I was doing for her, but because of how I was feeling inside. I was harboring totally ridiculous, completely irrational fears. For the first nine months after Todd died I was fearless. Nothing scared me, because I was so numb; I just didn't care if I lived or died. When I was in Costa Rica and was asked if I wanted to go zip lining through the jungle canopy, my response was "hell, yeah!" But as I emerged from my fog of indifference and pain, I realized that Brooke needed me, and that I need myself, to be full and whole and functioning. I wanted to live, and I found myself terrified of everything, even things that had zero chance of actually occurring. Although I was trying to find things that made me feel happy and enlightened, I was allowing those completely irrational and unfounded fears to paralyze my ongoing development and growth.

Remembering how amazing and transformative my trip to Costa Rica was, I thought another surfing vacation might help me continue on my healing path and figure out what to do about my work situation. This time the group of us from the first trip decided to go to Panama, and we added four more girls to the mix. Brooke was once again in the care of her grandparents—both sets tag teaming during my nine days away, so

I should have felt okay about being gone. But on day one of surf camp, all of my irrational fears came to a head, and I had a complete meltdown right before I was supposed to jump into the water.

The setup in Panama was completely different from Costa Rica. In Costa Rica, we learned to surf from shore and waded into a sandy-bottomed ocean with long, gentle whitewater and measured waves that you could see coming in time to judge their behavior. In Panama, we anchored offshore and were thrown into the middle of a churning washing machine of currents, waves, and whitewater swirling atop a jagged reef just a few feet below the surface. One bad fall and I'd be thrust downward under the power of the wave breaking overhead and then jettisoned back up through the current as the leash to my surfboard tore me back to the surface—all the while trying to avoid the razor-sharp coral formations as my legs and feet kicked and flailed to bring me back to the air. On top of this imagery, I envisioned sharks emerging from the depths to attack me. I got a minor reef scrape on my foot, but it was still a bleeder. Would the blood trail lead the sharks right to me? And despite the shore being within sight of our launch point, I still kept thinking that a current would sweep me away and I'd get separated from the group only to somehow lose my board that was tethered to my ankle, leaving me floundering in the ocean, eventually succumbing to my own lack of cardiovascular conditioning.

Why was it that the ocean that I loved to swim in, gaze at, and be around every chance I got turned into an evil monster, waiting to eat me alive when I was supposed to be surfing? I didn't want to die and leave Brooke without both parents—but I also believed that fate is fate, and when my time was up, death would still come for me whether I was braving the wild surf or cowering like a wuss in the boat.

As I sat wondering why I felt this way, I knew it went back to fear. While I was attempting to restart my life by trying new things and getting out of my comfort zone, the plain and simple truth was that I was terrified. I was afraid to be alone, even though I'd been alone for many months. I was afraid of being a single mom and having the responsibility of raising a respectful, successful, confident daughter on my own and having people judge and stereotype me. I was afraid to date again, knowing I'd have to "put on a show" and go through the long, tedious process of courtship. I was afraid of failing financially, so stayed in a job I hated for the security, yet I was afraid to stay in it because it was affecting me physically and mentally. I was afraid of being with people and hearing about the joys and milestones in their lives. I was afraid I was in over my head and the next wave would take me down for good.

But through this fear, I also realized that it's when I'm the most afraid that I discover the most about myself. Fear makes me reevaluate who I am and why I'm here. In *The Book of Secrets*, Deepak Chopra says, "Spiritual growth is spontaneous. The big events come along unexpectedly, and so do the small ones. A single word can open your heart; a single glance can tell you who you really are. Awakening doesn't happen according to the plan. It's much more like putting together a jigsaw puzzle without knowing the finished picture in advance." This idea of single moments—good, bad, scary, or exciting—all fitting together into something bigger is so powerful for me. It means that every time I am scared of those imaginary sharks out to get me, or every time I am astounded by something profound said by my two-and-a-half-year-old daughter, all of those pieces are going to be a part of me and a part of my journey.

Todd, I am so scared of being alone. What if I screw up? What if I am a bad mom? What if I never meet anyone who lives up to you and I spend my life lonely? I don't want to be the crazy old cat lady who lives down the street (although it would be dog lady in my case). I need to find a way to transform all of this fear into an opportunity to learn something about myself. You were always game for anything if someone else planned it. Well, I certainly didn't plan this, but I'll follow your lead and get in the game.

FORTY NINE

A week or two after I got back from Panama, something started to nag at my brain. I wasn't sure what it was, but I experienced an almost constant buzz of energy that felt like it was pushing me toward freedom from the prison I had been in for eighteen months. One afternoon when I sat at the computer in my kitchen checking e-mail, something in my subconscious moved my fingers across the keyboard, and I typed "heart health, Minneapolis" into the search bar on the screen. As the search results flickered onto the screen, the buzz intensified, and I knew I was taking the next step in my journey.

Among the search results was the web site for the American Heart Association. I had heard about the organization's work but had no idea how many people were supporters, how many volunteers they needed, or how many different areas there were within the association to make a difference. I just knew it was time to do something so that Todd's death wasn't in vain. I had to educate others about heart health so that no one else would lose their husband or wife or child way too soon. I immediately sent the local AHA chapter an e-mail telling my story, and I was invited to come and talk with them about volunteer opportunities.

At the first volunteer meeting I attended, there were so many people who had stories to share about how heart health has personally impacted their lives. None were exactly like mine, but they were all powerful, tragic, and uplifting. It was inspiring to see how they were turning a negative experience into a positive force in their lives. I knew that I was in a group of people dedicated to the same goal of making a difference, and I was excited about what I could do to help AHA with their cause.

I don't have a lot of time, but when I can, I continue to volunteer with AHA, and I share their message all the time. And when I have extra money to donate, it goes straight to them. It's been such a positive experience. Not only am I doing something worthwhile, but I'm also showing Brooke that volunteerism is important. I hope that as she grows older she understands that doing something for the greater good benefits everyone and is a key to a balanced, happy, and healthy life.

FIFTY

After getting involved in the American Heart Association, it felt hypocritical to be preaching health and wellness while stagnating in my own body. I had to do something to improve my health and my mind. My body was tight, my mind was coiled up, and I just wasn't the person that I knew I could be if I made a valiant effort to be more proactive about my physical, spiritual, and emotional health. Since sixth grade I've known that I have scoliosis, a minor curvature of the spine. For several years I had felt that my body was getting out of alignment, and I was suffering from severe stiffness in my hips. I have always had bad posture, and slumping over, lying in bed, curling up on the couch, and carrying a toddler around was wreaking havoc on my body.

I went to a chiropractor to get realigned and discovered the clinic also offered a service called Rolfing, which is manipulation of the connective tissue and can help alleviate the symptoms of scoliosis. It was not a relaxing, peaceful hour of bliss. The therapist pushed and pulled my body parts, and the ligaments and tendons that hold them together, into their appropriate places. But it was so worth it. After several sessions, I added half an inch to my height, and my new, almost-perfect posture made me look ten pounds thinner than I actually was.

Perhaps the biggest change I made was to start running to improve my cardiovascular health. I hated every second of it but knew it was good for me—and Cosmo loved it.

"Let's go for a walk, Cosmo," I'd call, grabbing my running shoes. He would dash over, tail wagging, knowing he'd soon be running free on the nature trails near our home. I tied my laces and grabbed the running belt—a wonderful invention that made walking my eighty-five-pound dog so much easier. Instead of trying to wrangle him with my arm and hand strength, he was attached to the belt around my waist so the full weight of my body controlled him. Cosmo turned into a pretty good companion, no longer dragging me down the street, but instead obediently trotting along at my side—until we got to the nature trails near our house, where he started to pull anxiously, wanting freedom from the leash to run and sniff and roll in all the stinky dead animal carcasses or excrement he could find. Most of the time he needed a bath when we got back home.

On our outings I listened to the same motivational songs over and over on my iPod. I felt as if Todd were walking with us, and I swear I felt him breeze by sometimes when I was talking to him. Yes, I did talk to him out loud. It was so nice to converse with him, even if he couldn't talk back. I think Cosmo felt him there, too. He turned off the paved path at the same places every time, right where he used to go with Todd. But I wouldn't venture there for fear, as irrational as it may be, of a murderer or rapist attacking me with no one around to hear me scream. Cosmo reluctantly turned around when he saw me bypass those tracks he was so used to treading for four years. He still missed Todd, always will until he leaves this world to join him.

The first day I attempted to run on our walks, my cardiovascular endurance only allowed me about half a block of running before I had to stop to catch my breath. But after a couple of weeks, I could run almost three miles. It may not sound like a lot to you long runners out there, but for me it was a huge accomplishment with my bad knees, stiff joints, lack of motivation, and dislike of physical exercise. Soon running became something I had to do. I ran, fast and furious, not sure if I was running toward something—hope, a new life, breathing room—or away from something—grief, the past, memories. Probably a little of both. I ran, as fast as my out-of-shape lungs and muscles could propel me. Cosmo was leading me, free from his leash, yet remaining close by, my guardian and escort on the trails through woods, ponds, and pasture. My body was purging the negative energy I had been storing inside to make room for something new. I ran, feeling the weight of my shoes and memories like lead on my shoulders, bogging me down, but lightening with every step.

I ran, hoping my two years of zero exercise wouldn't cause my heart to explode, which would be a pretty cruel joke of fate.

On one of those runs we approached a sharp curve lined with tall weeds and trees. I couldn't see around the bend, but no one else was there; I could sense we were alone. Or were we? Cosmo slowed, sniffing the air. From the weeds just in front of us, a large whitetail deer, a doe taller than me, leaped across the trail so close that the movement of air in her wake ruffled my hair, and I could hear her grunting breath as she sprinted to safe harbor in the trees. I stopped abruptly, startled and a little scared by her sudden presence. I watched her tawny body flee into the surrounding woods, Cosmo chasing after her, curious to learn more about this other being in what he thought was his domain. Where had she come from, this beautiful animal who had just crossed my path? Was she a sign that great things were waiting for me just around the bend? Was this a good omen of big things to come?

"Cosmo!" I yelled, my heart racing from the encounter with the deer, adrenaline and oxygen buzzing through me. I scanned the tree line but saw no sign of either dog or deer. I started to run again, and Cosmo darted from the weeds twenty yards ahead of me, hearing my footfalls on the trail, resuming his command post. I ran, faster now, toward whatever lay around the bend. I ran, smiling, knowing everything would be okay. Everything would be great.

SHIFTING

*"The important thing is this: to be able at any moment
to sacrifice what we are for what we could become."*
—Charles du Bos

FIFTY ONE

Clearing the dinner dishes and wiping off the kitchen island, I glanced toward the window, but found my view blocked by orchids. Five of them, all in various states of growth, all thriving, lined the kitchen windowsill, and another four soaked up the sliver of sunlight that peeked in the bathroom window. For several months, I didn't think they would make it. They stopped blooming, their leaves shriveled, and they sat in the water I gave them, taking days to drink it up. When I got back from Costa Rica, the orchids were barely clinging to life—just like me. I decided to try repotting them. When I pulled the delicate flowers out of their pots, all that remained were tiny threads of roots, barely sustaining them, yet somehow they managed to survive. A year later they were flowering again—just like me. It was as if we shared the same root system; the same nutrients and spirit were helping us grow. For a year I too had withered and faded and hung limp, showing any hope of survival only if you dug deeply to the threads of root maintaining the small bit of life and soul remaining. Somehow that small bit was able to sustain me through those dark days when I wanted to die, when I wished and prayed for anything to take me away.

There's a section in the book, *Orchids for Dummies*, called "Mission: Orchid Rescue and Resuscitation." It says, "If the orchid still has some healthy, firm roots, cut off all the soft mushy roots and repot in new potting material ... if the roots are almost all gone, emergency measures are called for and recovery is not definite ... this method has no guarantees, but following this procedure has saved orchids that were in the 'hopeless' category." This is where I felt I was at after Todd died, in the "hopeless" category. It took some tender loving care and patience, and now, like my orchids, I was coming back to life. Immersion into new surroundings and cutting away of dead parts is what it took to nurse me back to health.

I tried so many things to get me to that place of renewed spirit and life force. Individually, they seemed like nothing but futile efforts that burned up time and money, but together they led to this miraculous recovery. *Orchids for Dummies* says, "many people place much too much faith in fertilizers. They think fertilizer is some type of elixir that will save the day. Actually, if the orchid is in poor health, fertilizers are rarely the answer … fertilizers are most useful as a boost to help an already healthy orchid grow better." For me, the elixirs of traveling, shopping, and reading were fruitless at the time, but as I emerged from the fog of sadness, anger, and self-pity, they started to work. Those crazy, sometimes overused elixirs started to nurture my slowly healing soul.

Orchids thrive in warm weather. It took me a while to figure this out. I knew orchids grow naturally in rain forests but didn't make the connection that even a sunny windowsill in Minnesota is way too dry and cool for them to really flourish. Once I made that discovery, I started to follow the advice from the book to water with warm water, since cold water can shock the root, slowing down growth. After reading that, I decided to pour some boiling hot corn-on-the-cob water over my original four orchids, thinking maybe it would mimic the hot, humid environment in which they naturally grow. And you know what? It worked. The next morning they were standing taller, and one of them really looked as if it had grown an inch overnight. I too awoke that morning feeling as if I had grown an inch, as if I had new life. I guess both the orchids and I benefited from some extra attention.

That afternoon, I purchased six more orchids. Were these plants somehow mirroring my life force and spirit, and was purchasing new ones a sign that I was adding new depth and layers to my life? Would giving my original orchids six new friends make them happy and surround them with fun and companionship? Maybe I was reading too much into it, and I just like orchids. Caring for them did bring me enjoyment, despite the $240 price tag. Retail therapy at its finest; one more purchase to keep me feeling artificially happy.

Realizing that I too require the warm sun year round prompted some serious reconsideration of my living situation. I live in Minnesota, about the coldest place south of Canada. While many people here love the winter, I truly despise it. From November to April I am housebound, not venturing into the snow and cold unless I absolutely have to. I do not enjoy winter activities like skiing or ice fishing. I do not like having to wear boots, three layers of clothes, and hats and gloves just to go to the grocery store. I do not like getting up in the dark and leaving work in the dark. Brooke doesn't like the cold weather, either. She is a sundress and sandals girl, and it's a fight every time I have to dress her to go outside in the winter.

This lack of connection to the Minnesota lifestyle had me considering relocation to a more pleasant winter climate. Todd and I had talked about it before he died, and I thought about it even more seriously afterwards. But I was reluctant to leave my family and friends. I didn't know how I'd do it alone—moving to a new place with just Brooke and Cosmo with no one to watch Brooke, no friends to hang out with, no connections. So as a first step, I decided to adopt a temporary snowbird status and move to Los Angeles for three months during the winter to see how it felt. Luckily, I had the luxury of being able to work from anywhere, so why not from a place where it's seventy degrees in January instead of negative ten?

Besides the climate factor, I really needed a change of scenery. Both Minneapolis and my hometown had so many memories. I didn't want to forget them, but I also didn't want to have them thrown in my face every time I went to the gas station or a restaurant. Everywhere I went, something reminded me of Todd. I didn't expect that to go away if I moved, but I figured that in a new location, instead of being surprised by memories that arose when I least expected them to, I could selectively choose how and when to reflect on my life with Todd. As I started to wade back into society and the world and proactively seek out my next

229

move, I wanted to have control—and I really wanted to be warm while I did it.

So I found a place to rent in Los Angeles from January through March of 2010. I found a day care for Brooke and had a mental plan for how I would kick-start my life again while living in a new city that I loved so much. We would wake up with the windows open, even in winter. I would get my tasks done quickly each morning (easy, since I'd be working from home) and then put the job stress behind me while I enjoyed the rest of the day. I would take the dog for a long walk/run through Runyon Canyon. I would grab lunch at quaint cafes. I would reconnect with old friends who live out there. I would start to date again, escaping the traditional midwestern men who hunt, fish, and ride motorcycles for proactive guys who weren't already married with kids. Maybe find a guy who surfs and might actually have the balls to talk to me. Brooke and I would go to the beach, hit the playground, walk Cosmo, all while wearing flip flops in winter. I was ready to move on, and now I had a plan to get me there. But as often happened, fate had something else planned for me.

FIFTY TWO

Most afternoons I got the perpetually reliable after-lunch crash. One of the benefits of working from my home office was that if I needed to take a siesta, I could do it without a coworker catching me asleep under the desk. Sometimes I'd catch up on a recorded television show I missed and then doze for a bit, but if it was nice outside, I'd relax in my backyard hammock and think. The hammock wasn't one of those store-bought, mass-produced jobs with no slack or softness. It was handmade, woven in colorful, super-soft fabric that attached the old fashioned way, between two trees. When I kicked off my shoes and stretched out in it, it enveloped me like a big hug, and I was immediately transported back to where I got it—Costa Rica. I would lie there and wonder: If I hadn't gone on that life-changing trip, would I ever have gotten to where I was now? That trip kicked off my transformation, my evolution, my growth, whatever it was that led me to the life I was now starting to live. That trip gave me the perspective I needed to launch me into my new normal.

People would constantly tell me they didn't know how I did it all by myself—parenting, full-time job, writing time, me-time. I wasn't sure how I did it either, and most days it was still a struggle. But I did know that my self-development, that "me-time," is what grounded me and saved me. I'd grown so much as a person in my understanding of both myself and the universe. I realized that we are all a part of the same world and energy field, and that the boundaries between material and imagined things are nonexistent. They are boundaries constructed by our minds to give meaning to the energy and matter that surround us, but really we are all just masses of vibrating energy—molecules and atoms flowing between and within each other without the limits of time or space.

Everything that ever existed in the past and everything that will ever exist in the world is here at every moment—dying, regenerating, reforming, and recycling—all of the particles in creation all the time. Ervin Laszlo, the Nobel Prize-nominated scholar, describes it best in his book *Science and the Akashic Field*. He says that every second in our bodies, ten million cells are dying and ten million are regenerating. That means that as a cell in my toenail dies, a new one forms in my ear. When cells die, they may cease to physically exist, but their energy doesn't. So the energy in my toenail's dead cell disperses and is transferred to another cell somewhere else, maybe not even in my own body. Maybe that piece of me, my energy, floats through space and time to Russia, where it ends up in paint for a new school, and over time it flakes off and lands on the ground, where it decays into the soil, and is transferred into nutrients that are absorbed by the grass that a cow eats, and the energy then flows through the cow's body, maybe ending up in its eyes, which are then seeing the world from a cow's perspective. My energy is no longer in my toenail, but it still exists nonetheless. This concept is incredibly important to me because it means Todd is still here and his energy is still all around us. Knowing this has helped me to move forward.

Todd, I know you're out there, still existing somehow. Your energy isn't gone. I feel it so often when I'm thinking quietly, when I'm walking the dog, when I'm dreaming. Your body may be just ashes now, but that energy that gave you life hums along with the energy of the sunlight, wind, rain, and stars—and it hums along with my own energy. We are probably more in sync now that we've ever been, and it makes me smile to know we're connected with every breath I take.

FIFTY THREE

As more time passed, my inner peace and view of life continued to evolve, and I was seeing a much clearer picture of how I wanted to live. I knew my healing was still in process, but I couldn't imagine my perspective would revert back to how it was before. I could only see it developing into a lifestyle, further impacting my decisions and actions.

I started noticing how people make poor choices regarding their health and their relationships, and it just didn't make sense to me. I listened to my friends and family nag their spouses, I heard couples bicker about the stupidest things, I saw people suffering in bad jobs with unfulfilling career paths. I saw people eating huge, unhealthy meals or drinking themselves silly multiple times a week, and I wanted to find a way to help them. I was not judging—all of those things have been me at one time or another, and I have never been a model of perfection—but my eyes were now open. I saw things in a whole new light and tried to incorporate better habits into my life. But how can I help others? What can I do to use my story and experiences to benefit others? I need to figure it out and make it real.

Todd, your death has changed me. I am no longer even close to who I was before you died. I need to make my life worth something. I need to have something meaningful to leave behind when I die. I need to do something to make you and Brooke proud. I promise I'll do everything I can to fulfill this goal and make something of this life I have left. When we meet again, we're going to have so much to talk about!

FIFTY FOUR

As I began to feel my emotional and mental ideas about wellness and balance shift, I knew it was time to try to get my physical body back in order. This wacky adventure through grief had taken its toll on me. Not eating at all, eating too much, not exercising, experiencing panic attacks and major stress—it was damaging me, and I could feel it in my body and see it in my face. I looked several years older than I did in my post-pregnancy pictures before Todd died. Back then I had a glow and energy. I looked healthy, even with a few extra pregnancy pounds. Now I looked worn out, like a woman who has lived hard and suffered. Fine crinkles had surfaced around my eyes, and a deep furrow had formed between my eyebrows—my "bitch line" as I called it. Even when I was smiling, that furrow gave onlookers the impression that I was constantly crabby at the world, and maybe I was a little bit. I decided it was time to recapture my youth.

My first step was to figure out how to protect myself from the damage of stress. I hit the books again and researched stress and its effects on the body and brain. I kept running across articles on nutrition and health supplements for fortifying the body's functions. I had always been aware of what I eat and the nutritional value of food, but maybe it was time to take a more serious look. So I ventured out to the nearest Walgreens and started reading health supplement labels. Fish oil, vitamins A through Z, antioxidants, herbs—how could I even begin to make sense of all of that? I did what I do best—hit the bookstore for some retail therapy, buying every book I could find on health supplements and herbs. Then I started marking them up, flagging pages and jotting notes on which supplements were good for alleviating stress. When I was finished, I had a list of about fifty ingredients that were supposedly good for relieving anxiety, and five or so that I knew I wanted to try. I bought them and experimented with different combinations and dosages. After several months, I felt better. But I also felt that it was overkill. I didn't like taking so many pills every day, even if they were natural and over-the-counter. I started to wonder: Why couldn't I create a health supplement that combined all of this stuff into one? Why couldn't I make it easy for people to understand what that supplement would do for them by providing education and a label that spelled out exactly what it does for our bodies? But how in the world would I even begin to do something like that? My idea was ridiculous. Keep dreaming, Kristen, I told myself.

As I continued to read about stress relief and work/life balance, Integral Theory kept resurfacing. I read more books, did more research, and contemplated getting my master's degree at one of only two schools in the world dedicated to the study of Integral Theory. But should I add student loans to the debt I already had? Should I add the class load to my already hectic work schedule? I wasn't willing to compromise my time with Brooke. And it wouldn't leave me much time for my real passion, which was writing. But I continued to be drawn to Integral Theory and listened to lectures, read articles, and trolled the Internet to find all that I could about it. The ideas behind that philosophy were helping me to make sense of Todd's death, my awful job situation, my potential career path, and even parenting. After months of considering whether to purse a master's degree in Integral Theory, and after learning that the program was offered online, which made it even more attractive, I decided to apply. A couple of weeks later, I was accepted as a master's student at John F. Kennedy University in San Francisco. I felt empowered and finally back in control of my life's course.

FIFTY FIVE

A few months after Todd died, I had been sitting in my kitchen watching the news and saw a story about a company that specializes in concrete products made with cremation ashes mixed in. I had been looking for an alternative to having Todd's ashes just sitting on the shelf but hadn't found anything that seemed quite right. I investigated the concrete company and didn't like the fancy designs or artwork their products featured, but I still liked the concept, so I kept the idea in the back of my mind.

It was now the spring of 2009, and I was ready to take Todd's ashes off the shelf and give them a respectable place to reside where he wouldn't be alone. I asked Chad, a friend from my hometown who owns a decorative concrete company, if he would be willing to make a bench. I described what I was envisioning—nothing too fancy or feminine, something a little rustic and a lot Zen to blend in with my landscaping plans for the backyard. I thought about having the ashes mixed directly in with concrete that would be formed into the bench, but Chad suggested building the bench with a canister in the leg to hold the ashes. That way, if anything happened to the bench or Brooke or I ever wanted to remove the ashes, we would have that option. Chad drew up a few plans, and when I saw that he was going in the right design direction I told him to go ahead and build it.

A couple of weeks later, on a weekday afternoon, Chad's white truck drove up my steep driveway. I immediately stopped work in the middle of an e-mail and went outside to see his creation. I was anxious and apprehensive, wondering just what this final resting place for my husband would look like. The bench sat in the truck unassembled, much of it securely in the backseat of the cab instead of the open air of the truck bed. I smiled at the thought that Todd's bench had been kept safe from the elements on the drive over, even though it would sit outside for years to come.

"We have to assemble it here. I'm guessing it weighs over four hundred pounds all put together," Chad explained, walking into the backyard with his coworker to assess the setup.

I left them alone, not wanting to hover, but kept sneaking peeks out the window at their progress, anxious to see the work of art that would be a key fixture in this and any future backyard Brooke and I would have. I felt as if a stepping-stone in my journey were in progress, and that once this bench held Todd's ashes I could move on to the next step, whatever that might be. When I sensed that the assembly was nearing completion, I casually walked out the back door "just to check in." There the bench sat, exceeding all of my expectations. I ran my hands over the earth-hued seat, its smooth, flat surface warm to my touch and a sharp contrast against the rustic, inverted-pyramid legs aged to a smoky gray. On one side of the bench was a "tower" of sorts, about four and a half feet tall, in which the ashes would be placed, along with a space for a light covered by an antique bronze roof. I peered inside and felt a warmth rise within me, flushing my neck and face. I smiled and blinked back my tears. The bench was perfect. It captured everything I had been visualizing: the Zen-like lines, the perfectly faux-aged legs, the patina-frosted bronze details, all perfect.

I tentatively sat on it, not sure what I expected to feel, just wishing Todd was there to see it—then remembered that if he were there, I would have no need for the bench in the first place. I was so grateful to Chad. He didn't know it, but he had just completed the most important project he would ever work on, giving a little family a lifelong memorial to the person who had been the center of their world and left them too soon.

I walked back to the house. It was time to face a bigger task— determining how to move Todd's ashes from their current home into the canister in the tower of the bench. I had never opened the black plastic container that held the ashes. It was nestled inside a reddish wooden box that sat on a shelf in whatever room I felt he needed to be in at any given time. If I needed Todd around, I would put the box in the dining room, where I walked past several times a day. If Brooke was having a bad day or doing something fun that I thought Todd would want to witness, I would put him in her bedroom. Funny, but in all that carrying between rooms and all the gentle caresses and hellos I gave it as I walked by, I had never investigated the contents within that pretty but simple wooden box. I didn't feel like I should invade his privacy by peeping inside, and I wasn't emotionally ready to see him in that state—a pile of charred ashes like what was left of my dad's campfires on mornings at the lake after the flames burned out.

Now, with the bench installed and awaiting its resident, I had no choice but to open the box and retrieve the ashes. I gently took the box off the dining room shelf and carried it the ten feet into the kitchen, anxious to give Todd a more comfortable and appropriate home. I carefully placed the box on the island, unsure of the tools I might need, but knowing I would likely find them nearby if I set up shop there. Slowly easing the top up, I bent down to eye level and peered inside. The edges of the box were covered in a fine layer of dust, which wasn't surprising, considering the contents. I dusted the outside daily just through rubbing and carrying it but had never thought about cleaning the interior space. The black container inside was about seven inches wide, six inches deep, and eight inches high, a compact rectangle that almost looked like some sort of electronics device. From moving the box all the time I knew that it was heavy, and I had assumed that was due to the weight of the wood. But upon removing the container from its chamber, I discovered that it and the wooden box were relatively light, that it was the contents within that weighed so much—eight or nine pounds. Still, that was a fraction of Todd's weight of a hundred and ninety. The difference had been lost somewhere as the cremation flames evaporated any liquid from his cells, leaving less than ten pounds of Todd Brown in the physical world.

I gently lifted the inner black box, inspecting it from every angle, my body tense and my mind temporarily blocking the emotional weight of the task I was undertaking. The box was one of those infuriating contraptions where you can't find any loose edge to pry it open, like those receptacles that hold batteries or electronic accessories. Do they really need that much safekeeping? In this case, yes, the contents required the utmost in safety and care. Yet my frustration increased.

"How do I open this damn thing?" I cried, my hands tightly grasping the container that housed my former other half. Assessing the implements in the kitchen, I decided a butter knife would do perfectly, and I grabbed one from the utensil drawer that overflowed with toddler spoons and forks. The knife worked, and I opened the black box to find yet another form of containment—a large, clear plastic baggie secured with a twist tie with Todd's name on it. It looked like the gallon-size bags I used to store my homemade bread in. I chuckled, feeling like I was opening one of those presents where inside the box is yet another, smaller box, and another and another, until you get to the smallest box you can imagine, and in it is a tiny piece of precious jewelry. Only in this case it was something else, but no less precious than the most expensive diamond ring or strand of pearls. The containers I had to go through to get to the ashes were nothing fancy, nothing special. Not that I expected there to be a gold leaf box with a bag made of fur and leather, but it was amusing to see the actual contents housed so simply. Todd would appreciate that; the simpler the better, and a clear plastic bag was about as simple as you could get.

I'd seen cremation ashes on television and in movies (recall the scene in *Meet the Parents* where Ben Stiller's character accidentally pops a champagne cork into the urn holding the ashes of Robert DeNiro's character's mother, and the cat proceeds to pee in them), but I had never seen them in person. Gazing at Todd's for the first time, I didn't feel sad or upset like I thought I might. Instead, I thought how they weren't really Todd, but just what was left of his physical body. And while they represented so much more than that, for a moment I was compelled to investigate the bag of gray soot further to see how he had ended up, not spiritually, but physically. What did his presence in this world look like now after being engulfed in flames?

I lifted the bag from the plastic shell, in scientist mode instead of widow mode for a change. I observed the contents as they shifted around, appearing more "chunky" than I thought they'd be, not the fine dust I had envisioned. A little morbidly, I wondered if those chunks were little pieces of bone. There was also a random piece of wire in there, and I was not sure what that could have been, but my analytical mind started to go through various scenarios of why there would be wire in the ashes. Maybe it was something the "fire crew" had used to keep the body in place while he was being cremated, or maybe it was from something they had used to keep his body "puffed up" for the funeral visitation. Because they had taken so many of his tissues for organ donation, the funeral director told me he had to be "stuffed" in order to look somewhat normal. It was a gruesome thought, but that was what I was thinking as I analyzed the ashes. I was driven by a weird fascination to examine the scientific facts of the matter, to see what had become of Todd.

There were more ashes than the canister in the bench would hold, and I realized that I would somehow have to transfer a portion into another bag that would fit inside the bench. I stepped back from the counter, feeling a bit of fear and apprehension. Looking at the bag of ashes was one thing, but handling the contents was another, as if by making contact I would be releasing his spirit into the air or losing some of his life force or something silly like that. When I opened the bag, it did indeed release quite a large cloud of dust into the air. But instead of cringing or trying to prevent losing any, I found it comforting to see Todd's particles physically floating and dispersing into the air of our home, surrounding us with his molecules. I actually took a deep breath, willing some of them into my lungs, but as I should have expected, that just made me cough and sputter; they were ashes after all, and had no business in my lungs. I know Todd had a part in that coughing attack; he was always good for a prank and a laugh right when I needed it.

Returning my attention to the task at hand, I tried to figure out how to transfer the ashes from one bag to another. Do I use my hands? A measuring cup? A spoon? Some sort of holy vessel made for ash transport? Do I just pour them out but risk the entire contents spilling out too rapidly, causing me to have to either sweep or vacuum up the overflow? And is that even legal? I thought I had read somewhere that ashes can't just be sprinkled or scattered anywhere. After much pondering, bouncing between using a soup ladle, mason jar, or measuring cup, I ended up choosing a stainless steel one-cup measurer—nice and sturdy (to support the weight it would hold), not too cheap (as if that mattered), and the right width and height (size was key to easily maneuver in and out of the two bags). I felt that Todd was laughing at me, thinking, "Just dump it in the bag already. It's not like it's really me in there." What should have taken about thirty seconds instead took me half an hour of analysis, planning, and execution to be sure I was doing my husband justice and paying him the respect he deserved.

Finally, the deed was done. After tenderly sealing both bags and replacing the original back into its black plastic case inside the wooden box, I walked out to the yard to inter Todd in his new home. I approached the bench, appreciating its craftsmanship, knowing how much Todd would love it. Gently and lovingly, I eased the new bag of ashes into the canister in the bench's tower. Looking at Todd's new resting place, I felt the familiar pangs of sadness building in my chest. I again stroked the smooth seat of the bench, turned away from this newly dedicated memorial, and went back into the house, my stomach lurching and my eyes unfocused, each footstep outweighing the last.

Walking into the kitchen, I saw a light coating of dust covering the surface of the island where I had just completed the transfer. The sadness I had been holding at bay broke through, and familiar tears filled my eyes. Did I really just hold my dead husband's ashes in my hands? I had actual, physical contact with him, yet he was nothing but soot and lifeless matter. Was it really just two years ago that we were planting flowers and raking leaves, our infant daughter playing on a blanket in the grass, our whole lives in front of us? Now he was again in our yard where he belonged, but his life was over, and it felt like mine was behind me—that only in looking back would I be able to be with him again.

Somehow I managed to get to my bedroom. I pulled the curtains shut to block out the light and crawled into bed. The act of splitting Todd's ashes had been so much more than my waking mind and physical body could take; out of sheer emotional exhaustion, my body shut down, plunging me into sleep for five hours. When I woke up, I looked out the window at the bench. It sat in all its glory under the pine trees, surrounded by the memories of the blood, sweat, and tears we shed to get that backyard into shape after buying the house six years before. It was a perfect place for Todd's ashes to reside, a place where more blood, sweat, and inevitably, tears will be shed for that man who would now reside only in my memory.

The bench was installed. Todd's ashes were interred. It was now time to whip my backyard into shape. I love gardening; something about it soothes my soul and gives me energy. I love digging in the dirt and planting new shrubs and flowers. My favorite thing is growing vegetables that I can reap after watching their progress throughout the season. But this makeover required more than just planting; it required a major overhaul— new borders, new fencing, everything. Thankfully, my brother was willing to help. He was going to school for architectural drafting and had some great creative ideas and the manpower to help me with the heavy lifting.

We worked for several weeks throughout the spring and early summer, transforming the yard into a relaxing, Zen-inspired sanctuary. We put up reed fencing to cover the hideous chain link fence that was threaded with red and white metal strips. It had to stay up to keep the dog contained and I couldn't afford to replace it with wood. We installed new borders around several plant beds, rehung my Costa Rica hammock between two trees, put in several new plantings and shrubs, and landscaped the area around Todd's bench with river rocks, making the bench the focal point of the yard.

The day we finished I took Brooke outside to see the work that we had done. She immediately ran to the bench and started playing in the river rocks. Her reaction was exactly what my goal had been by having that bench made for Todd's ashes. I never wanted him to be all by himself in a depressing, lonely cemetery surrounded by other dead people and he wouldn't have wanted that either. Now he would always be near us. Brooke would be able to play near him and talk to him whenever she wanted, just by going out to the backyard.

"Brooke, do you like the new bench?" I asked.

"Yeah, it's pretty," she exclaimed, climbing onto it.

"That bench is where you can go to talk to Daddy anytime you want to." I felt myself tearing up but didn't want her to see any sadness when I talked about the bench. I wanted her to feel happy and close to Todd when she was out here, so I blinked the tears away and sat down next to her.

"This is Daddy's bench?" she asked innocently, trying to process what I was telling her.

"Yes. Any time we want to be near him, we can always come back here to his bench." I hugged her closer to me, again fighting back the tears.

To this day, the area by the bench is Brooke's favorite place to play in the backyard. She can spend hours there, rearranging the rocks, making tracks in the gravel, playing with the plants and flowers that surround the area, and of course climbing all over the bench. Mission accomplished: Todd is not alone, and neither are we.

FIFTY SIX

My job was making me crazy. I had just had an awful meeting with my boss and was outside taking deep breaths, trying to control the panic constricting the airflow to my lungs. I cursed to myself, talking to the spirits and to Todd. He never spoke back, but I knew he was there, silently witnessing and "signing off" on the decisions I made when I'd hash things out with the universe. That day, I was conversing and fighting with that spirit voice in my head about my life and what to do with it.

"I don't know how to get out of this career path," I sighed, my shoulders slumping as I sat heavily on the steps.

"You need to find your 'thing,' what you love to do, that you can do for hours yet it feels like no time has passed at all," the spirit voice replied.

"But I need the income to support Brooke," I argued.

"Do you need as much as you make now? You could get by on less. If you were doing what you love, you could get by on less."

I absorbed that statement for a moment. It was true. I could get by on less. Was I willing to compromise the lifestyle I'd grown accustomed to—travel, restaurants, shopping, movies? Would a more rewarding career be enough to fill the void I was trying to satisfy with my retail therapy?

"I am so scared to make a move, and I don't even know what the move would be," I said, closing my eyes and lowering my head into my hands.

"What do you do that overflows your mind and makes your spirit soar?" responded the voice. (The voice is always so corny.)

Without a moment's hesitation my head popped up. "Writing!" I said excitedly. That's when I heard Todd's voice speak to me for the first time.

"Do it," was all he said. Do it. Do it. Such tiny little words. I sat silently for a moment, hoping Todd would speak again, but he didn't. I closed my eyes, visualizing what my life would be like if I didn't have the stress of my job any more and had time to breathe and write and figure out my next steps. I looked up, feeling excited.

"I should do it. I should write. I would love to write. But no one will think I'm interesting."

"They don't have to think *you* are interesting, they have to love your writing," said the voice.

"What would I write?" I asked, but already my mind had started to bubble with ideas.

"What have you been writing about all these months?"

"That's just for me, to heal and prove to myself I can make it through this shitty situation," I countered. A vibration was buzzing through me. I knew I was onto something.

"Don't you think others would benefit from that story? You are a survivor. You made the best out of one of the worst things that could ever happen to someone. Others need to hear about it and you can help people."

I sat, shocked by the significance of that statement, saying nothing, letting the excitement build. Could I truly help people in a real way?

The voice spoke again.

"Kristen, you have stories to tell."

FIFTY SEVEN

Most days at about four o'clock I would start to feel anxious and excited, knowing I'd soon be making the six-minute drive to day care to pick up Brooke, my little monkey. If I finished my job-related work early, I would do a few chores around the house and take the dog for a walk, then be off to pick her up. I couldn't drive fast enough. I pulled into the lot, parked in the first open space, walked briskly to the door, punched in the security code, signed her out on the computer, and headed to her classroom.

I liked to sneak in and watch what she was doing in that environment where I couldn't interact with her or keep an eye on her. She would usually be holding some security object—a doll, stuffed animal, something to ease her separation anxiety—but always looked happy and was having fun. When she spied me, she instantly dropped, and sometimes threw down, the toy.

"Mommy!" she yelled, sprinting toward me, her big blue eyes beaming and her tooth-filled mouth grinning at me with that welcoming smile I waited all day to see. She clambered up into my arms and hugged me tightly, and we gathered her things, said goodbye to her teachers and friends, and headed back home, where just minutes before I'd been pacing, waiting for this moment of perfection when I forgot my problems. I knew only this perfect little human being who I was responsible for loving and raising into the best woman she could be—and that was the only thing that mattered.

Now the spirits were kicking me in the ass, saying, "Figure things out and get yourself together." And they were so right. I wanted Brooke to look up to me and remember me as a mom who was happy and always put her first. I didn't want to be the mom who was always stressed and working, who hated her job. I wanted to be the inspiring mom who had a love of life and worked for something she was passionate about. I needed to get my act together.

THE BEGINNING

"Life begins on the other side of despair."
—Jean-Paul Sartre

FIFTY EIGHT

M_y heart pounded against my chest. Fumbling in my pocket for my hotel room key, I lurched toward the door, struggling for breath. This was worse than all the other times. Surely I was having a heart attack. I slid the key into the slot, trying to catch my breath and hold down the sob threatening to burst from my throat. Breathe in … 2, 3, 4, 5, 6, 7, 8. Breathe out … 2, 3, 4, 5, 6, 7, 8. My chest began to unclench a little but my stomach quivered, the anxiety of the last six hours of work meetings taking their toll—as had the majority of my work interactions with my boss that year. I lay on the bed in the dark room, breathing in and breathing out, trying to quiet the throbbing in my chest and rush of blood in my ears. How had I let it come to this?

The voice came. "Yes, you let this go on too long."

"I know. I've tried to convince myself that it's just a job, that she's just another boss, that neither has any effect on my life or my livelihood," I explained.

"So why are you lying here now in a panic again?" the voice asked.

"Because I need the money and health insurance to support us, to support Brooke. I can't be irresponsible and be unemployed." The throb was getting worse as my anger grew.

"But would you be unemployed? What about all of those ideas you have? What about the health supplement you want to develop? Or the book you want to write? Or the speaking you want to do to help others?"

I closed my eyes to try to calm my mind. "Those are just crazy dreams. And even if I did consider it seriously, it will take months, even years before I would make any sort of return on the investment. I can't be an irresponsible parent and do that to Brooke." I was justifying my inaction to myself as much as to the voice.

"But can you afford to have panic attacks? To be on edge all the time? To risk your health? Does Brooke need to lose both parents?" the voice asked pointedly.

I saw a vision of me in a hospital bed dying, Brooke next to me just five years old. Was that my fate if I stayed in a job that affected me mentally and emotionally, causing my body to manifest physical illness? Did I need as much money as I made? Couldn't I get my own health insurance and make it work with my savings for a while?

"You're right. I need to make a change. But maybe I should just wait a little longer and hold out until Christmas bonuses? They're just three months away. And what about my house rental in Los Angeles?" My heart faltered even as I said it.

"Is it worth it?" the voice asked.

I stood up, shaking my head to readjust my vision to the light in the room. Looking at the phone by the bed, I saw the message light blinking. It was from my boss, who was still working downstairs and already suggesting new action items for the agenda in just the ten minutes we had been on our afternoon break. I cringed, my heart rate increasing, shoulders tensing, breath faltering as panic attacked me once again.

"No. It's not worth it," I announced loudly to myself and the voice, thinking of Brooke at home with her grandparents. I walked back down to the meeting, knowing that instead of taking pointless pages of notes and trying to figure out what my boss wanted, I would be planning my exit strategy. I wouldn't let my spirit get eroded any further by the work situation I had been suffering. It was time.

FIFTY NINE

"10, 10, 10, 10, 10," I repeated silently. You know when you find one of those rare, life-transforming books that you go back to over and over again? For me, that book is the self-help tome *10:10:10* by Suzy Welch, which I had discovered while researching work stress. Sitting in my work meeting, I tried to appear focused and engaged but was really working through scenarios in my head. If I do this, if I really do this, how will it affect my life in ten minutes, ten months, and ten years? How will quitting my job impact Brooke's life in ten minutes, ten months, and ten years? What appeared to others as feverish note taking and deep thinking was indeed that—but not about the teams' strategies for 2010 or what our next projects would look like. I was making lists of the pros and cons of my decision. Drawing quadrants from the Integral Theory masters program, I starting looking at how my decision would interact with my environment, my relationships, and the bigger world. All the while, one simple answer kept resonating in my head, the one word that crystallized my decision: Brooke.

The next day, I drove the four hours back to Minneapolis, my mind buzzing with excitement as I wrote my resignation letter in my head. I was terrified. I was nauseated. But I knew this was the right decision. I pulled up to my parents' house, where Brooke had been staying, and walked inside.

"So you survived?" my mom asked, knowing I had been dreading the trip. She had also been on the receiving end of a frantic e-mail I had sent as the panic attack set in the previous afternoon.

"Yep, but I also made a decision. I'm quitting," I announced. I picked Brooke up, reassured in my decision.

"Mom, I missed you while you were gone," Brooke said, hugging me.

"I missed you, too," I said, hugging her back. I settled onto the couch to talk through my plan with my parents. I was going to start my own health supplement and work/life balance company. I would start telling my story to inspire others to overcome challenges. I explained my fear, and also my need to do something for myself and for Brooke that would make me happy again. My parents were completely supportive. They agreed it was time for me to make a move and escape the work misery I had been in for so long.

When I got home, I drafted my resignation letter. The next day, a Friday, I e-mailed it to my boss. As soon as I hit "send," I smiled—quite possibly my first genuine, non-Brooke-related smile in two years. And I knew that this moment would end up in a book someday to show people how I made it through and found the courage to do something crazy for my own health and well-being and the good of my daughter.

SIXTY

I sat in my home office, notebook in hand, brainstorming ideas for my new life as my own boss—no marketing constraints, no supervisor to keep me down. All I had was me to make things happen.

First: Company name, business registration, and trademark—Happy Hour Effect. Done.

Next: Speaking engagements—Follow up on inquiries sent. Done.

I started pacing, working through potential scenarios in my head, trying to fight the fear and self-doubt that threatened to paralyze me. I had been going it alone in my personal life for over two years now. I could do this! Couldn't I?

"Spirits, did I do the right thing?" I asked.

Silence.

"I'm unemployed. Oh, crap. What did I do?" I sat on the edge of my chair. The familiar panic was rising in my chest—but I noticed that it felt different this time.

The voice finally spoke. "Calm down, Kristen. It will be all right."

"Okay, you're right, as always. I'm self-employed, not unemployed. Right?" I tried to convince myself things would be fine.

"Right. What's the worst that can happen? You'll have to get another job down the road if things don't work out? You have years of experience and tons of contacts. You have thought about this for a long, long time. You have done the research and analysis and finances. You will be fine. Take a breath."

"Oh, crap. What did I do?" I repeated. My mind raced, but the panic didn't overtake me. Instead, I looked down at the notebook pages filled with ideas and plans, and I felt energy—true, strong, potent energy—surging through me from my scalp to my toenails. I had already been asked to tell my story at a couple of events. Plans were in motion to start Happy Hour Effect, my very own work/life balance company. I had contacted an FDA-approved lab and had a formula of natural ingredients to start me off in developing my health supplement. I had done more market research than was probably necessary. I had written almost all of the manuscript for a book. I took a deep breath.

"Yes, Kristen, you are ready. One step at a time," the voice said, easing my fear and amplifying my energy.

"I can do this," I announced, sliding my chair back up to the desk and picking up my pen, another list forming in my mind, another idea that would help me inspire others and myself. But I still felt anxious.

"Spirits, can you give me some sort of sign? Something to prove I'm doing the right thing by launching a business on my own in this awful economy. Is risking Brooke's financial security to chase down this dream a good idea?" I hoped for an immediate sign like a box of money falling from the sky onto my lap. I looked to the ceiling, but all that was there was a cobweb.

When I woke up the next morning I went to my computer, as I had been doing for years. But I no longer had to check for to-dos from the boss, dial in to a conference call, or read company memos about new processes. With a newfound feeling of freedom and hope, I clicked open my calendar and e-mail box. And there they were—three messages, each one asking me to speak at upcoming events.

There was my sign. I *can* do this.

SIXTY ONE

"GNC loved it! They want to carry it and just have to figure out how many stores," I exclaimed to my mom on the phone. I was at the Pittsburgh airport, having just pitched Happy Hour Effect stress-relief health supplement to buyers at GNC four months after taking that crazy leap of faith and quitting my job. I actually did it—I developed a product, and the world's largest retailer of nutritional supplements loved it. Pacing around the airport, I could hardly contain my emotions. I called my parents, sister, brother, and best friend. But it still didn't feel like I had told everyone who needed telling. That lingering compulsion to talk to Todd still arose at times. That deep-down instinct to share life's big and small wins with him hadn't burned out. Maybe it never will. Maybe I'll be old and gray or even remarried and still want to talk to him when something life-changing happens. I sat down near my boarding gate and pulled out my notebook.

Todd, I did it! I really, really did it! I don't have any money coming in, but I'm so damn happy. I just wish you were here to share it with me. But none of this would be happening if you were here. It's so bittersweet. I am going to an Academy Awards event in a couple of weeks to share Happy Hour Effect with celebs and media. I just met with a huge retailer about a company I started myself. I speak to hundreds of people about work/life balance and stress relief. I'm going to be on the cover of a national magazine. And I have you to thank for all of it. This crazy journey you sent me on has been the worst thing I will ever experience, but your light has propelled me through it and made it the best thing I could ask for in my situation. Thank you for guiding me and being here.

GNC was the latest in a series of big victories for my new product, but that didn't mean money was coming in yet. It was money out all the time. Paying for ads. Paying for events. Paying for marketing materials. Paying for postage and shipping. I was seeing my savings and home equity line of credit slowly erode, and it was terrifying—but it also felt good because I was building something I could call my own. I was finally my own boss, creating my own path in life. I was a role model for Brooke, and now others, proving that you *can* overcome challenges and find balance in your life no matter how crappy things have been in the past.

There was a downside—I couldn't afford to rent the house I found in Los Angeles for the winter. But soon, very soon I hoped to get to California to take the next step in my journey.

SIXTY TWO

A few weeks later, I was standing onstage, staring at the faces of hundreds of people applauding, crying, smiling, and some even standing—*for me*! I smiled and waved, slightly embarrassed, to the group of women who had come to hear me speak, trying to hold back my tears and my laughter, mentally reviewing the rollercoaster ride of the last few years. A new baby, a rocky marriage after the baby came along, a death, a rebirth, a dream realized—how had all of this unplanned craziness happened to me? As I stood there taking it all in, feeling like I had finally taken a step toward happiness again, a strange thought arose: What if I had died and not Todd?

If I had been the one not to wake up that morning, the lives of those I loved would be so much different. Brooke would probably be living in Montevideo because Todd would have needed to be in a small town with more support from his family. His parents would see Brooke more often, and mine would be wanting more time with her. I would never want Brooke to have a life without me. Of course I wished no one had to live without Todd either, but that's not how things turned out. All I could do is think about what advice he would give me if he were here. What would he say to me? Would it be the same things I would say to myself? I think so. I hope so.

Dear Kristen,

How you made it through this horrendous experience is still a mystery to me. I cannot believe you found the strength to continue living when all you wanted to do was curl up and die. I am so proud of you for your resilience and your bravery and your courage to face each day—and for putting on a happy face for Brooke who, despite her young age, was no doubt confused when her dad, a constant presence for the first nine months of her life, suddenly disappeared. You kept things calm and safe for her, even when it took all of your strength to get out of bed.

In those months of suffering not only did you find yourself, you found Todd. You found his true nature—a man who was the best friend anyone could have asked for and whom you were fortunate enough to have known for six years. Six years—it isn't a long time, but it felt like a lifetime as you lived it; it felt like a life. As you continue on your path without Todd, I hope you can find a way to let yourself smile and laugh when you think of your life with him. That's what he'd want—to be remembered with a grin, not with tears. He'd want you to be happy and productive and energetic and hopeful for the future, not locked in your house, afraid of moving on, afraid of life without him. He is always here. He knows you're feeling lonely sometimes. He knows you're scared of a future without him. But he also knows that you have great things ahead of you.

Your life is far from over. Your fate isn't to live out your days as a sad, lonely widow who still listens for her daughter's breath in the night. You will take this growing confidence in yourself, and your newfound hobbies and interests, and use them to enrich others' lives, to reach out to those who are suffering through grief, loss, or loneliness, and to help people learn not to take a single thing for granted.

You will love again—and be loved—by another man, by more children. You will always have Todd to turn to when you're feeling that wall of grief rising up. He'll provide you with the strength you need to climb over that wall, to stand on top of it and look across the vastness of the future and know that things will be okay—more than okay, that your life will be great. I have faith in you, and so does Todd. You will make it through this best worst thing that happened to you and be a stronger, more resilient, more loving person who is so very much loved—trust me, you will. You are already well on your way.

Warmest Regards,
Kristen

A dear friend since elementary school sent me a note and included a quote by Elizabeth Kaye that perfectly captures the way I feel and think so much of the time now.

I no longer expect things to make sense. I know there is no safety. But that does not mean there is no hope. It simply means that each of us has reason to be wishful and frightened, aspiring and flawed. And it means that to the degree we are lost, it is on the same ocean in the same night.

Sometimes I think these last couple of years have been one long day and night and that one morning I'll wake up and things will be okay again. That I'll miraculously open my eyes after finally sleeping through the night and feel happy and healthy, with no regrets and no fear. But this long day isn't over yet. All I can do is carry on and remember how lucky I am to have been given six wonderful years with Todd; to keep his memory alive by living life to the fullest each and every day; to instill happiness, respect, and wonder in our daughter by being her role model—for both of us. That is all I can do and everything I will do, and I know that Todd is helping me guide her from wherever he is now.

Dear Brooke,

Your dad was a great man; a man who was loved by many and who loved you more than you'll ever know. His eyes look back at me from you every day, and that curly, crazy hair of yours comes from him, too. As you grow up you'll miss having him as your dad, but know that he'll always be around. You can talk to him any time you need to, and he'll guide you on the right path. He may not physically be here, but his light is always shining, making our dark days disappear and giving us the perspective we need to see things clearly.

If he were here, he'd teach you to be laid back and relaxed, not to stress about too much in life, and to be a good friend to everyone you meet. That was your dad—the best friend a person could ask for, that guy who made you feel better just by being around. That's what he was to me—my best friend, the one person I could talk to any time I needed a pick-me-up, the one person I'd call when something funny happened, when I had good or bad news to share and just wanted someone to listen. He is still that for me, and he can be that for you, too. Just tell him things; he'll be there listening in the silence, imparting his wisdom and advice, not through words but through his spirit and the lessons his life taught us.

As you grow up and go through life, I want you to live right by treating others with respect, not judging other cultures or religions, being kind to animals and the environment. I want you to choose the spiritual path that enlightens you, be it Christianity, Buddhism, or nothing at all, and to respect others' spiritual choices. I want you to have an inner strength that drives you to take action in your life, to be brave, to make others feel valued and loved. Most of all, I want you to feel loved and to know that all the days of your life I only want the very best for you. I will always, always, always be your mom and your best friend, just as your dad will always, always, always be there for you, an unseen entity with whom you'll forever be linked in spirit and in heart. We will always love you, no matter where we are.

Love,
Mom

In the movie *The Curious Case of Benjamin Button*, one of the characters says something like, "we lose those we love so we know how much they meant to us." Todd meant more to me than any other person I've ever met, but I didn't realize it until after he was gone. The love we shared, and now the loss I've suffered, have given me a broader understanding of the universe and of those demons Sadness and Anger, and how they play out during times of heartache like I've endured the last two years.

And finally I come back to Regret. How do I reconcile my past wrongs against someone when he's dead? That's the question that has kept me awake night after night since Todd died. I go to bed wondering how I can possibly move forward, knowing that I wasn't the best wife I could have been to him and that he wasn't the best husband he could have been to me. How can I ever find the words that I didn't get to say before he left so unexpectedly?

Dear Todd,

Your life has left a permanent imprint on mine. Not an hour passes when I don't think of you. I know that as time goes by the pain I feel will ease, but that imprint you left will never go away. You made me a better person through your life, but it's your death that's changed me forever. It's been the best and worst thing that could ever happen; such a terrible loss has caused such a tremendous change in me. I now know how important it is to live for today and appreciate what life has to offer every moment. I now know how paramount self-discovery is to living a continually enriching life. I now know that truly knowing, respecting, and loving myself is the first step in loving someone else well. And that balance is so very, very important.

When we were together, I was focused on being with you, on making you happy, on thinking about what we would be together, and I never spent any time doing things for myself. I had no hobbies, no strong drive to learn and grow. But now I am focusing on me. I have spent the last months living selfishly, learning what makes me tick, makes me passionate, makes me want to keep on living. Losing you taught me that life is precious. You never know when death will come, so you have to embrace every experience as if it might be your last.

I'm so terribly sorry for not being the best wife I could be. I'm sorry for nagging you for golfing too much. I'm sorry for every criticism I gave you. I'm sorry I didn't kiss you the night I left the wedding dance and talked to you for the last time. I'm sorry for not being with you in bed the morning you died so I could try to save you. I'm sorry we didn't get to spend six decades together instead of just six years.

And I'm thankful to you for making me so joyfully happy—and so heart-wrenchingly sad. Only through this excruciating ordeal have I been able to see how important it is not to take anything or anyone for granted; to prioritize those people and things in my life the way they should be; to not let work, other peoples' ideas, or fear of failure allow me to get sucked back into the rut. I know my journey is far from over, and I know that with you guiding me I will stay on track.

You will always be my best friend. In fifty years I will still be talking to you. It was because of you that I was able to find myself and make a life again—a life without you, but with you more fully a part of it than ever before. I will always miss and love you, and I promise to be a good role model for our daughter. I will tell her all about you and show her pictures and videos of you so that she knows your face, your voice, and your laugh. And not a day will go by when I won't send you my love, that powerful life force that's driving me now—love for you, love for Brooke, love for myself, and love for life.

Until we meet again,
Kristen

I have finally found the words. To reconcile Regret and my past wrongs, and to tell Todd what I didn't get the chance to say when he was alive. Even though he is gone in body, he's still with me in spirit every moment. He's heard what I have to say, and I have heard him. This long day is over now. I can finally sleep.

EPILOGUE

*"After all that's happened, I like to say now that
I may be money-poor but I'm happiness-rich—
and that's all that really matters, isn't it?"*
—Kristen Brown

RECONCILIATION

Every memory I have automatically gets classified into one of three buckets: Pre-Todd, With-Todd, or Post-Todd. But for many moments that occurred after Todd died—like Brooke's birthdays and weekends at my parents' lake cabin, which they didn't have when he was alive—my mind still places him there, and I unknowingly fabricate memories. I have very specific, vivid recollections of events that occurred Post-Todd, but something in my subconscious is still set to With-Todd, and in my recollection he is there with me, as he had been for so many years. Then I stop and realize he couldn't have been there, and my brain moves the memory to the right bucket. I always feel a twinge of sadness mixed with a smile and a clenched fist as I simultaneously miss him, laugh at him, and curse him, and think about how things might have been in my world if I were still With-Todd.

In my first journal entry after Todd died, I wrote, "I always thought I wanted the fairy tale, and now I realize I had it all along." Todd was my knight in shining armor who saved me from the cold that first night we met by tucking a blanket around me. He saved me from sore, smelly feet the next day by taking off my boots. He saved me from a life of selfishness by giving me Brooke, making me a parent. He saved me from myself these last years by guiding me on my journey through this awful grief and sadness. I am so lucky to have had a man who has supported and loved me and will continue to love me, flaws and all, even in his absence.

When facing tough decisions, I don't ask myself what Jesus or God would do; I ask, "*What would Todd do?*" Todd has been my strength while I've struggled with my spirituality and view of the world during this journey. I believe there's a God, but not a guy in the sky, a king who presides over heaven and doles out judgments to those on earth and to newcomers entering the pearly gates. That just sounds ridiculous to me. In all the research I've done on religion, spirituality, science, and the universe, the theory that makes the most sense is that we are God. The energy that connects us to everything else is God. The emergent property that allows molecules, chemicals, and nerves in our brain to interact and give way to thoughts and emotions is God.

My perception of the universe is that everything I see, feel, and touch is created by me and for me in my own mind, and that all of us have the same capability to create our own lives. I have discovered that the power of the mind is a great thing. I have personally witnessed my own transformation—not just witnessed it, but driven it. I have made my choices and found ways to make them a reality. I am God, harnessing the power I hold over my own life and finessing it into the existence I want. Does this mean I've renounced my Lutheran upbringing? No. I believe that if people need a way to connect to each other in an organized manner, then they should do what they have to do in order to find that connection. For me, it is the idea that I am God and God is in me that holds the most power and comfort. We all have control over our own destinies; we just need to know what our endgame is so that we can continually chart our course and create our own past, present, and future every second of every day.

But if we have so much control over our lives, why do we get sick? Why do we die? Because biology makes it so. Just like we are our own God, a cancer cell is also its own God. It wants to fulfill its endgame. The plaque building up on the walls of our veins and arteries has its own endgame; it wants to stick to itself just by its natural properties. The plaque isn't out to get us, and neither is God. If we eat poorly, adding to that plaque, if we don't exercise to keep the blood moving to sweep the plaque away, if we have skinny veins that will clog up faster, it is likely that the endgames of those scientific processes will trump our own plans, because science is a very powerful force. We can't fight millions of years of evolution and think we'll change it in just our short life spans here on earth. All we can do is slow the processes that are at work in our bodies by living a healthy, balanced lifestyle in hopes that we can extend the time it takes us to reach our own endgame.

In Todd's case, his death was tragic and untimely. So many people have said to me, "everything happens for a reason" or, "he's with God now." I have always hated both of those phrases. What possible reason would God have for taking away a young man just starting his life with his wife and infant daughter? The explanation for Todd's death is that the plaque in his left descending artery built up faster than his body could counteract it. He didn't do anything wrong. I didn't do anything wrong. God didn't "take him" from us. That time bomb in his chest exploded, plain and simple.

Of course the fact that it didn't have to happen still makes me beyond angry. There are screenings and preventive measures that Todd should have done when he was alive, but we didn't know about them. A young, healthy guy with no risk factors isn't the first person who gets sent to a heart clinic for a stress test. I want to help change that. No child should grow up without a parent because he or she died of a preventable disease. No wife or husband should spend sleepless nights wracked with guilt, wondering what they could have done to prevent their spouse's death. Todd's story needs to be told so that the public is shaken into awareness that heart attacks don't just happen to elderly, overweight, sedentary people with high blood pressure and cholesterol problems.

As for "he's with God now"—yes, he is, because he is God. I am God. We all are God. I believe that even after we die we still have that emergent property of being able to think and interact with the world, even though it's at a much higher level of consciousness. That's why there is evidence of ghosts. That's why there are psychics out there (the real ones, not the quacks) who can communicate with the "other side." That's why I've felt Todd guiding me so many times. He is here and still actively participating in his life. We just can't see him.

While there's no "good" reason Todd died so young, the best reason I can come up with is that it's led me here, to a place where I have finally found my path in life—to help people through my writing, my words, and my ideas. Todd's death will not be in vain, and my story can help others become more aware of those scientific forces at work whose endgames may not correspond with our own.

MOVING ON

March 2010. It's snowing—big, sharp flakes frozen crisp by the Arctic air that's settled over Minnesota since Christmas. But happily, I'm not there. Instead, I'm strolling along a sunny street lined with palm trees, the sun slowly thawing the permafrost of my heart, and I am falling more and more in love with Los Angeles. Some people say they dislike the crowds, the vanity, the pollution, the impending doom of an earthquake that will cause California to fall into the ocean; but for me, this is the land of dreams. California has been calling my name for years, and the call got louder and louder as my professional endeavors kept bringing me back. Now I'm in L.A. mixing business with pleasure as Happy Hour Effect sponsors a pre-Oscars event and my friend Rachel and I once again celebrate our love of movies.

The Oscars are in four days, and the center of the action is at Hollywood Boulevard and Highland Avenue, which sparks with excitement as workers erect bleachers and roll out the red carpet inside a fenced enclosure. The barrier is to keep the "outsiders" away from the stars and Hollywood elite who will rub shoulders inside. Someday I will find a way inside that fence, but this year I will settle for being a step closer. For three days, I will greet a steady stream of guests as they visit the celebrity and media gifting suite in the Beverly Hilton's penthouse to hear more about my health supplement and listen to my message of work/life balance. Happy Hour Effect is the official sponsor of the event, and our logo is everywhere. Just six months ago, this idea was just that, an idea. But now, here I am in, feeling like I'm living a dream.

As the start time for the event draws near I visit with representatives from other companies who are also showing their products, and a buzz rises. Who will be the first celeb through the door? Will we get any news coverage? Will this event be worth the time and money it took to get here? The door to the suite opens, and in walks Johnny Hollywood—not an A-lister, but someone I recognize nonetheless. We all scamper back to our "stations," ready to wow the celebrities enough that they spread the word to others.

"Hey! What have you got here?" Johnny asks, approaching the Happy Hour Effect display. His charming smile causes a surge of adrenaline to jangle my nerves, but I don't want to come off as a giddy, star struck, annoying fan. This is my chance to impress people, and I don't want to fail. I take a deep breath and put on an air of laid-back professionalism.

"Hi, I'm Kristen, the founder and president of Happy Hour Effect. It's a health supplement I developed to help support the body and brain from the damaging effects of stress." I sound confident. I can do this.

"Well, I definitely need that. Tell me more," he says, picking up a bottle of my supplement and inspecting the label.

"Who doesn't need it these days?" I reply. "I developed it after a tragedy in my life. My husband passed away in 2007 when our daughter was just ten months old. Two weeks later I got a new, challenging boss at work, then the economy tanked, and there I was in corporate America, terrified I would lose my job as a newly single mom."

"Oh man, that sucks. I'm so sorry," Johnny says, looking at me with empathy.

"Yeah, it did suck. But I had to move forward, especially because I had a child. So I started trying different natural supplements to help support my body and mind. I could see and feel the damage that was happening and knew I needed to do something, but I didn't want to go down the prescription drug route." I try not to fidget with the blue dress I had chosen to coordinate with my logo colors.

"Good for you. That is cool. So how did you figure out how to make a supplement?" He picks up a brochure from the display.

"Well, a lot of the things I tried worked really well, but I didn't want to take fifteen different pills every day. And there wasn't anything on the market that actually supported the bodily systems that are affected by stress. Most just change your brain chemistry. So I found an FDA-approved lab to help me make it and make sure the ingredients I wanted to put in it wouldn't make your head explode. And now here I am," I finish, not sure what to do next.

"Wow, that is a crazy amazing story. I definitely want to try it." Johnny looks me in the eye, smiling.

"Cool. Here's a bottle, along with what I call the Red-Carpet Revival Kit. It comes with a wine opener, meditation cards I put together just for this event, a Mike Swoop CD, and chocolates—because who doesn't need good music and chocolate to relax."

"Awesome, thank you so much. I'm going to try it, and I'll tell my friends about it, too. I know a lot of people who could use this." He reaches out his hand to shake mine.

"That would be great. I'm just a little startup, so any help you can give is much appreciated. Thanks so much for stopping by."

"No problem. Good luck. See ya later," Johnny says, walking away.

I take a deep breath to calm myself after the first celebrity interaction of the day. I spend the rest of the event chatting with more stars, media types, and the other company reps in the suite. It's great exposure for my company and a fun way to get a glimpse into the other side of life, the Hollywood life that I love to fantasize about participating in someday.

Three months later, I'm in Los Angeles again sponsoring another celeb and media gifting suite for the MTV Movie Awards and I even go to the show. My love of the city and the beaches has solidified now, and it's just a matter of finances to get here on a semi-permanent basis. Fortunately, GNC is now stocking my product, and it's selling more and more every week. I am still money-poor but happy, feeling the momentum of my business goals moving toward something big.

One of my goals has been to develop a talk show called "The Happy Hour Effect with Kristen Brown." In June I pitch my idea to the Oprah Winfrey Network contest, "Get Your OWN Show," feeling that it's the logical next step in bringing all of my hard work together into something that encompasses my new way of living and views of the world. Out of ten thousand people who entered, I am one of those who make the first cut and move on to the next round. I am elated, envisioning my future helping others in a meaningful way—and just as quickly I'm crushed when I learn that I don't make the top forty. But I remind myself that I can't dwell on the future, I can only control what's in front of me at this moment. So I bounce back, ready to pitch the show to other networks and television programs in the hopes that I can get even a one-minute segment about work/life balance and stress management out into the world so that others can learn from the wisdom I have acquired over the last three years. That is my goal now: To help people live less stressed lives—in balance, like I have learned to do—and realize that you can overcome even the worst things in your life. Sometimes it just takes a leap of faith to discover your potential.

MOMMY-ING

Brooke and I have found our groove. It may not be most people's idea of the ideal parent/child relationship. I let her watch movies and television. I indulge her love of fashion by buying her more shoes and clothes than I have. I fall prey to her manipulation in the grocery store checkout lanes and in Target's toy section. I've tried to change her sleep patterns with no success; she continues to go to bed late and sleep in late. Todd was the same way; he stayed up late while I would crawl into bed early, and I would be up at the crack of dawn while he lazed away the morning in bed. As with him, if I try to wake Brooke before she's ready, it's not a pretty scene.

"Mommy, get out, light off," she commands, pointing me toward the door. Her normally sweet-as-sugar politeness has no place in her just-waking vocabulary. Once she's up, she has breakfast in bed almost every day. She goes to preschool whenever we're both ready, and sometimes she doesn't go at all.

"Please, Mommy, I prooomise I will just play and not bother you while you're doing your working. So I don't have to go to school today." She pleads in a matter-of-fact, this-is-how-it's-going-to-be voice while looking up at me with the sweetest angel eyes she can muster.

Independence is one of the few of my genes that she inherited. She doesn't like to go to school and would rather play at home, even if it's by herself. She is a little introvert just like me, preferring to play solo or in small groups instead of in crowds. But it breaks my heart a little to have her home with just me and no playmates her own age. She doesn't have any siblings, and there aren't young kids that she's friends with in our neighborhood. She likes my friends' children, but we don't get together with our kids very often. Her cousins are still babies, and her preschool friends are just there to help pass the time until I come to pick her up again. She is all about me—which makes sense, since I am all about her. Maybe when she gets a little older and starts school, I will consider adopting another child—a three- or four-year-old who needs a good home. Or maybe by some miracle I will meet another Mr. Right, and he will want a child of his own. Who knows? The future is such an odd and unpredictable thing now. So I try not to dwell on it and instead take time to appreciate the moments as they happen and enjoy the ride.

DAYS

One day. That's all it takes to change a life. We have all had days that leave an indelible memory for us to savor or loathe. I've had a lot of days that have changed my life—some for the better, others for the worse. And in between, there are all those other regular days that make up a life.

I remember one of those, during the summer of 2002. It was the summer of twelve weddings and the beginning of a courtship. I was living in a two-bedroom suburban apartment in Apple Valley, Minnesota. With the apartment came access to the community pool, a giant rectangle of chlorine-y blue water that on the weekends was overridden by screaming kids but during the week was a refuge for those lucky enough to have a day off from work. Todd and I had been dating for six or seven months and both found ourselves with a day off, so I invited him to laze by the pool with a cooler of beer, snacks, and no one around to interrupt us. It was that day when he noticed my toes for the first time. Or maybe he had noticed them before but hadn't felt comfortable enough to say anything, since our relationship was relatively new.

"Hey, beaner toe, get over here," Todd called to me from the opposite side of the pool where he was lounging, drinking a beer. I was mortified. He had spied my weakness, my weirdly shaped pinkie toes that look strangely like giant beans. But I knew my toes weren't a deal breaker after all the sarcastic teasing that we were both masters of and loved to partake in. The rest of the day passed uneventfully, but it was representative of those that were to come with Todd during our life together. Days filled with fun, teasing, beers, and toes.

That random day always surfaces when I think of the best days of my life. Nothing special happened; it was just a simple day full of simple joys—a perfect day.

Today was another one of those unremarkable but perfect days. It's ending with both Brooke, now three-and-a-half, and me covered in a layer of dirt and sunscreen. Her short, bouncy, blonde curls have tiny pieces of boxwood stem woven into them from her adventures in her "fairy wonderland" in the backyard, while my dark brown hair is a sweaty, greasy mess from planting our window boxes. We are both in sundresses but too soiled and unfit for any place requiring a dress. I am stretched out on a lawn chair in the backyard, my dirt-covered legs atop Cosmo, who is perched at the foot of the chair. He is eighty-five pounds of soaking wet fur from the kiddie pool he made his own today. Brooke sits next to me, my arm wrapped around her, her head resting against my chest as we watch the birdbath she has just filled up with water, the birdbath my high school classmates gave me after Todd's funeral almost three years ago.

"Mom, we have to be quiet so the birds come to take a bath," she says, putting her finger to her lips and scolding me for being too loud. We sit silently for a few minutes, staring at the birdbath and the trees and structures around us. Power lines run overhead. Our small tan garden shed sits close by. Suddenly a robin swoops down, not to the birdbath but to a tree branch four feet above it. Hanging from the branch is a small bunch of orange berries—a feast for a bird and a feast for our eyes as we sit here quietly watching. I hear an intake of breath from Brooke when she spots the robin. I whisper to her, "Brooke, do you see the bird?"

"Ssshhh. We don't want to scare the mommy robin away," she says so softly I almost can't hear her. She's right. It's a female, her breast not nearly the red of the males who constantly frequent this berry-covered tree. We sit for another few minutes watching the robin eat the berries as another one, a male, lands on the power line just feet from the branch. There they sit, the mommy robin eating, the daddy robin watching, protecting from afar. Brooke gazes intently at the scene, enthralled as I am by the simplicity of nature and the perfection that our day has been.

Suddenly, both birds take off, startled by something unseen and unheard by us as our little family watches theirs.

"Mommy, did you see them? That was neat," Brooke whispers, with wide eyes.

Not wanting to disrupt the peace, I whisper back, "That *was* neat. Maybe they'll come back."

"Well you have to be quiet then," she murmurs, settling into position to intently observe the birdbath and the trees and bushes she has spent the day underneath.

There are the best days, and there are the worst days, and there are all those days in between. The best days are like robins, providing us flitting moments of joy and then flying away before we can grasp them. The worst days are like the birdbath, reminders of things that we wish forgotten but that define us in countless ways and give us perspective on our life. And then there are all those days in between—days just like this one. Days like the one I spent by the pool with a man who flitted in and out of my life like the robin, but of whom I am constantly reminded. By the birdbath that sits proudly in my garden. By the daughter who sits on my lap, pressing her blonde curls against my chest while we watch those robins. Reminders of what I had and what I have.

Today was nothing special, but oh so special, because I let myself be aware of its specialness. It was an ordinary day, but extraordinary, because I spent it with Brooke. It was a day in between the best and the worst, but how I want every day to be—one that I remember and that makes up what will become my life.

Todd's heart ran out of beats, but mine is still going strong. I want to make the most of the beats I have left, whether it's for one more day or twenty-five thousand. I will live well through the best and worst days, and all the days in between.

Not the end...

ACKNOWLEDGEMENTS

Thank you to you for taking a chance on this book and giving up a few hours of your life to read my story.

Thank you to my many editors, teachers and reviewers. From the earliest drafts to the final edits, your insights and encouragement were invaluable: Sheryl Sieracki, Nancy Raeburn, Dena Bjorklund, Carol Riley, Kate Hopper, Connie Anderson, The Loft Literary Center and all my class members. Thanks especially to Mary Carroll Moore whose classes profoundly changed my writing life.

Thanks to Balboa Press and Hay House for your commitment to this book.

Thank you to my surf camp ladies for the trips that inspired so much of my transformation!

Thank you to my book reviewers Peggy McColl, Lauren Mackler, Theresa Rose, Julie Bauke, Jeff Cohen and Senator Holland Redfield. Your early reads and praise are very much appreciated!

Thanks to Erin & I Photography for your amazing cover and bio photos.

Love and appreciation to my writing group for your feedback and encouragement: Lee Blum, Shannon McCartney-Simper and Prinna Boudreau – your books are next!

Lifelong thanks to my friends for your support during such a huge transition period in my life you know who you are!

To all of you out there friends and strangers alike who have sent me notes, emails and positive vibes through this crazy journey through grief – thank you.

Thanks to Todd's family for keeping his memory alive every single day and embracing Brooke and me.

Every day thanks to my big, shaggy companion Cosmo. You've been an excellent bedfellow, dog hair and all, and kept me company during many dark nights.

Eternal thanks to my family for encouraging all my crazy ideas, pushing me to move forward and your unconditional love.

Love to Brooke, my pillar of strength. I hope I can be a role model for you as you grow up.

And finally, thank you to Todd, my first soul mate and my forever friend. I am grateful for your presence in my life--past, present and future. I will miss you always until we meet again.

All my gratitude and love to all,
Kristen

READING GROUP GUIDE

QUESTIONS FOR DISCUSSION

1. Discuss the topic of losing a significant other. How does Kristen's relationship with her husband impact her reaction to his death?

2. How do you feel about the title "The Best Worst Thing?"

3. Kristen writes about feeling extremely protective of her daughter after her husband's death. How do you think her experience would have been different if they had multiple children? What if they hadn't had any children yet?

4. Despite the sad and tragic circumstances, Kristen maintains a sense of humor in her book. Do you believe it changes the tone and message of the memoir? How would the book be different if she didn't include some of her funny thoughts?

5. Kristen shares multiple experiences of "visits" from her husband from the other side. Do you believe in ghosts or that deceased individuals can contact us from the afterlife? Does it comfort you or disturb you?

6. In the opening chapters, Kristen shares the story of her courtship and early marriage to Todd. Do you think this gave you more empathy for her than if she had started the book the day he died? Did their early relationship evolve similar to typical relationships? How did it change over time?

7. Kristen shares her insomniac tendencies and how it worsens after Todd's death. Yet she has many transformative

experiences in those sleepless hours. Do you think her sleep habits (or lack of sleep habits) impacted her healing process?

8. Kristen shares her initial feelings of embarrassment over being a single mom and feeling judged when she doesn't wear her wedding ring on her left hand. Do you think those feelings are valid?

9. One of Kristen's "therapies" was shopping. Why do women use shopping as a band-aid? Have you used retail therapy to feel better? Do you think it was an irresponsible way to react considering she was a single mother with a daughter to take care of?

10. The book leaves the reader with some unanswered questions about how Kristen's business started and progressed. Do you wish she had included more about her professional life? How do women's identities tie to their career?

11. Kristen felt like Todd's life insurance was cursed money but necessary for their financial security too. What are your thoughts on life insurance and were Kristen's feelings valid about the money feeling cursed?

12. Kristen shares multiple stories about Todd's and her own experiences and skill at dancing and singing. Do you think Kristen was too self-conscious about her dancing and singing? Why is the thread of dancing and singing important to the book?

13. In the book, Kristen mentions her need to be alone to heal and her "me-time" as therapy. Women often forget that me-time is important every day, not just during times of stress. How do you build in me-time?

14. Kristen weaves in her spiritual growth journey and feelings on religion throughout the book. Do you think she would have eventually come to the same conclusions/feelings if Todd hadn't died?

15. Put yourself in Kristen's shoes. If you had young children and a seemingly healthy husband with a full life planned, how would you handle a similar situation?

16. Todd died in 2007 and Kristen started writing just three months later writing the book real-time as she experienced her grief. Many people believe you should have some distance between yourself and an event so you have a broader perspective. Do you think Kristen wrote the book too soon after her husband's death?

17. Kristen stretched beyond her comfort zone and went to surf camp (twice). Do you think it's valuable to get out of the box sometimes? Why? How does it contribute to our growth? What is the craziest thing you've done?

18. Do you think Kristen would have started her own business if Todd hadn't died? How did her growth lead her to find a new career path?

19. Kristen mentions being money-poor but happiness-rich. How does the shift from a financially-focused measure of success differ from being happy with our life despite our material worth?

20. Grief is a journey of a lifetime and the feelings never go away – they just change over time. Do you think if Kristen were to write this book in 20 years, it would be the same, different or a little of both? Why?

TOPICS FOR DISCUSSION

Death of a loved one
The process of grief
Retail-therapy
Life insurance
Single-parenthood
Spiritual growth
Entrepreneurship
Writing as therapy
Karaoke
Dancing
Change
Stress
Accepting help from others
Taking chances
Surfing
Getting out of your comfort zone
Living in the present
Learning from the past
Self-motivation
Leaps of faith
Understanding others
Money vs. happiness

CONNECT

Want to get Kristen's Twitter, Facebook and Blog posts including news, FREE e-books, newsletters, meditations, and daily stress relief tips?

Visit me online for more information on my writing:

Website: www.kristenkbrown.com
Facebook: Kristen K. Brown Writes the Up-Side of Down
Twitter: KristenKBrown

To learn more about Happy Hour Effect* please visit:

Website: www.HappyHourEffect.com
Facebook: Happy Hour Effect
Twitter: HappyHourEffect

EVENTS AND MEDIA

Want to inspire your audience with stress management advice or to see Kristen's media coverage? Go to the Newsroom: http://www. happyhoureffect.com/newsroom.html

Want Kristen to speak at your event or company meeting about stress management and overcoming change both personally and professionally?
Contact her today at: speaking@kristenkbrown.com.

Mention this book and get $100 off speaking.

Discounts available on bulk book orders.
Perfect for reading groups, events and more.
Contact support@happyhoureffect.com for more information.

ABOUT THE AUTHOR

Kristen Brown, 34, is a widow mom, writer, speaker, radio host and founder of Happy Hour Effect®, an award-nominated stress management and health supplement company. She inspires people using her professional expertise and personal story to demonstrate ways to manage stress thus improving wellness. She is a certified member of the Women's Business Enterprise National Council, a member of the National Wellness Institute, has been nominated for multiple American Business Awards and is a volunteer for the American Heart Association. She showcases her company at Hollywood events and has been on the CBS news, featured on the cover of March magazine and on television, radio, print and online. She offers multiple training and stress management products on the Happy Hour Effect website and *The Happy Hour Effect Balance Plan*, a stress management and goal-setting program she developed based on her own personal experience, professional expertise and education is being adapted into a book series. She is pursuing her master's degree in Integral Theory and lives in Minneapolis with her daughter and dog. Her key message: Stress Management…Made Simple!